Acting fr
the Heart

Australian advocates for asylum seekers tell their stories

Edited by

Sarah Mares and
Louise Newman

FINCH PUBLISHING
SYDNEY

Acting from the Heart: Australian advocates for asylum seekers tell their stories

First published in 2007 in Australia and New Zealand by Finch Publishing Pty Limited, PO Box 120, Lane Cove, NSW 1595, Australia. info@finch.com.au. ABN 49 057 285 248

11 10 09 08 07 8 7 6 5 4 3 2 1

The publisher and editors wish to thank the contributors to this anthology, all of whom have donated their creative work without payment. The royalties from the sale of this book are being donated to the Bridge for Asylum Seekers Foundation.

National Library of Australia Cataloguing-in-Publication entry
Mares, Sarah.
Acting from the heart.
ISBN 9781876451783 (pbk.)
1. Refugees - Legal status, laws, etc. - Australia. 2. Detention of persons - Australia. 3. Asylum, Right of - Australia. 4. Emigration and immigration law - Australia. 5. Social work with immigrants - Australia. 6. Australia - Emigration and immigration - Social aspects. I. Newman, Louise K. II. Title.
325.210994

Editorial selection team: Karen Cornish, Michael Dudley, Winton Higgins, Gaby Mason Michael Wall and Sally Zwartz
Edited by Sean Doyle
Editorial assistance from Rosemary Peers
Text designed and typeset in Galliard 10.5/14 pt by Emtype Desktop Publishing
Cover illustration and design by Natalie Bowra
Author photos by Paul Walker, NSWIOP
Printed by Southwood Press

Notes The 'Authors' notes' section at the back of this book contains useful additional information and references to quoted material in the text. Each reference is linked to the text by its relevant page number and an identifying line entry.

Disclaimer Every effort has been made to ensure that the contributors' experiences described in these stories have been depicted as accurately as possible, and that the words and actions of the people mentioned have not been misrepresented.

Advance praise for this book

'The heart breaks in silence to read these stories of courage and endurance in a struggle against cruelty and indifference. These are true stories - stories which capture a shameful period in Australia's history, stories which record the efforts of ordinary Australians to resist the callous policies of a heartless government. I knew many of these stories already before I read the book, but I was moved to tears of anger and shame reading them, remembering them. The authors of these essays exemplify the very best of Australian values; the government policies that made their efforts necessary exemplify the very worst. We will be remembered for this.'

Julian Burnside QC

'There have been many brave people involved in placing the refugees' plight in front of the public and challenging the politicians' thinking. I have always believed an important part of the process of changing people's minds is to hear the stories of the refugees themselves. Equally important ... is to hear of the work that so many people do ... that takes courage and a generous spirit. That is why this book is an important part of Australia's history.' *Ian Chappell*

'In the Anne Frank Huis in Amsterdam, Australia is shown as unwelcoming to "reffos" in the 1930s. Today, many advocate protection for the deserving. This book illustrates a welcome change of heart.'

The Hon Michael Kirby AC CMG, High Court of Australia

'An illuminating and at times harrowing reflection on the treatment of asylum seekers in Australia, *Acting from the Heart* is a reminder to each of us that individual action does make a difference. The inspirational stories give voice to those who have suffered under and those who have fought against, unfair and indiscriminate government policy. Compelling reading for all Australians as a reminder of a continuing injustice that demands attention.'

Rev. Tim Costello, World Vision Australia

'These personal stories ... give a real sense of what a policy of harming some people in order to deter others does to people, both to those who suffer and those who try to help them ... This important work records the genesis of an extraordinary citizens' movement in Australia, and it does so by making vivid the pain and injustice of what Australia has done.' *Dr Eva Sallis, Australians Against Racism*

'It'll make you cry. Sometimes it'll make you laugh. It's the untold story of Australia's own underground railroad ... Where disparate individuals decided they wanted to make a difference, no matter how small, because they felt it was the only moral choice ... it's the inspirational story of a swelling grassroots movement ... These accounts open a bleak window on mandatory detention and show how ordinary Australians can make extraordinary inroads into a callous and seemingly impregnable Government policy.' *Chris Rau, journalist and sister of Cornelia Rau*

To all those who seek refuge on our shores
and those who welcome them

For those who've come across the seas
We've boundless plains to share;
With courage let us all combine
To advance Australia fair.

From Verse 3, 'Advance Australia Fair',
Australia's National Anthem

First they came for the Communists, and I didn't speak up,
because I wasn't a Communist.
Then they came for the sick, the so-called incurables,
and I didn't speak up,
because I wasn't mentally ill.
Then they came for the Jews, and I didn't speak up,
because I wasn't a Jew.
Then they came for me, and by that time there was
no one left to speak up for me.

Pastor Martin Niemoller 1892–1984

Contents

Foreword

A group of Australian people who wished, in the most imaginative way possible, to show their solidarity with asylum seekers locked up in the infamous Baxter detention centre took kites to fly high into that vivid and relentless sky above the centre's enormous walls. But even this small gesture, this symbol in the sky designed to tell the detainees that Australians knew they were there and felt fraternity with them, could not be permitted. Police arrived, kites were smashed, Kafkaesque threats of prosecution for violating air space were made. This, in good old, laid-back, easy-going Australia.

As one of many, many advocates' tales in these pages, the incident encapsulates the absurdity and the ruthlessness of our policy on asylum seekers. This book needs to be widely read not only because it has the capacity to grip the attention of any reader, but also because its story tellers are the ones who stand up for compassion – that now-despised virtue – on the days the rest of us are too busy looking at gross domestic product to pay even mental attention to gross national crime.

Take, for example, Frances Milne's involvement in a life-and-death struggle to prevent the brutal deportation back to a future of imprisonment and torture of an African she calls Kassabe. Or Michael Dudley's account of a woman who escaped detention on her third anniversary behind the wire and now stood on a cliff ready to throw herself into the sea. Her baby had been taken from her the week before. 'The small mother had shouted, so they put her in solitary ... they carted her off to an asylum, but she was angry, not mentally ill, and this was no true asylum but a prison.' The press and the public took up her case and suddenly asylum was granted. We are left to ask why it was not granted earlier, and with less torment?

In our Australia it is not only the asylum seekers who have been scapegoated, but anyone who dissents from the policy of mandatory detention, and particularly advocates like the people whose stories we read here. They are, as depicted by some of their detractors, people with nothing better to do with their lives except cause a stir about people with whom, thanks heavens, the government is taking a firm hand. The reality is that the advocates represented here, a number of whom I know personally, are frantically busy people who have either given up other potentially lucrative business to devote themselves full-time to the victims behind the wire, or who fit their work for asylum seekers somehow into their full-time professional career. They don't necessarily have time to take on an administration that consumes innocent humans, but, as one advocate's husband explains it, even while he cries, 'Christ Almighty! Not another refugee!' the moral imperative of fighting for the freedom of another human takes over, even if the fight might be futile. 'Occasionally, a refugee is saved notwithstanding the best efforts of the Australian government to destroy them, physically or psychologically. Not much time to celebrate, however, because there is always another unfortunate refugee on the doorstep, figuratively speaking.' In fact, to help asylum seekers under the present system is to take on their frustration, their anger, their racing pulse, and their pain which has so often led to self-mutilation and suicide.

In the world view of the government, there is nothing wrong with the system, so 'Ed Mund' wrote to his local member of Parliament:

If there is something wrong
What kind of evidence do you believe?
Letters from the sufferer or
Letters from their advocate or
The tears of the sufferer or
The sweat of their advocate or
The blood of the sufferer or
The corpse of the sufferer or
A message from God?

We don't need a message from God because we have the stories told here.

I honour the people who write in these pages, and when at last the better angels of Australia begin singing again, so will Australia honour them. But that hope is coloured darkly by the ongoing battles these story tellers are engaged in right now, some of which, sadly, they will lose to a stubborn government and a criminal policy.

Tom Keneally
Australia Day, 2007

Introduction

Since 2001, thousands of Australians from all parts of the country and all walks of life have been moved to act in support of asylum seekers and refugees, and against our government's immigration policy and practice. For some, the 'refugee issue' has become a defining personal stance, one which has engaged and divided families and communities. It is an issue on which it has been difficult to remain neutral. Some of those who chose to engage with this issue tell their stories here.

Australia has had relatively few asylum seekers compared to most other Western countries, but has implemented an increasingly harsh response to those who arrive without valid visas. For example, from 1990–1999, 92,800 applications for asylum were lodged in Australia (with 14.6 percent granted protection), compared with 374,000 lodged in the UK (34.9 percent granted protection) and 245,000 in Sweden (46.6 percent granted). The policy of indefinite mandatory detention of all 'unauthorised' arrivals, both adults and children, was first introduced by the Keating Labor Government in 1992. This has been elaborated on as the central platform of immigration policy, intended to deter further arrivals and to send a clear message to the international community, regardless of the cost to those seeking asylum. Elaborations of this policy include the development of Temporary Protection Visas, the excision of numerous islands off the coast of Australia from the migration zone, and, most recently, attempts to legislate for the offshore processing of all arrivals on Nauru, a small, desolate, bankrupt Pacific island state.

These policies harm the most needy – those fleeing political oppression and persecution in countries where there is no formal process for seeking refuge and no access to UN processes. Of the 9500 unauthorised arrivals in Australia between July 1999 and December 2001, most were political refugees from Iraq and Afghanistan. From 1992–2004, over 4000 children arrived, 300 of whom were unaccompanied, without adult care and protection. These children were detained along with other adults and families in a range of metropolitan and remote detention centres, often for years.

The Australian Government's response to these arrivals was dramatic, deliberate and divisive. Echoing a century-old fear of invasion from the north, the language of immigration politics pandered to this fear: 'illegal aliens', 'invasion', 'hordes', 'flotillas of leaky boats' and a 'tsunami' of hungry refugees. It seems all measures were justified in the fight to protect 'the Australian way of life', whatever the human, ethical and financial costs. Enormous political and financial resources have been spent implementing and justifying the policy to the Australian people. Australia's human rights record and our sense of ourselves as 'the land of the fair go' were two of the casualties.

This divisive national discussion dominated the lead-up to the 2001 Federal election. A group of asylum seekers on a sinking boat were accused of throwing their children overboard to further their entry to the country, remembered as the 'Children Overboard' affair [*see Timeline of events*]. Another group was rescued by the Norwegian freighter, the MV *Tampa*, but was refused permission to land in Australia and forced to sail to Nauru. The representation of the asylum seeker as manipulative, greedy and dangerous – and, above all, as 'un-Australian' – was complete. Little matter that these accounts were inaccurate and manipulated for political gain.

One story above all others appears to have been pivotal in countering this demonisation of asylum seekers and initiating the upsurge of protest against these aspects of government immigration policy. In August 2001, after a camera was smuggled into Villawood Detention Centre, film of a silent, listless, six-year-old detainee, Shayan Badraie, was shown on ABC television's *Four Corners*. The shocking evidence of his trauma and withdrawal, his resuscitation in hospital followed by decline when returned to detention, highlighted the predicament of children and parents in detention. It also highlighted the callous determination of the government to allow harm and damage to vulnerable individuals in the name of so-called 'border protection'.

Members of the community, in increasing numbers, found the detention of infants and children intolerable, even if they remained fearful and ambivalent about the *bona fides* of adult asylum seekers. The ensuing campaigns and debates have brought together individuals with no previous history of political involvement. This is a 'suburban', grassroots political movement rather than a centralised or organised campaign. Opposition to government immigration policy has taken many forms. Individuals came together with a common sense of disbelief and outrage that acts of cruelty were undertaken by elected representatives in their name, and that 'Australian values' now seemed to include callous self-interest and a disregard for human suffering. The refugee question has essentially become a moral debate and, for some, a way of redefining not just Australian values, but what are essentially human values. The crisis of identity suffered in Australia has been profound. The loss of our respected international reputation has perhaps had less impact on the general community than has the erosion of our self-image as the land of the 'fair go', with opportunity for the underdog. The detention of over 4000 children cannot easily be seen as fair or necessary.

Stories of conditions in the detention centres and the psychological damage done to asylum seekers were circulated by concerned groups and individuals from churches and religious organisations, professional bodies, legal groups, human rights and child welfare groups. Journalists were provided with information and evidence, and just as importantly, countless individuals acted from conscience and a sense that to be a passive bystander in the face of evil is to collude and support it. The feeling was, as Edmund Burke famously put it, that 'The only thing necessary for the triumph of evil is for good men to do nothing'.

As TS Eliot wrote, 'After such knowledge, what forgiveness' – there was no easy way to forget once the reality of the treatment of asylum seekers was made public. Actions have taken many forms: writing letters, visits to detainees, organised protests, pro-bono professional reports, legal representation and psychological research – all intended to support those seeking asylum and to protest the harsh immigration regime.

The stories and experiences in this collection speak to the profound emotional impact of this social movement. Advocates have experienced extremes of frustration, anger, sadness and some joy. There is sadness at the loss of Australian moral innocence and of identity; sadness at the pain and damage inflicted on vulnerable individuals; frustration at dealing with a political and bureaucratic machine intent on detention at all costs and operating within a punitive model where all are guilty; and occasional joy at those victories of release and freedom.

Each person involved in the support of asylum seekers has had to confront the reality of their own thoughts about Australian history and national identity. To help an asylum seeker who is being harmed by flawed and morally bankrupt government policy is a political act. Many have had to rethink their assumptions about professional roles and responsibilities.

About this book

The editors of this collection are both child psychiatrists. We became involved in response to the obvious and apparently deliberate harm occurring to the mental health of children, adults and families as a direct consequence of government policy. The hypocrisy of concurrent government campaigns aimed at prevention of child abuse, suicide reduction and mental health promotion alongside immigration policy and practice appeared to indicate that some human beings were worthy of care and protection while others were not. Harming the latter could be justified in the name of deterrence. Such hypocrisy has dangerous historical precedents, and required protest.

The idea for this anthology arose out of a series of writing workshops run in South Australia and NSW that were originally intended to assist advocates and professionals to deal with the stresses and vicarious trauma resulting from ongoing work with incarcerated families and with unsupported refugees in the community. The stories generated were a clear testament to the wrongs of immigration policy, and also to the strength, determination and grace of asylum seekers, refugees and their advocates. We then invited contributions, starting with a small list of known advocates – and the network did its job: within four weeks, we received over 90 written submissions and 50 illustrations. As you can imagine, the editorial process was difficult.

The stories form an historical record of this significant period in Australia's social history. They also make compelling reading.

Sarah Mares and Louise Newman

WELCOME* TO AUSTRALIA*
*(NOT NECESSARILY)
aweldon.
14·11·03

Part 1

Remarkable people – on both sides of the wire

These stories are about everyday people responding to extraordinary circumstances. The stories of asylum seekers and their advocates are at once ordinary and remarkable. These are the stories of individuals who found it impossible to be passive bystanders or to remain blind to human suffering. They felt moved to speak out, to act, to visit and support. The stories are many, from widely different places and perspectives, but all share a common humanity. The stories of asylum seekers are, after all, the stories of us all – parents saving their children, individuals seeking freedom and dignity, the power of the will to survive. Perhaps the advocate is open to the universal nature of these ordinary human needs.

These are stories of life-changing relationships, of love and heartbreak, of courage and perseverance; stories of intense feelings and commitment to the values of an Australia that has become a receding memory. Australia – the place of fairness, equality, support and caring for the underdog – has increasingly given way to the callous and mean-spirited self-protectionism of the comfortable yet anxious majority. The media and political discourse represents the asylum seeker as foreign, other and abject, capable of dissimulation and even child abuse. In the face of this, ordinary people telling human stories of escape and determination can have a powerful impact. These personal stories of decision making and commitment, which humanise the asylum seeker experience until they are 'people like us', are simple, political acts of resistance.

It was the boy

*Former journalist **Ngareta Rossell**'s harrowing visit to Villawood would go on to shake the foundations of immigration law and practice*

This is a story about Villawood - about why I went there, what I found there, and why I'm still going there today.

Once a hostel for newly arrived migrants who dreamed of a better life, today Villawood is an immigration detention centre for displaced persons, where any thought of a better life is lost in the effort it takes to keep breathing. Villawood is bad. Just how bad is glimpsed fleetingly when somebody kills themselves. Villawood is not high on the public consciousness.

When I think of Villawood, I think of many things: a Grimm's fairy-tale, Hansel and Gretel and the Keystone Cops all rolled into one. Happy endings? There are some. But dress it up or dress it down, Villawood is a nightmare movie with an R rating. So long as detention remains indefinite, nothing will really change, because locked up is locked up.

Yet in spite of everything, I'm not sorry I went there. No-one forced me. How many times do you have the opportunity to observe the entire human condition in all its manifestations? Villawood has caused me great grief. It has lost me friends but it has made me new ones.

It's also had its side effects. My family and friends looked on in astonishment as I disappeared beneath a sea of legal documents and late-night phone calls. All of a sudden I had no time for the minutiae of other people's lives. Resentment all round ... they were hurt. I was hurt because they didn't understand that I was busy saving lives while they were busy saving frequent flyer points. It was difficult to find a meeting place. With some I never did.

I first went there because a friend invited me. As simple as that. I kept going because the more I went, the more convinced I was that a great injustice was being perpetrated upon a small group of displaced persons fleeing the Taliban and Saddam Hussein. The continuing claims by politicians that refugees were 'gold diggers' and 'terrorists' seemed way off the mark. The raggle-taggle bunch of 'boat people' I was meeting, in their thin, hand-me-down T-shirts, were as poor as church mice. Most had arrived with only the clothes they stood in.

So why the fear-mongering and deception emanating from Canberra about refugees? It was simply not true. Whose purpose was being served by this misrepresentation? I kept visiting Villawood. There was much to learn in Villawood and the stories there were legion.

The first thing I learnt about Villawood was that summers there were hotter than anywhere else. In January, hot winds from mountain bushfires sweep through, mingling with the sweat and anger of those facing yet another year behind the wire. Summers in Villawood are when fires blaze up and detainees break out.

Winter in Villawood is the season of depression, when the coldness of temperature is matched only by the coldness of heart, when the damp rises up from the ground, when the orange floodlights cast weird shapes on the wire, and when the potted plants and new-look landscaping stand stark and geometric against the fence. Winter is the season of Valium and television, when detainees save medication – because this year, they might just 'do it'.

To remember what life was like before Villawood is a challenge. Whatever I was doing before appears trivial. The halcyon days, when motorways led to country holidays, have long since gone. Today the M4 and the M5 are simply roads to Villawood. Pollution goes with the territory.

Villawood lies one hour west of the Sydney Harbour foreshores, away from the city, the golden beaches and the afternoon sea breezes. Villawood belongs in that other land, out west. It's an hour and ten minutes from where I live.

I still remember that first day, jammed in between high-octane semis, as, grinding and braking, they hurtled themselves at the open road to burn rubber all the way to Melbourne. Before the T-junction, where the semis turn, in there somewhere among the eucalypt trees, among the scattering of brick veneers and fibro cottages, are the prefabricated admin buildings, the run-down, dark, brick dwellings that are Villawood. There are no signs.

This is the land of the battler with the dream, who is moving ever-further west to the big house, the big mortgage, the lifetime of bank repayments and Saturday afternoon football. This is the land of cheap housing, where the unemployed look for prescription drugs or an easy mugging at a train station. This is the land where the meat pie has given way to the kebab, where the scent of lemongrass pervades the open marketplace at midday in Cabramatta. Villawood can be found after Auburn but before Cabramatta. Villawood is migrant country.

It was pre-*Tampa*, pre-September 11, pre-'Children Overboard' and the sinking of the boat known as the SIEVX when I first went to Villawood. As insignificant as it sounds, it was curiosity that led me there. I had just been to Iran. I had on my mind all things Persian: perfumed gardens, hand-woven rugs and fine miniature paintings. I wondered if there might be Iranians in Villawood.

Iran was different and beautiful, with its high mountains, desert landscapes and ancient cultures. I loved it. Other things were not so attractive. Life under strict Islamic rule was fraught with danger. Conspiracy theories were rife. The eyes and ears of the government were everywhere. You could taste the fear. It was there in the eyes of those brave enough to speak to foreigners. Clearly, Iran was not a country for free spirits. Many people were trying to leave.

At a pizza shop on the corner of Gurney and Woodville Roads, we turned. There it was. You couldn't miss the wire, so much steel glinting in the sun. At the end of a cul-de-sac lined with factory warehouses were the gates. The lettering was in black, on a white sign inside the entrance: 'Property of the Commonwealth of Australia. Welcome'.

As we approached the gate we could see the queue snaking along a razor-wire fence, through a gate and along a concrete path to the visitor processing area inside. The waiting time to get in was one-and-a-half hours. This was the old Villawood, before the age of the new pop-up tickets, before designer smiles were pasted to the faces of the Villawood staff, who today enjoin you to 'Have a nice visit'.

Then it was all savage voices and unrelenting orders to 'Get outta the doorway. Get back from the desk. Youse won't get in if youse don't get back from the desk!'

If this was how it was for visitors, how was it for the people inside?

'They're from the prisons,' someone behind us whispered as we watched a guard refuse entry to someone with incorrect ID. Why prison guards? I didn't think the people inside were prisoners. My query was left unanswered as we slowly shuffled along, until finally our turn came to be processed.

A sour-faced woman confiscated car keys, licence and wallets. 'Youse'll get them back when youse come out,' she said.

Only one more lock to go. As we waited for the last gate my friend told me to prepare myself. Even today the hairs on my neck stiffen when I remember. That day I hadn't the slightest idea what she meant.

The last gate was opened and slammed shut behind us. But at least we were in. No camera in my hand, because cameras were banned. But the 'camera' in my mind was complete, with a brand new film and a recording device. A low hum of different voices in different languages mingled with the sound of clanging gates as we walked in. The compound was crowded. Some people had managed to bag a table to sit at with their friends. Those who were not so lucky paced up and down while small children ran in frenetic circles, round and round like mice in a maze with no exit. Guards were patrolling the perimeter fence; hard on their heels a pick-up truck circled the compound at intervals. So this was detention..

But it wasn't the guards, the wire, the intrusive PA system or even the runaway children that made me swallow hard. It was what I saw on the other side of the compound. It was the boy. At least I thought he was a boy – an emaciated bundle of bones in the lap of a man seated at a table near the fence. The man was dressed in tracksuit and thongs. The woman beside him was in headscarf and long coat, Iranian style. Memories of the fearful faces in Iranian streets came flooding back. The couple sat like two shop dummies, the stricken child between them. I could not take my eyes from the boy, a bizarre sight in a First World country.

At first I believed he was a fake boy, a child made to look like a boy, a fundraiser for famine in Africa. You could not look like that and still be alive. But as we drew nearer, the bundle twitched, stretched and reached out a stick arm to turn over. So great was that effort that the feeble body fell back limp. Limp but alive.

I took a breath, looked away; pretending I wasn't staring. Thoughts ricocheted through my brain. Why wasn't he in bed, on a hospital drip? Why was he out here among the crowds? I looked to my friend for an explanation, but already she was moving forward to greet the seated couple. It was them we would see.

'Don't get up,' she said, signalling to them to stay put. They had saved a seat for us at one of the plastic tables. They were Iranian. As we took our places, a short, dark man in Bermuda shorts whipped over from the other side of the compound – another detainee. He had come, he said, to act as interpreter for my friend, who would take a statement. The child was not mentioned. It was as if he were invisible to everyone.

My friend produced notepad and paper; the interpreter translated. I vaguely heard what they were saying. My eyes kept straying to where he lay. Comatose. The trouble was, the father began, they had no lawyer. Their case was finished, failed. They'd had 28 days to appeal, but they hadn't. Why? Don't know. Just didn't. Too tired, too sick. The boy? Too ill. Their case simply slipped from their grasp.

My friend looked up from her notepad. 'Deportation?' she asked pointedly. The man nodded. Yes. All through this dialogue the boy had not moved. I was half-listening, but then I heard 'deportation'. I shrank at the thought of anyone who had left Iran without papers being sent back. The interpreter paused. He had something of his own to say about deportation.

'None of us know when,' he said. 'Yesterday him. Today me.' His gaze swept around the compound and came to rest upon me, the newcomer. 'How do you think we feel being here? Did you ask that?'

I did not ask that. He was reading my mind. He looked hard at me. 'I'll tell you anyway. We thought we were coming to a democracy.'

I squirmed.

He spoke urgently, as if he had only one chance to convey what he had to say. 'The boy can't drink. Can't eat. He is dehydrated. His system is shutting down.' I stared at the small, pale face with the shock of dark hair. 'Why?' I asked. 'How come?' The interpreter shrugged. 'What do they expect when they lock a six-year-old in the desert with crazy people who want to impale themselves on wire?'

My friend wasn't finished. We had actually only just begun. She asked the interpreter if we could get back to the family story. But I couldn't hold back.

'Why isn't he in hospital?'

The interpreter laughed a laugh that wasn't a laugh; more a scornful explosion of air. 'Hospital!' Beads of perspiration had broken out on his forehead. 'He'll be back there any minute. He is admitted to hospital, re-hydrated, and then returned to detention, only to deteriorate again. You'll see.' He raised his voice. 'You tell them outside what's going on inside here.'

My friend looked at her watch. The couple sat silent. The boy lay still. I felt ill.

The interpreter went on with the story. The family had been sent to Villawood from Woomera because of the boy's illness. 'A blast furnace in the desert,' he said. 'That's where they keep the kids. Forty degrees in the shade. You know Woomera? Let me tell you then.' He was working himself up. 'Woomera is a place where they do what they like, where police douse children with water cannons, and sewage flows on the ground where children play.'

Wasn't he confusing Australia with Iran? I moved in my seat and looked down at the boy. His breath was coming fitfully. His parents were oblivious.

'You don't believe me, do you?' The interpreter was as jumpy as the parents were passive. The interpreter raised his voice: 'You think it's not true.'

'I didn't say that.'

'Look at him.' He pointed at the boy. 'Can you see him? Is he true? That's Woomera. Look at me.'

I looked away. I wished he wouldn't speak so loudly.

'My hair's falling out. My teeth are rotten, I can't sleep nights.' He was determined to be heard. And I heard him. Nobody else seemed to hear him. 'That's Villawood.' He sat back. He'd had his say.

My head was spinning. This was not the afternoon outing I was expecting. I half-stood but then sat down because the mother had begun to speak. Her face was blotched and pink. For the first time I noticed she had a baby. She held the baby close. She spoke in a low monotone I had to strain to hear.

'Doctors in hospital say, let us out. Detention makes him like this.' She blew her nose. She looked to her husband whose eyes were red. 'But Minister say no. "No release".'

My friend kept scribbling.

'Minister knows,' said the woman. Her face was impassive. 'No release for us.'

The full impact of what she said did not hit me until later. Did she really say the Minister knew? I refused to believe it. I had seen starvation in Third World countries. But in Australia we don't do starvation.

A guard was shouting at people to get away from the wire. In one corner, guards were creating a racket with two-way radios. Meantime, the parents had reverted to their shop-dummy pose. Later I learnt that many people in Villawood were on antidepressants and tranquillisers.

Dusk had come to the compound. Visitors were packing up and heading to the exit. The interpreter had gone. My friend put down her pen. I was relieved. She stood, I stood, the family stood, we looked at each other. So much to say but I found no words.

We said our goodbyes and watched as the family trudged into the gloom of their quarters – mother, baby, father with dying son slung over his shoulder like a parcel of laundry. We walked our separate paths, through separate gates, back to our very separate lives.

We left the compound and the camera in my mind switched off, the credits rolled. 'To be continued,' it said. By the time I reached my front door, culture shock had turned to steely resolve. The iron had entered my soul. We would get that family out. And how many others? What of Woomera? Maybe there was truth in what the interpreter had said. Did politicians really know about this family?

That was it. My involvement with refugees began on that day: 14 July 2001.

Postscript 'The boy' is Shayan Badraie, whose case became prominent after the family's story appeared on the ABC's *Four Corners* in August 2001. [*See also the stories by Junie Ong and Jacquie Everitt.*]

The ARAB and the JEW

***Judy McLallen** forms a bond with an Iraqi detainee that transcends ancient racial enmity*

Villawood I had been visiting Villawood weekly for about six months when I saw a man crouching behind the wire and staring into the visitor area. No-one visited him, so he stayed inside the detainees' compound. Dressed in a long, white gown, he looked blindly straight ahead, still as a rock.

'Who's that?' I asked.

'Ah, that's Hassan,' Kerrie [Lee] said. 'Come, I'll call him out. Help him, will you? He's got no-one and he's lost his family.'

She introduced us, and immediately he launched into a tirade of complaints that lasted, I swear, a good 20 minutes.

He's mad … Jesus, what've I done?

Suddenly he just stopped talking. I looked at him for the first time and said, 'No wonder no-one talks to you.' He blinked as if he didn't hear me, then laughed.

'Will you visit me again?'

'Yes.'

'When?'

'Next week.'

'What time?'

'Oh I don't know what time. What's with this time thing?'

I came to realise that time was the only commodity he had.

That day I stepped into a world I'd never seen before; a friendship built on dead men's shoes, a sense of protectiveness that overshot all my Jewish mothering attributes.

Why? I asked myself millions of times as I drove in the searing heat of February and then sat outside for hours in the damp darkness of August enduring that ghastly hell-hole of Villawood IDC.

Often Hassan was silent, broken. He would shuffle toward me carrying his trusty electric kettle, prepared for our tea-drinking ritual. He started the habit of making me tea when I arrived. Visitors usually bought food to share, and the simple gesture of returning the hospitality made him feel 'somehow whole again' (he said). I could make him laugh, and see a light flicker just for a minute in his eyes, and think, *Ah, he's only dead on the outside*.

Coming home from visiting him was really weird. I'd lie on the couch, staring, just like he did, not budging for hours. My real life stopped, friends simply dropped out. My family became invisible.

Hassan was difficult. 'I'm in a maze … I can't get out.'

Occasionally I saw another Hassan. This Hassan was articulate about world politics and current affairs. He could reason and interact as if we were somewhere else. His sharp observations about how we, the advocates, behaved were often funny and insightful.

He was raw and absolutely unrepentant about being intolerant of small talk. Not a good way to get out of Villawood, especially for long-termers. Getting out of Villawood depended on building a relationship with an outsider to help you, but how to talk small when you don't exist? Hassan didn't and doesn't do small talk.

It was the shop that kept him from crumbling completely. He ran it from his bedroom in the detainee compound. His window was the shopfront. I'd bring in supplies: cigarettes, phone cards, noodles, soft drinks – the stock changed depending on which nationality was being targeted in the weekly raids – one week I'd be doing Chinese noodles, the next lots of chocolate bars for the kids, who seemed to arrive in unexpected bursts. And just as suddenly they'd disappear, be deported or released, and he'd be stuck with a pile of stuff no-one wanted. I knew the little bit of money he made from this exercise he sent to his father-in-law to help him find his family for him. He knew it was futile but it kept him busy. He's a trader, after all.

'Go on, tell me a story,' I'd ask.

'History, religion, or a myth?' he'd say.

'Arab stories, your life, I want to hear about your life.'

'Baghdad …' he'd sigh, 'charcoal fish in cafes by the Tigris, sleeping on the roof because it's so hot in summer, listening to my uncle talk politics into the early morning. Moving, we were very poor, there were so many of us, we were always shifting house. I had to live with my grandmother.'

'What about your mum? What did you do after school? Tell me about your dad, how come you can sew and cook?'

He couldn't bear to say the names of his kids without tears rolling down his face. Such ordinary questions for such a dreadful place.

It came on me suddenly like a rash, a sickness that wouldn't leave me. I jumped into the abyss of blind faith. I would change his world. I had no idea how, but I felt a bubbling rage that drove me. I stopped sleeping. Six years later I still can't sleep.

I was the first Jewish person Hassan had met; I confused his belief system. We became as familiar as old school mates. It could have been me locked up in there. Sixty years ago it was me – six million of us in the ovens. I had no choice.

My journey Every hour now was devoted to Hassan, or so it felt. My family were horrified, annoyed and irritated. I changed into a person I didn't know. She was 55 but unknown to me. My annoying indecisiveness disappeared. I became self-assured, confident and totally convincing … well, that's what I showed Hassan. He tested me over and over. He still does. I won his trust.

I started small. First, the physical test: I smuggled into detention a mobile phone inside a whole cooked chicken … a huge coup for my self-esteem. I gloried in that achievement for days. Next, the brain test: I've never been good at networking, but somehow I worked my way through the minefield of asylum seeker advocate roadblocks. You know, the people who know everything and refuse to share?

I started gathering contacts and knowledge and tools that could help Hassan get out of there. Determined for Hassan to have his day in court, I spent 12 months chasing his files, which were scattered all over Australia. I called lawyers with an air of knowledge that I didn't have.

'You walk out of here with a halo of freedom,' he said to me one day. 'Don't be bullied by the gatekeepers …' he spurred me on.

Hassan doggedly called me early morning, mid-morning and late at night on his new, forbidden mobile.

'Where are you?'

'I'm on the window … I'm in the cupboard … I'm under the sheet.'

We talked for hours, me wasting time, he filling it.

'I can't bear it. I'm banging my head on the wall. The noise won't stop. They want to move me. They're talking about me, they whisper when I walk into the dining room. They make me open my mouth to put in the pill. I'm drugged, I can't walk, I can't breathe. I won't be here tomorrow. They are taking me somewhere. My stomach, the pain, my back, my legs, my knees, my chest … how much more do I have to endure?'

Another time: 'Don't worry, I won't kill myself, 'cause then it'll all have been for nothing, I came for my children. I came to save them. My life is finished but for them there's hope. Has Saddam taken them? Where are my kids?'

My phone bills were stupid. I spent months looking for pro-bono lawyers, made dozens of appointments with barristers, solicitors, and for every one who agreed to meet me 10 would refuse. 'The case is hopeless … the case has no legs … he lied.'

Hassan changes before my eyes. The raving slows down. We talk about things he could never imagine: the Holocaust, living without fear, saying what you think. I tell him things I've never told anyone before. He's funny.

'It's the Arab and the Jew,' I tease him.

He started talking to me on my radio program, the voice from detention. I interviewed others, an Afghan doctor about to be deported after being locked up for two years, a young boy who'd sewn his lips together. I became an activist.

Hassan needed an identity. He needed to improve his English, engage his brain, and I needed an activity to focus on when I visited him. He wrote – his letters were published in the daily press, 10 in total. He started a garden inside the detainee compound that gave him a new name. Now he was The Garden Man, not The Tea Man, and no longer was he Detainee 8159. Letters and seeds and bulbs and pots arrived from all over the country, from strangers who'd read about him. Hassan became quite famous!

I too was transformed. Who is the person who stands patiently in a queue in the searing heat for three hours, who sits in the icy damp winds in the visitor area in the dark, shivering, with no hope of getting warm? I lost myself.

Me, the epitome of impatience. Me, who'd rather miss out than wait. Me, who waited quietly while alien hands rifled through my bag, undoing boxes and sniffing my food, reading my diary, snooping through my belongings like a tomcat at a garbage can. Me, who can't bear to tell myself where I'm going, let alone let someone look inside my bag. It was like being strip-searched each visit. I learned to shut up.

And then his day in court came. 'I want them to hear my side of the story. I don't care if I fail, they have to hear my story.'

The day fizzled before sunrise. The barrister jumped ship at the last minute. Devastated, we licked our wounds.

'I'll die in here.' He sank into the black hole that captured him more and more frequently. Not eating, not moving, not talking for days and days.

Two more failed attempts to be released from detention through the doctrine of *habeas corpus* (unlawful detention) convinced us that seeking judicial review would not get Hassan out of detention.

'I give up.' Again he said, 'I'm dying. I will go anywhere in the world … please, Judy, get me out.'

Now this tack needed money, lots of money. I don't have money, but in my old life I made money. I've been a corporate caterer, a marketer, a teacher, a restaurateur and a mother.

'How much?' I asked him.

'$10,000.'

'OK, I'll do it.'

'Sure, like you'll get me a visa, eh?'

'Jewish promise: I'll get you out of here somehow.'

I explored the possibilities: Canada, Malta, Fiji. Dozens of international phone calls, form-fillings, Internet searches all proved dead ends. Meanwhile I shifted my focus on how to get Hassan his promised $10,000. Whatever happened, he would need money. I set up ASNA Inc. (Asylum Seekers Network Australia), a non-profit organisation, together with a couple of fellow advocates. It was and is a liaison organisation connecting people in need with appropriate professional support.

The process 'And you're from …?' receptionists would ask when I called a government agency.

'ASNA,' was my terse reply, as if they should know. No-one asked what it was.

We had one fundraising event at my place with an amazing auction, high-profile contributors, plenty of publicity, generous guests and terrific live music. I recorded and played to the audience a 'thank you' tape from Hassan. We reached his target.

The Minister for Immigration has the discretionary power to release a detainee on humanitarian grounds. This was my new goal. I gathered information for a huge s417 humanitarian submission [*see Glossary*] that covered every aspect of the Minister's guidelines that would lead to Hassan's release. Hassan was not convinced, but occasionally he would allow himself to hope.

The purpose of my visits to him now shifted ground – long sessions of forensic-style interviews took place in the corner of the visitor yard. I unravelled the knots, found the gaps, unpacked the unverified assertions, backed his claims with academic evidence, sourced country reports the government had not. I felt a surging power sweeping through me when I discovered something vital that might be the missing piece that would give him his freedom.

I was peddling the best product in the world: life. Academics, famous writers, local film and television heroes, retired judges, rabbis, priests, high-profile members of the Jewish community, media personalities and people I knew who were influential all became my target for support. I lost my fear.

I reported my every movement to Hassan. His standard response was, 'What's the result?' I knew his every movement: what he ate, how he slept, who he talked to. He couldn't conceive of what I was doing.

After about eight months the submission was ready. I then found that special politician whose compassion and tenacity helped me get Hassan out of there. Four years and three months had passed with Hassan locked inside the wire of Woomera and Villawood.

On March 11, 2003 I turned on my email and saw the following: '… the minister has granted him a PPV.' I sobbed at the noiseless screen; it was a Permanent Protection Visa. Tomorrow Hassan was going to the dentist for the first time in over two years. I called him. 'Hassan, please don't go to the dentist tomorrow.'

'Why not?'

'I want to come visit.'

'Wait till I come back.'

I said nothing.

The following day the psychologist from Villawood called me. 'Will you pick him up?'

'Of course.'

The queue felt different; I could hear my heart singing.

Hassan was a wreck. He'd returned from the dentist. The psychologist had him put in a room alone so he could tell him quietly that he was to pack his things. He believed he was to be deported. He had a migraine. 'Let me stay one more day, please,' he begged.

'No, you have two hours – get going.'

He ran to his room – it was packed like a tip, with over four years of stuff: the poignant, plaid, plastic bag filled with toys for his kids he'd bought in Bali on his way here four years ago, the now-useless stock for his shop, the throw-outs of other refugees who had been deported or released. He was a hoarder of the worst kind.

Next to me in the car, the stranger was silent. What did he see as we went into that enormous tunnel on the F5, all the way across the Harbour Bridge? His second journey was just beginning. Neither of us could speak. In the car his mobile kept ringing. Grinning, he answered it without sitting on the window or in the cupboard.

We made a film, I wrote a play. He lived with Ric, my husband, and me for six months. I started to heal; he gardened, he studied, he lost some of his fear. He'd lost himself in detention; I'd lost myself, too. Neither of us has recovered – the Arab or the Jew.

I kept my promise.

Postscript I'm now studying second-year law and Hassan is doing a bridging course for accountants at TAFE. There is so much more to tell.

No forgiveness: they *did* know and they didn't care

Early childhood professional ***Trish Highfield*** *describes her confrontation with officialdom over children in detention*

It was hot yesterday. Everyone's face was flushed after we wrote and talked about our experiences with detention. I hate that heat. I always feel that terrible heat after dealing with DIMIA in Canberra, or the Prime Minister's office, or when I leave long, angry messages on my local MP Tony Abbott's mobile.

That heat is only relieved by a swim or working in the garden. I think it's poisonous – I know it's not good for my body, but I need to go to that place to be able to lobby. You have to be on alert; ready for the sick mind games these distant bureaucrats play. They don't have to deal with the late-night phone calls from children saying farewell, afraid enough of their own despair to share it with me, leaving me powerless to protect them from themselves. Messages delivered with such chilling certainty that it robs me of sleep. My imagination distorted in the dark hours before dawn, hoping the callers will still be with us when I wake.

Memories, of an exquisitely beautiful young mother with skin like alabaster, now in the locked ward at Glenside Psychiatric Hospital. So severely wounded and left to waste in detention, she could no longer walk or speak. Memories, of waiting in the Visitors Area at Villawood IDC with Aamer, an Iraqi doctor and a detainee for too long. Supporting so many and helping me to understand the damage of detention.

I hurried to Villawood early this morning because I had heard there was a young girl alone. I grabbed coloured pencils and glitter pens, drawing pads, a bracelet, a storybook and a small, soft seal made with foam pieces, moulding to any shape you want. The seal is beautiful, with large, sorrowful eyes. I enjoyed playing with it on the train trip this morning.

I am feeling anxious about this child. Will I be able to connect with her? Does she speak English? Are the gifts, the treats (I did include some sweets) enough for a child suffering such deprivation? Will she like them? The constant dilemma. Am I trying to buy their forgiveness for the sins of my country? The cruelty. A few cheap trinkets to salve my conscience. How can any of this ease their pain? I'm stumbling along, trying to help without knowing where to find others willing to listen and to act. A hundred phone calls, but no-one will move. Not even those supposedly delegated to protect the children.

I ask Aamer to bring the child, the one who is alone. I feel sick. I want to cry for this little girl. I cannot begin to imagine how frightened she must be feeling. I want to comfort her, cuddle her – but I can't impose myself on her just because I have a need to make it alright.

Aamer saying, 'Trish, there is not just one child, there are four of them. The older boys are working in the kitchen but I will get the two young ones. The young one, she needs some warmth.'

Now I'm alone in the Visitors Area. It is cold. Aamer is coming out of the inner compound with a boy about 11 years of age and a small girl. My God, they are so small. Dr Rahmin, a community paediatrician who has examined many asylum seeker children, is right: children *don't* grow in detention. So pale, so frightened, bewildered as they walk slowly towards me. I want to weep, but I must be cheerful, welcoming. Poor little darlings, this is unbearable.

Aamer urges the girl towards me, with reassurance in her mother tongue that I am a friend. I am a stranger. With Aamer's urging, she sits next to me. I slowly reveal the contents of the bag. She is smiling, interested. But I am feeling terrible because I fear I have nothing for her young brother. I am apologising, saying I didn't know he was here. Then I remember, I have some magic glitter pens – and yes, he would like them. He is now looking through the bag and finds the toy seal, and with such tenderness he strokes his sister's cheek with the soft cuddly creature.

I reach out and touch her hand, gently stroking it. Too soon she is moving closer – I am a stranger. I rub her back and she is cuddling into me. My heart is breaking. Her need is so great – but his is greater. 'Would you like a soft animal? There are lions, tigers, giraffes.'

'I would like a tiger.' But he needs so much more.

I say goodbye. I am shaking as I wait for the officer to open the outer gate to freedom. Another visitor approaches. She had been watching me with the children. She looked as distressed as I felt. I shall never forget her words: 'What is happening in our country? You must know someone who can help. You must do something.'

But I've been trying and trying – none of them will listen.

Some months before this I had read a story buried at the back of the news pages about a riot at the Port Hedland IDPC. It revealed that two adults and two of their teenage children had been removed to prison. They were forced to leave behind two younger children – a brother and sister. On reading this, I contacted a senior officer in the Western Australian Department of Family and Community Services. At first she refused to discuss the matter with me, saying it was confidential. I persisted, ringing each day until they accepted my sincerity as an early childhood professional and member of the Social Justice in Early Childhood Group. An assurance was given that there was a care plan in place for the siblings left without family to care for them. I reminded them that the centre manager had been charged with assaulting a detainee, and I was deeply concerned about tolerance for a management culture where children were separated from parents.

These children now in Villawood were the same two who had experienced the riot-equipped officers with their batons charging through the Family Compound at Port Hedland. Their parents removed, their older brothers beaten. The little ones left to cry alone at night. They later told me that the young girl, barely six years of age, wandered each night from bed to bed seeking comfort from other detainee women, longing for the mother taken from her by Australian officials.

For years I rang Howard's office, Ruddock's office, senior staff at DIMIA, the Opposition Leader's office, confronting them with the suffering of the children. They did nothing. They can never, ever say they didn't know. They *did* know – and they didn't care!

People with pure hearts preach forgiveness. I cannot forgive, and I hope those responsible are forever haunted by the horror of what they have done.

Kassabe's story

Refugee advocate ***Frances Milne*** *chronicles the life-and-death struggle to stop a man being unlawfully deported*

I felt weary but very relieved when I got home that afternoon after being in court with the Iranians all day. Shane Prince, their barrister, had just argued successfully that the 11 Iranians subject to forcible deportation should be allowed to await the outcome of an application for leave to appeal to the full bench of the Federal Court. The Iranians, he argued, faced a real chance of torture and persecution in Iran.

It was a cold July day in 2003 and, as I climbed the stairs, I was looking forward to a cup of coffee. The phone was ringing. Do I answer that now or get a coffee? I asked myself. Some days the phone rang almost constantly. My long-suffering husband had given up answering because it was usually some desperately worried asylum seeker wanting reassurance or help. Nothing much can happen at this time on a Friday afternoon, I consoled myself as I reluctantly picked up the phone.

'It's Ali, Kassabe's (not his real name) friend. He is gone. They take him this morning. We try to ring you all day. They take him away. No-one knows what is happening.'

'Ali, how do you know he is gone? Where has he gone? Is he still in Sydney?' I tried to collect my thoughts.

'This morning Immigration took him away very early. No-one allowed to see him. He is gone. We think he was taken to airport.'

My world stopped – I could not believe what I'd heard. I checked the messages on the answering machine: all confirmed what Ali had said. My mind went blank, I started walking mindlessly backwards and forwards, backwards and forwards across the living room. My brain just ceased to function – I could feel it shrinking up into a tight ball. It was completely inconceivable that this terribly tortured man could be taken by Immigration and returned to Africa, where he would certainly be tortured to death. I was too numb to panic. Perhaps this *was* panic. I had never before in my life experienced such total shut-down. I could scarcely breathe.

Stop! Stop still and start thinking! You have to do something! You have to save this man's life! So think how you will do this right now! You always find solutions. You must find a solution right now! Forget consequences – focus on solutions.

I stopped in the middle of the room and slowly my brain uncurled and thoughts started flooding back. Where do I start? What do I do next? My first reaction was denial. It couldn't be happening. Then I suddenly remembered last week's court case. It is not possible that Kassabe is being deported because the Minister's counsel told the Federal Court last Friday that Kassabe would not be deported until his request for the Minister to review his case was decided. Shane Prince, also Kassabe's barrister, had insisted on that assurance, otherwise, he told the judge, he would seek an injunction against removal immediately.

The request to the Minister was a detailed submission containing new evidence of Kassabe's claims of torture and continuing danger. In the submission, Kassabe was requesting his case be reopened and reviewed. Death, medical and hospital certificates verified Kassabe's account. Letters from family members, one of whom directly observed the murder of his brothers by the paramilitary, were among the new evidence.

At last my mind was starting to race. I must find out what was happening. Unless I can get absolute assurances to the contrary, I must assume that Kassabe was being removed. If he was being removed he will have been flown to Perth. First, ring the airlines and find out what flights are leaving for Johannesburg today and tomorrow. Then ring Immigration and demand to know what's happening. Next, phone Shane Prince to get an injunction from the Federal Court to stop Kassabe's removal if he has not already been deported.

I was told a plane left Perth for Johannesburg at 12 noon each day. I rang the head of Immigration in Sydney and said if Kassabe is being removed, then the Minister's commitment has not been respected. The secretary took the message and very soon a senior officer in Sydney rang back and said she knew nothing about a request to the Minister, and would contact Canberra. She refused to say what was happening, which further confirmed my fears that Kassabe was in the process of being deported.

Having alerted the Sydney Immigration office, I contacted the Minister's office and tried to contact the 'removalists' responsible for deportations. My message was: this man's 48B (shorthand for the request to the Minister) had not been finally decided by the Minister. Who had the submission? The Minister's staffer in Parliament House checked on the computer, to find it had only just been entered. He hastily assured me the submission was 'in transit to Sydney', where it would be assessed on whether it met the guidelines.

'Well you had better do something,' I told him. 'Sydney is removing the man right now from Australia even though your Minister's lawyers assured the court last Friday he was safe while the Minister was considering his case.'

By now it was 5 p.m., and I was scared both the Canberra and Sydney offices would close. I was determined to keep chasing them until I knew Canberra and Sydney had made contact. More importantly, I was fairly certain that Kassabe was still in Australia, or there was no point in Immigration scurrying around to find the submission.

I then phoned Shane Prince. In spite of a very full day with the Iranian case, he said to meet him at the court at 9 a.m. on Saturday and he would seek a Federal Court injunction against Kassabe's removal. He contacted the office of the Minister's legal representative to tell him to be on stand-by for a hearing at the Federal Court on Saturday morning. Meantime, I was to try and find out whether Kassabe was still in Sydney or Perth. No-one would tell me. I assumed he was in Perth. I did not trust Sydney and Canberra to make contact with each other. So I faxed Sydney my copy of the Ministerial request I had put together for Kassabe, and rang back to ensure they were waiting by the fax to receive it. What I had not bargained on was that Sydney would immediately set an officer onto making a decision that night.

My panic returned. This could only mean Immigration was determined to refuse him protection so they could deport him tomorrow. The excuse would be that the request did not 'meet the 48B guidelines'.

This, in turn, meant that a single Immigration officer had the power to reject the request without it going to the Minister. So Kassabe's last lifeline would be snapped that night, 25 July 2003, by a single bureaucrat making a life-and-death decision.

I kept phoning the Sydney officer and found she was at dinner with friends. So what – a man's life is more important than dinner with friends. However, her mobile was turned off at 7.30 p.m. No-one answered the phone in the Sydney office. I contacted Rev. Rosemary Miller of the Uniting Church in Perth and asked her to check whether Kassabe was in Perth Detention Centre awaiting removal. That finished anything I could think to do that night except tell everyone who had left messages what I knew.

Shane Prince and I met at the Federal Court early Saturday morning, and he prepared and lodged the application for an injunction. The duty judge, Justice Branson, heard the application at around 10.30 a.m. and ordered a hearing to take place at 12.30 p.m. It was not until we were about to walk into the hearing at 12.30 p.m., Sydney time (10.30 a.m. Perth time) that we learned from the Perth refugee advocates that Kassabe was in Perth Detention Centre and in a suicidal state. It was not until we were in court that we learned from the Minister's lawyer that Kassabe was indeed being removed at noon today from Perth. In fact, it was the same lawyer who gave the Minister's commitment that there would be no removal the previous week. He apologised to the court about the lack of communication within the department.

It was increasingly tense in the court as the lawyers put their arguments why Kassabe should or should not be granted an injunction against his removal. The hands of the clock moved on and on towards noon (Perth time). The judge realised everyone's attention was fixated on one thing only – the clock. She asked, 'What time does the plane leave?'

When Justice Branson heard '12 noon', now only 30 minutes away in Perth time, she acted immediately. There was a gasp of relief throughout the court when she announced she intended to issue a Restraining Order to prevent Kassabe's removal. She said she would now order the Minister's solicitor to leave the court to take whatever action was needed to prevent the removal. He and I walked outside together. I was anxiously trying to get through to Kassabe at Perth Detention Centre to tell him he would not be removed, but, as I later learned, he had already been forced through the check-in gates by the South African escort team, who had flown in from Johannesburg the day before. The noon flight was loading passengers as the Minister's representative finally made contact with Perth Immigration. At 11.40 a.m. the injunction took effect and an utterly shocked and traumatised Kassabe was half-carried back to the detention centre.

Kassabe's own tale was even more dramatic. He'd been told to report to the Stage 2 interview room at Villawood at 8.45 a.m., Friday 25 July. There he was told he was being removed. He immediately asked to phone me. His Immigration case officer refused to let him phone.

He had a large sewing needle inside the lining of his coat in case something like this happened. He started slashing into his arms so they would get a doctor, so he could get the doctor to ring me. Instead, they sent in about eight male guards and a male nurse, who forcibly held him down, hurting his back and demanding he either take sedatives or receive an injection. He kept yelling that that this was unjust, and screaming, 'Not this one', meaning the injection. He said, 'If you inject me, I will break the needle in my body'. He later recounted: 'God then gave me the strength to fight them'. He struggled, and they could not get the needle in in spite of him being forcibly restrained. Desperation gave him an unbelievable strength. However, the legacy of his struggle is ongoing, intense neck pain.

One guard filming the whole episode said, 'I don't agree with this but it is my job'. Kassabe answered, 'This is your job – to hurt people and break a body?' That guard continued filming throughout the struggle at Villawood to the boarding of the 11 a.m. charter flight to Perth. It was a small plane, with only a pilot and one crew besides the escort staff. At Bankstown Airport Kassabe shouted, 'This is injustice! You don't understand. They will kill me at the airport in my country, just like they kill the Iranians'. But there was no-one to listen.

Kassabe was accompanied by two guards and the male nurse, who had been the most brutal. They strapped him in with a big body harness, which had handcuffs on it. These were left on him from the time he left Villawood to the time he arrived in Perth some 10 hours later. Because his wrists were bleeding, he begged for the handcuffs to be 'easy' (loose), but the guards tightened them and Kassabe was in agony. The plane stopped to refuel in Whyalla, but no-one let Kassabe go to the toilet or loosen his body harness or handcuffs.

When I talked to Kassabe on Saturday night, he had slept for several hours from sheer emotional exhaustion. He later found out he had been sedated for some days prior to the trip.

Months later I obtained under Freedom of Information legislation all Kassabe's documents held by Immigration. They contained some interesting information. For instance, the Villawood psychologist reported on Thursday, 24 July:

I have been in having daily therapeutic sessions with [Kassabe]. The current mental status reveals that he is clinically depressed with intense negative emotions. Considering this and his personality structure, it is certain that he will have behavioural outbursts when he realises he is being transferred from VIDC [Villawood Immigration Detention Centre]. When the outbursts occur he will be in a state whereby the officers will not be in a position to board and travel on a commercial flight.

If the transfer has to happen, it is highly recommended that he be transferred in a chartered flight where he can be closely monitored and not disruptive to others around him.

It is also important that once Detainee [Kassabe] arrives in Perth IDC he be constantly monitored because he will portray acute and severe tendencies to self-harm. This becomes significant because his personality will propel him to try and come out with successful harm attempts. Due to his current status I would believe that the nature of the self-harm could border on fatal if the opportunity was to present itself.

This gives credence to the report of a visitor to the Perth Detention Centre that there was a body bag in the corridor, which he surmised was in case Kassabe committed suicide on the plane.

Two years later, when the Minister allowed his case to be reviewed, Kassabe was granted a TPV. His claims had been finally accepted. However, this was not before he experienced more cruelty in Baxter where he was sent next … too awful to report in a story which is now ending well.

Three years later, Kassabe is much sought after in Perth for his fitting and turning and welding skills. The Western Australian mining industries are screaming out for such skills. At last Kassabe can hold his head high, knowing he is desperately needed by Australia. He is still terrified for the safety of his wife and son, but he is rebuilding his life with determination so he can bring them to Australia when he gets permanent protection.

There are some positive signs. The Minister seems more determined to improve the primary assessments, with the issuing of new guidelines. These would, we hope, result in refugees being recognised by the first immigration officer who assesses their case, or at least by the Refugee Review Tribunal [*see Glossary*]. It might also mean Australia is becoming more concerned to have a proper protection process, instead of using the deportations of failed asylum seekers as a warning to others that Australia does not want you here even if you are a refugee.

But I have a final dilemma. Do I allow this article to be published? I have not asked Kassabe because it will precipitate all the anguish and terror of things best forgotten, and I cannot contact him at the moment – all his phones have been disconnected. I have talked with his other supporters but they have no definitive advice. What I fear is retaliation. I console myself that no-one can identify this man because I have not revealed his country and I have changed his name and family details. Therefore, there cannot be any retaliation against him and his family by his own country.

But what about retaliation from the Australian government? He is only on a TPV. Australian officials can punish him and, indirectly, punish me by not granting him a PPV in a few years' time. Then we would have to mobilise massive support, and his mind might crack this time. Do officers still use their anonymity and power to 'get their own back'? Or has the Palmer Report [*see Timeline of events*] changed the culture of the Immigration Department? My gut feeling is that there is real change, especially at senior levels. Officers are definitely more accessible, and many more are bringing humanity to a system they secretly disagree with. Change among middle-level officers remains very patchy.

I do not know the answers. But if I continue to live in the shadows of this most evil system of unjust imprisonment and wrong decisions, I become party to that evil. I love my country and I know what has happened and what is happening to asylum seekers. In the end I hear one refugee cry above all others, 'My country destroys the body but Australia destroys the mind'.

MORNING COURAGE

Librarian and teacher* Helen Tait *reflects on life in detention after visits to Woomera and Curtin

This morning
when I walked
early
in the exuberance of new green
and the gaiety of new spring
I was transfixed for a moment
by a tiny poppy
in a tiny gap
in the pavement
flowering red
It is hard to receive
mail from prison
It is hard when words
wrung red from prison
run the grief
from the cracks
of mental breakdown

WHAT KIND OF ASYLUM?

Child and adolescent psychiatrist* Michael Dudley *condemns the callousness that sent a mother to the brink of suicide

The police brought me to the coast. I have nothing to do just yet, loitering, crunching my boots on gravel, looking over the blue straits to Cook's Landing, where the *Endeavour* beached. Bare Island, a high, cloudless day and deep blue light, light of my eyes, where else but Australia.

They bundled me out of my office like a fugitive. She'd bolted, I'd called them, and now they'd found her rocking on a clifftop, in flight from her land but not yet safe from her battles, refugee without refuge, pursued by the Furies. And here, while I'm waiting in the stark light, is the ABC on the police phone, wanting to talk about Virginia and daughter Naomi, locked in Villawood for the three years since her birth [*see Timeline of events*]. No place like home and no place for you. Today is her birthday.

The small mother had shouted, so they put her in solitary. When other detainees protested about their removal, she spoke to media from the rooftops. They carted her off to an asylum, but she was angry, not mentally ill, and this was no true asylum but a prison. Naomi disappeared, maybe fostered, a whole week missing. How can they tear the child from her mother? Everyone saw, no-one intervened. Since then, Naomi turned from laughter to tear-soaked and listless, not consolable even in her mother's arms. We are the ones shouting now, into the light against the sea breeze, in sight of the woman standing there on the clifftop. This has to stop, no-one has listened. They must listen now.

In the dying light, the police have coaxed the woman back from the edge. They take her to a true asylum. She will square off with her demons, give the sop to her savage god. Another call comes through. The department has backed down, the letter campaign and the story of the third birthday in jail have worked. They promise papers, visas. The tide seems to be changing on the straits. No place like home and a place for you. *Asylum Granted.* A moment of sweetness in the sea breeze.

But what kind of asylum, and for how long?

RIMANA

Physician* Michael Douglas *describes the mutual benefits that flow when a regional community embraces refugees

Rimana's voice carries her soul. As she speaks, one can hear the anguish and the strength she has drawn on throughout her short life.

She shares the terror of the night when, just 12 years old, gunshots echoed around her village. She saw her younger sister succumb to a gunshot wound. She ran into the darkness, clasping the hand of her five-year-old brother. She was separated from her mother and other siblings. She walked through days, through countries, through heat, through war, through fear. After three years, she stopped, with a cohort of thousands, in Kakuma [*refugee camp in Kenya*]. Her life in the camp was arduous, and she lived in constant fear of rape and starvation. It is there that she spent her next 12 years. As her departure from the vast refugee camp was announced, another brother, whom she had assumed to be dead, wondered, 'Could this be our Rimana, my sister?' Her mother and brothers furtively tried to find her, but their first contact came as Rimana was stepping onto the plane bound for Australia.

Rimana has become the face of a refugee – demythologising any caricature that may have crept into our national psyche. She has revealed the pain and sadness, and the reciprocal determination and strength that emerge with the name 'resilience'.

Her story continues to unfold. She learnt the painful reality of her mother's journey, mutilated in that night of war. As if to drive home the cruelty, Rimana and her mother lived in the same refugee camp for those 12 years – never knowing the other was there. Rimana now seeks desperately to bring her mother to join her, but these attempts have been unsuccessful. More than anything, this has eroded her heart.

It has been extraordinary and gratifying to observe how a small endeavour to assist a handful of refugee families has been embraced by the wider community of a regional locality. And as the community, young and old and of all persuasions, has mobilised in response to their need, a commitment has grown to ensure their welfare is nurtured. This commitment has not been an isolated phenomenon. Services clubs offer support; business leaders provide fundraising and employment opportunities; schools seek to involve refugees in their social justice programs; and many hundreds of people continue to involve themselves in small ways to provide assistance at a one-on-one level – helping with appointments, driving lessons, support schooling, or simply having time together. Service organisations, both government and non-government, have extended themselves to reach that need, chiefly driven by compassionate champions within these agencies.

Rimana is testimony that the greatest ambassadors for the refugee program are the refugees themselves. It is the refugees that build the momentum of community support, who stand as tangible evidence that vast numbers of people in the world – people with the same hopes and disappointments, the same loves and hurts, dislocated from home and family – seek stability and a future. It is the refugee who will transform the landscape of Australian consciousness, and convert it to a greater compassion. Such influence, in at least some communities, has rightly placed refugee settlement as a humanitarian concern that transcends political or geographical bias.

The lines have become distinctly grey in assessing who the real beneficiaries of settlement are. No longer is it simply the case that we, with plenty, will help you, with so much need. It is you who enrich us with your humility and grace, with your culture and your ambition; it is you who teach us of hope and strength. We sought to reach out to the needy, and yet it is us, in our comfort, who have equally benefited from that reaching.

Married to a refugee advocate: the worst-paid job in the world

*Long-suffering husband **Frank Hetherton** learns to accept refugees into his life and his home*

I am married, for my sins, to Margaret, a refugee advocate and supporter of most other deserving causes that put their hand up. Margaret was reared a Catholic, as I was, and has been unable to shed the moral imperatives that that uncomfortable background burdened us with.

Christ Almighty! Not another refugee, you might say. Even so, we follow Christ, although he doesn't look all that Almighty any more as I survey the refugee scene.

Bruno Bruno was out to please everybody in sight and particularly me, the husband and titular head honcho – my wife being his advocate for refugee sanctuary in Australia.

He bounced up to me one sunny morning in a Balmain park. 'You will be my Australian father, Frank,' Bruno said enthusiastically, 'I will call you "Dad".'

That settled it for Bruno, and who was I, a 70-something-year-old, blue-eyed Celt, to deny paternity to a 30-year-old Nepalese refugee?

'I can do many things for you,' he said, casting an eye over the neglected foliage that passed for our garden – 'for nothing,' he added emphatically.

The 'for nothing' bit caught the ear of a nearby contractor who was redoing the park for the local council. He promptly befriended Bruno – on terms and conditions, I suspected, heavily favouring the contractor. But c'est la vie for refugee seekers in Australia.

Bruno stayed with us for a few weeks, sometimes making it home at night, sometimes getting stranded on ferries or trains that had finished for the night, but always bobbing up the next day, trying to make a life. He was a nice man, puppy-like in his willingness to please. Probably getting exploited, stranded in Australia, unable to go back to his own country but likely to be deported anyway. Very sad, very depressing.

We have so much. Bruno had a lot, too – of uncertainty and fear, and a desperate energy.

Rajab's lament 'If I am killed, no-one will ask who is killed and why.'

So said Rajab to Philip Glendinning, a social researcher. Glendinning had gone to Pakistan to discover the fate of refugees that the Australian government had deported back to their home country. Rajab fled Afghanistan at the age of 20, when his brother was murdered – Rajab was next on the list, caught up in murderous tribal conflicts. The infamous MV *Tampa* rescued Rajab, briefly, only to see him shipped off to Nauru, the island speck on the equator, a hell-hole of heat and depression. He told us his young friend died on Nauru.

Rajab was deported back to Afghanistan. By that time his family had fled Afghanistan to nobody knew where. Glendinning found Rajab in a miserable, dangerous squat, living day to day from occasional labouring wages, most of which he used to pay off the police. He is without papers, and is likely to be denounced. Rajab's only 'crime' is his minority religion, his only asset and his greatest liability. He said it is only a matter of time before he is killed.

'She died, in pain, at the hands of "persons unknown"' (hospital report) Maddy came to the calm waters of Johnston Bay, East Balmain from strife-torn Africa in 2000 – to the children playing on the swings in Peacock Point Park, overlooked by world-class restaurants filled with Sydney's beautiful people.

Maddy, a striking woman, struggles out of the taxi and hobbles to the front door of a stylish Glen Murcutt-designed house on the Point. She hobbles because a bomb thrown into her African home mangled her foot – the best thing that could have happened to her, as it turned out. Mangled feet don't matter that much in a swimming pool, and Maddy was a champion swimmer – good enough to swim well in Sydney's 2000 Paralympics.

The Olympics arrived as a lifeline for Maddy. She had to escape her homeland. She had fallen foul of the repressive regime when she refused to do their dirty work. They came looking for her, and when that failed they took her mother instead. Her mother was tortured. She didn't die of sleep deprivation, the kind of torture okayed by our Immigration Department. But she did die, of injuries inflicted '... by persons unknown', according to the Congolese hospital death certificate. One thing leads to another, doesn't it?

Five years later, Maddy is still not an Australian citizen, but she is alive, and lives in hope.

The Bridge for Asylum Seekers Foundation takes Maddy under their wing, orchestrated by Frances Milne [*see her and Virginia Walker's stories*] through the Balmain Uniting Church. Maddy takes up temporary residence with us, with enthusiasm. She says to me, one day, 'I'm going to call you "Dad" from now on. I'd like that, wouldn't you?'

It seemed like a good idea at the time. At other times, occasional visitors looked a bit startled: a black, 20-year-old beauty fathered by yours truly.

Maddy and her mentors got on with the exhausting, lengthy, refugee application process – two steps forward, one step back, for years on end. She got on with her precarious life in Australia with courage and good humour – a remarkable woman – with her ultimate ambition to become a nurse. Pro-bono medicos used their best skills to repair her mangled foot, followed by a long and painful convalescence.

But she made friends, she did voluntary work, her refugee application seemed to be progressing. We all looked forward to Maddy getting the protection and security of Australian citizenship.

And then the blow falls. I heard a cry, a heavy thud and rushed downstairs. Maddy had collapsed on the floor. Her breath came in short punctuated gasps, her eyes rolled up, the whites showing. She was in deep shock.

In her left hand, a crumpled letter from the Immigration Department. Instead of a letter of acceptance, Maddy had got a rejection from the department, and faced possible deportation back to Africa, back to the secret police that had murdered her mother, to the bombing that had mangled her foot. It was too much – after five years of work, uncertainty and hope it was more than body and soul could take. She closed down to unconsciousness.

The ambulance came – they resuscitated her and took her to hospital, to make her fit enough to be deported to Africa.

What hope for Maddy? What had gone wrong? Why the refusal? Who was doing this to Maddy? After five years! The department said they didn't know whether the sworn affidavits about Maddy from well-known African lawyers were genuine. They didn't bother to check, they just consigned her back to Africa. To what? To death? They didn't care; not their problem.

A plea was sent to the new Minister, Amanda Vanstone, from a prominent Liberal parliamentarian and others restating the obvious merits of Maddy's case. The department couldn't admit a mistake, so they gave Maddy an employment visa, not a refugee visa. Not at all generous: Maddy is not eligible for social services or for HECS, so she can study nursing only if she pays the large fees upfront. And I have to guarantee the Commonwealth of Australia against any Centrelink costs Maddy may incur for two years. How flattering! I'll probably get a mention in the Federal Budget budget papers next year. Or be kept awake by an 'operative' in case I have some vile secrets to reveal.

But Maddy is alive and kicking and looking forward to an improving future in Australia, which will be improved by her presence here. The people who wanted to deport her should be sent to Africa, to the lawyers who sent the statutory declarations they dismissed so lightly and callously, to give them some understanding of the consequences of their thoughtless actions.

My pleasure and honour always

*Researcher and refugee advocate **Sue Hoffmann** shares the highs and lows of helping the families of the SIEVX tragedy*

I spent October 2005 in Damascus, with my dear friend Mohammad. He'd arrived in Australia in November 1999, spent a year in immigration detention, then five years with a Temporary Protection Visa. He'd finally been granted a Permanent Protection Visa, which allowed him to travel overseas and return to Australia. His mother and brothers made their way from Iraq to Syria to see him for the first time in over six years … and I was invited to stay with them.

When he'd first asked me many months before, I assumed it was one of those generous offers people make spontaneously but later regret. So

I didn't give it much credence or thought. Until he got his Permanent Visa.

'I will go in September. When you will come?'

'Are you sure, you really mean it? You want me to come to Syria?'

'Of course, Sue. Why you not believe me?'

So I booked my flight, to arrive in Damascus a few weeks after him.

Among many powerful and moving experiences over more than five years of involvement with refugees and asylum seekers, the trip to Syria was a highlight for me. Twenty minutes after leaving the airport, we entered a *souk* (a market) with hundreds of small shops and stalls, where people and cars jostled for space in the narrow streets. I so wanted to get out of the taxi and walk, experience it for real.

'Can we come back here and explore?'

I didn't realise then that here, in the heart of the Shia district of Damascus, where thousands of Iraqi refugees live, was where I'd be staying for the next three weeks and would come to know parts of it well.

I loved the sights and smells and mountains and history of Syria, the overwhelming beauty of the mosques – one in particular, a few minutes' walk from the flat. With its golden dome dominating the skyline, and intricate mosaics made from predominantly blue tiles, it was at its best after the sun went down, backlit against the night sky.

Away from the tourist haunts, I was the only Western woman, the only woman without a *hijab* (head covering). It didn't matter. When, as a family group – Mohammad, his brothers, his mother and myself – we visited shrines and mosques, I would don a *hijab*. The brothers struck up conversations with other Iraqis, always introducing me, including me, their guest from Australia. Mohammad would translate: 'This family comes from Basra' – or Najaf, or Nazariyah, or Baghdad, all seeking safety in Syria from the violence in their homeland. I could do little more than smile and say, '*Salaam Alekhum*'. It seemed to be enough.

At one family gathering, the grown-ups were talking and the children playing. Unable to join in the conversation, I played with the kids. I got on all fours and took them for rides. They picked the large, pink, scented roses from the garden and adorned me with them. Mohammad told me, as he had many times before, how glad he was that I was there with his family, how much he appreciated all I had done for him. For my part, I feel I have done very little beyond make myself available to him when he needed to talk, and extending friendship to this sensitive, intelligent and complex man who has suffered perhaps the most profound of losses: the death of his beloved wife and children, who drowned when the asylum-seeker boat, the SIEVX, sank [*see Timeline of events*].

I first met Mohammad when I worked for a refugee support agency in Perth, and maintained sporadic contact with him and other Perth-based men who had also lost their wives and children. Whenever I heard of events connected with SIEVX, I let them know. I found this quite hard, as I never really knew what to say. What do you say to someone whose entire family has died? But I felt it was important they knew when something was happening so they were able to choose whether to be there or not. Three of us went to Sydney in late 2004 for a SIEVX memorial art exhibition, organised by Steve Biddulph and others based in Tasmania [*see Steve Biddulph's story*]. Mohammad and I sat next to each other on the plane journey and talked non-stop. That marked the real beginning of our friendship. We had a lot in common – how we thought, approached life, dealt with problems. We had our disagreements, too – not surprising given the difference in our ages, gender, religion, background. It all makes for fascinating conversations and discussions. Sometimes we talked about normal things. But the uncertainty of his TPV cast a shadow, and SIEVX was never far away. Few people carry burdens of such magnitude.

In April of 2005, Marg Hutton of the sievx.com website contacted me. Did I know that the trial of Khaleed Daoed, charged with people-smuggling in connection with SIEVX, was to start in Brisbane in a few weeks' time? I knew immediately the SIEVX next-of-kin had to be given the opportunity to be there. I phoned Mohammad. He said later it was as if an explosion went off in his head – he wanted to go. I started making arrangements, fundraising through refugee networks to cover costs for three Perth-based Iraqi men and myself; it was inconceivable they could go without support. I posted a request on Brisbane lists for accommodation. The response was fantastic – so many offers of places to stay, but once I heard Deborah's voice, the choice was made. I don't know how I would have coped without her and her husband Richard, who opened their home and their hearts to four strangers. Some mornings, before leaving for the court, the men would bring out the photos of their dead children to show me.

Shortly after arriving in Brisbane, an ABC reporter rang, wanting to interview me; the men travelling from Perth for the trial had captured the interest of the media. I made reference to the unanswered questions surrounding the sinking of SIEVX. He asked me what they were, so I told him.

'You can't say that!' he said.

I got the impression he knew very little about it. In court the next day before the jury came in, defence counsel expressed concern at the publicity surrounding the case. He wanted to play to the court the ABC interview with Sue Hoffmann that had aired that morning on 'AM' as an example. Not a lot throws me. That did. I was appalled, dumbstruck, shocked. I don't know if there is a word to describe how I felt at that particular moment. I was there to observe, now my name's mentioned in court. What if they aborted the trial because of something I said? Unlikely, as I'd been briefed about this, plus the reporter had said he'd get the ABC legal people to check his story before going to air. But … for the few minutes it was playing, and my voice – with my funny accent and slight lisp (which others can't hear, they tell me, but I can) – was all that could be heard in the courtroom, I wanted to sink through the floor, be anywhere but there. Yet I recall a part of me remained detached enough to be impressed with the quality of the sound system. The moment passed, the judge merely agreeing to address the jury about the publicity surrounding the trial.

I'm sure it helped the survivor-witnesses – Iraqis flown in from Norway, Finland, New Zealand by the Australian Federal Police – to see Arab faces in the public gallery as they gave evidence. This was how the Perth men learnt the details of the journeys undertaken by their wives and children before they met their deaths in the seas between Indonesia and Christmas Island.

The period of the trial was intense and painful: two of the witnesses collapsed in court and were hospitalised. A journalist cried. The Iraqis wanted justice for the deaths of 353 people, but the trial didn't address that. In the café opposite the courthouse, I drank coffee with three different men on three different days, each of whom told me their story and showed me pictures of their families as we cried into our coffees. Literally – tears dripped into our cappuccinos.

The first day of the trial, we'd run the gauntlet of a media pack keen to get footage of Iraqi survivors, the bereaved. Back at Richard and Deborah's that evening, we surfed the TV stations to watch ourselves. 'I/you look fat/short/tall/untidy/ugly …' – it was a light-hearted reprieve from the emotional roller-coaster of those few weeks. I should say, too, the men were fantastic. In appreciation of the work I'd done in arranging the trip, they'd decided they would do all the shopping and cooking. Good cooks, all of them. In the third week, Mohammad pointed out that I hadn't once made tea or coffee for anyone.

'No,' said I. 'That can't be true.' But when I thought about it, it was. They'd spoilt me rotten.

During the trial, I took copious notes and typed them up in the evenings, emailing them to various people around the country. The trial lasted almost four weeks, and I was at the court every day. Some days, the area outside the courtroom, between the witnesses, interpreters and the Perth men, was full of Iraqis. One of the barristers asked me to try and keep my friends away from the witnesses. Impossible. It was only polite that they introduced themselves to each other. Plus, the survivors knew the families of the next-of-kin. They were able to describe how they died – the little boy who was hit on the head by a piece of wood as the boat broke up, already unconscious before he went in the water …

The men returned to Perth at different times, but all before the verdict came in. It took a couple of days for the jury to reach a decision, and for this high-profile case the public gallery was packed. I sat next to a woman I hadn't seen in the courtroom before; we started talking.

She said her friend was clerk to the court or assisted the judge, or something, and had told her how upsetting, how awful this case was. The court proceedings seem so sterile, I'm glad her friend was touched by them. The tragic outcome of SIEVX had barely been acknowledged during the trial. Whenever witnesses started to talk about the 353 dead, as some did, they were shut up.

The jury was back: Daoed was found guilty of assisting in bringing people illegally to Australia on SIEVX.

My constant presence at the trial and connection to the Iraqis gave me credibility with the journalists. As we left the courtroom, one of the reporters said, 'We'll wait for you downstairs'. Then, as an afterthought, 'Is that okay?' With the Iraqis gone, I was the obvious person for them to interview.

I made a couple of phone calls to pass on the verdict and left the building to where the journalists were massing. I knew this would happen. This isn't something I'm used to, by any means, but I accepted the inevitability and necessity of it. Any chance to get the message across. Plus, I had a written statement from Mohammad to read out.

That was an odd time for me. It was like living in a bubble, those few weeks – a harrowing, emotional, intensely sad bubble. I don't believe I've ever cried so much.

It's now October 2006. In recent weeks, much of my free time has been spent in preparation for another momentous occasion in the SIEVX story, this time a memorial ceremony in Canberra, marking the fifth anniversary of the sinking. It's a project of mammoth proportions and vision, involving thousands of people across Australia, from Christmas Island to Tasmania, and years in the making. My role in this is relatively small, coordinating the making of 22 poles to remember the relatives of the three Perth men, Mohammad being one. He and his brother-in-law lost 14 family members. We've got 15 pine logs 1.8 metres long, and seven 2.4-metre logs. The big ones are for the adults, the small ones for the children. They're heavy. Each pole gets three coats of white paint. For the decorated bands near the top of the poles, the men have chosen a simple but effective design: the name of their loved one in Arabic, with a border depicting the symbol seen everywhere in Islamic art, the eight-pointed star. Mohammad has written each name in Arabic script. Once printed, we painstakingly cut around the letters with a blade to make stencils, using a similar technique for the borders. Using the stencils, we spray-paint each name onto a pole. The whole exercise takes many hours, spread over a number of weeks. It takes an emotional toll on the men. The Arabic writing to me is just Arabic writing, but to them it's the names of their wife, their child, their brother, and the pole is the nearest they'll get to a headstone. The final touch: two metal plaques per pole, bearing in English the name of the person the pole represents and the name of the people who made it:

'In loving memory of the beloved family of …'

It's a difficult project to coordinate, stressful; emotions are raw and the logistics are challenging. But we do the job, and the poles are decorated and on their way to Canberra to be erected with hundreds of others on the shores of Lake Burley Griffin to mark the fifth anniversary of the sinking. I'm relieved the poles have left Perth.

A week later and we're back from Canberra. It was a fantastic weekend, very sad at times, certainly moving, powerful and utterly inspirational. I know the SIEVX story will never die now; that's important to me.

The ceremony was very special. Picture a grassy slope leading down to a large lake, with over 250 poles laid on the ground a metre apart, wending their way down to the water's edge. All the poles are white with a deep band of decoration, most in bright colours. Each pole represents a person who died, but we don't know all the names, so the plaques for some read 'Name unknown'. The poles in the centre have been arranged in two arcs to form the shape of the SIEVX boat. One arc is made up of 25 poles named for the loved ones of next-of-kin present at the ceremony. Our group in Perth have made 22 of these. With their black on white design, they stand out. I am so pleased we made them.

Sometimes, in this SIEVX journey, I'm aware of a sense of rightness about what we've done, and this is one of those times. This is where we should be, with these poles as the centrepiece of the occasion, surrounded by hundreds of people who have come to remember and honour the dead of SIEVX.

A drumbeat starts. A procession of 500 people walks slowly to take up positions next to poles, until there are two people standing by each one. It takes some time, maybe 20 minutes. Only the arc of 25 is left unattended. The drumbeat stops. Silence. Then a drum roll. The 500 lift the poles so they're upright. They wait. The drumbeat starts up again. The Iraqi men who lost wives and children walk to the 25 poles. They take their place by a pole named for one of their loved ones. Other people make their way forward until there are now two people at each of the 25 poles. The drumbeat stops, then a pause, then a drum roll. The final 25 poles are raised.

The poles are held upright as a choir sings, their voices and the song hitting just the right note. Time is suspended. Then the music stops. A brief pause, another drumroll and the poles are gently set down on the

ground. The dead of SIEVX have been honoured, remembered, laid to rest. Even as I write this, the tears well up.

I've been immersed in the SIEVX story for many years. It's taken me to Sydney, Brisbane, Damascus and Canberra. I've written about it, spoken about it, researched it, met and cried with survivors and next-of-kin. Why do I do it? How can I not? There've been times in the last few years when I've thought, if I don't do this - write this letter, make this comment, arrange this event, contact this person - no-one else in the *entire world* will. Not because I'm clever, or special, but simply that at this point in time, with regard to this particular issue, I'm the only person with the connections, the knowledge, the understanding. I've had to follow my instincts and intuition many times as to the best course of action to take. My life has been almost totally submerged in the world of refugees and asylum seekers for the last five years, and particularly SIEVX. My friends are either refugees or advocates. So many other causes, why this one? My own family history, which is full of refugees, no doubt contributes, as does a sense of sameness and compatibility with those from the Middle East. I can't abide the inherent cruelty and injustice of a system that impacts on those who've already suffered greatly. But for all the tears, drama, pain, grief along the way - and there's been plenty of those - I don't have an iota of regret about the direction my life has taken.

My friendship with Mohammad continues as strongly as ever. He sent me this text message after we got back from Canberra:

'Thank u very much great SUE THANK U THANK U THANK U MANY EVEN IT'S NOT ENOUGH from MOHAMMAD xxx take care.'

I replied: 'Dear Mohammad. It is my pleasure and honour always x.'

Just about sums it up.

HELL has no holidays

Retired social researcher ***Libby Turnock*** *laments that release from detention did not end one family's ongoing struggle*

[*Names have been changed to protect identities.*]

'Can you come and see me?'

Mariam's invitation was all I'd been waiting for: within minutes I was on the Internet, booking my flight to Adelaide. Mariam, husband Danush and 13-year-old son Nouri had been released from Baxter a few days before, and I was anxious to personally welcome them to the outside.

Some kind people from a state welfare agency had organised for them to stay in a holiday house at the beach, facing the Strand. Knowing that Mariam's family had experienced a particularly toxic time in detention, they wanted to give them a treat – a holiday by the sea. I hoped the family would be able to appreciate this 'time out' and allow the healing to begin.

Yet from personal observation, when you go on holiday, you take yourself with you, including the emotional baggage: if something in your life is seriously wrong, it's hard to get in the holiday mood. I've enjoyed my own holidays less since becoming aware of this family's suffering. I've struggled with feelings of contempt for myself as I escaped to places of peace and beauty while Mariam languished in the hell-hole that was Baxter. How guilty I felt telling her I wouldn't be around for a few weeks! I avoided using the word 'holiday', and hoped there would be no emergency while I was away.

Now, at last, it was Mariam's family's chance for a 'holiday'. 'The house is very nice – and *big*!' Mariam exclaimed over the phone. 'There are three bedrooms – you can come and stay with us.' But she added that the three of them were having trouble sleeping in the strange new surroundings, and that her husband was still to settle down after the trauma of the move. (DIMA considered the family too disturbed to travel by bus, and had arranged for a charter plane to fly them from Port Augusta. I suspect DIMA wished to avoid a public spectacle.)

I thanked Mariam for her kind offer of a bed, but later rang back to say I'd found accommodation nearby. From my 18-month friendship with Mariam, I knew privacy was an integral part of the family's need for security. Many times during their three years in detention, when they felt most threatened, they would simply close the door on the rest of the world and refuse to talk to anyone - guards, fellow detainees or friends outside - and this isolation sometimes lasted many weeks. Heaven knows what mental torments they experienced during such times; none of us on the outside will ever know.

There was also some cowardice in my decision not to stay with the family. I had never met Danush or Nouri, but knew that both were suffering serious mental illness. Mariam, too, was unstable. By contrast, witnesses from their early days in Woomera have described Danush as 'the life of the party' and Nouri as a bright, well-behaved boy with a thirst for learning. Then, Mariam had the energy and magnanimity to care for unaccompanied minors as well as her own family. In less than two years, all three had changed beyond recognition. Danush had twice hanged himself and was now an almost-catatonic wreck of a man who rarely left his room (although sometimes he wandered out, naked and unfocussed, into the communal part of the detention centre compound). Nouri also self-harmed (cutting his arm many times and emulating his father's hanging attempts) while becoming angry and hostile towards everyone outside his family. The family unit that arrived in Australia in April 2001 was a happy one - close, but not unnaturally so. Now the family was pathologically inward-looking, feeding off each others' various psychoses. With no first-hand experience of people with mental illness, I was unsure how to best relate to them, and thought I would sleep easier at arm's length.

During my flight over, I tried to imagine what I would find. I'd met Mariam face to face only once, a year earlier, in the bleak Visitors Centre in Baxter. All our other communication - and there was a great deal of it - had been by phone and letter. I recalled her sorrowful young face, framed by a brown scarf. She had worn no make-up and needed none to highlight those dark, expressive eyes. Would she have changed since that meeting? What would Danush and Nouri be like?

Rosemary, convenor of the family's Circle of Friends support group in Adelaide [*see Resources*], met me at the airport and kindly lent me a car for the three days of my visit. None of the Friends had seen the family since their release: they were waiting for an invitation to visit, as I had been. Mariam had difficulty understanding the purpose and motivation of the Circle of Friends, and it disappointed all of us that she so often misinterpreted our best intentions. Cruel treatment at the hands of the Department of Immigration and guards at both Woomera and Baxter meant she trusted no-one. We understood this, but it was still disappointing when some offers of help and friendship were suspected by Mariam as being part of a DIMA plot. Resistance became her primary method of survival, even when this was counterproductive.

Over the time of their detention, the family's story became known and their plight attracted a wide circle of sympathisers. Even the late Steve Irwin sent Nouri two of his books after I wrote to tell him about the boy, including the fact that he was one of Steve's biggest fans. I was but one of many people committed to trying to get the family, by whatever means, out of the environment that was destroying them. Nothing worked, not the Human Rights and Equal Opportunity Commission's (HREOC's) hearings into children in detention in December 2002, where a number of health professionals painted a graphic picture of the family's mental health and urged their immediate release; not personal representations to the Minister by the Human Rights Commissioner or by Amnesty International; not even reports from DIMA's own detention centre staff. All were ignored. A dark cloud of hopelessness was enveloping me.

The transcript of the HREOC hearings made such shocking reading that I hardly slept for the following six months. I was already writing to Mariam, but this transcript really brought home to me the depths of the family's suffering and the evil of those running DIMA. Obsessed by the injustice of the situation, I felt compelled to *do* something. In desperation, I considered shaving my head and staging a one-woman sit-in outside my local Federal Member of Parliament's office (but decided against it, as it was so out of character I believed it would just lead to embarrassment all around). But unlike Mariam and family, at least I was free, with a sane and supportive husband and good friends. I organised letter-writing campaigns, visited my MP a number of times, and encouraged others to do likewise. Letters lobbying the Minister for Immigration were sent from every state in Australia. Nothing seemed to penetrate or even dent the callous carapace of DIMA. All there were deaf – wilfully deaf – to all entreaties, and allowed the family's season in hell to continue for a further 18 months after those hearings.

One of the greatest frustrations experienced by the family's supporters was Mariam's refusal to accept a Bridging Visa, holding out instead for a Protection Visa. This meant she probably stayed in detention six months longer than she needed to – meaning additional damage to the family's mental health and chances for recovery. She believed her family's survival depended on the strength of her will, and her judgement was often warped by this belief. In the end, we had to accept that it was her decision, and that we needed to continue to support her, despite her difficult behaviour, which included regularly hanging up on friends – occasionally after a stream of abuse.

That they were finally out was an enormous relief for everyone. It was a moment of great emotion when I stepped inside the door of the house and hugged my friend Mariam. Inside the house she wore no head covering, and thick, dark hair cascaded over her shoulders. I thought she looked stunning. Now she was smiling, her large eyes sparkling, reflecting a kaleidoscope of emotions. We talked and talked. She laughed at jokes and took obvious pleasure in cooking me an Iranian meal, now that she was free to do so. But there were still tears, especially when her attention turned to Danush and Nouri – tears full of love and grief.

Danush did not leave the house; he spent almost all his time in bed. He couldn't comprehend that he was no longer in prison. While I was present he appeared only once, passing by in the hall. Mariam called to him and introduced us, but he paused only briefly, turned towards us without expression, then continued on his way. My impression was of a shuffling ghost of a man, bearded, thin and very pale. Someone who met Danush before he became ill described him as 'drop-dead gorgeous, with movie-star looks'. Then, he and Mariam must have made a handsome couple indeed.

Of course I was interested to get to know Nouri, with whom I'd spoken a number of times on the phone from Baxter (and been struck by his intelligence and adult conversation). In appearance, Nouri was in much better shape than his poor father. With his mother's features, Nouri would soon grow into a good-looking young man. However, the emotional damage was obvious after a short time in his company. He was generally surly and negative. Since, at 13, he was in the throes of adolescence, this was hardly surprising, but in Nouri there was another layer of turmoil beyond that normal teenage angst. I didn't witness the rages that worried Mariam so much, but I did see glimpses of the underlying anger. He was reluctant to think well of anyone. Although polite most of the time, he was also inclined to express his opinions very strongly. I felt it was going to be difficult for him to make friends his own age, as in many ways he had leapt into adulthood without going through the normal experiences of late childhood.

Mariam and I were both pleased that Nouri was quite willing to come out with me, leaving her to attend to Danush. On the second afternoon of my visit, we set out together to walk along the seafront. I thought he might like to see where I was staying, a distance of a bit over a kilometre. This June day in 2004 was windy and overcast, the white-capped water grey and forbidding. Nouri avoided looking at the sea, saying that it reminded him of the scary time on the boat from Indonesia to Ashmore Reef. However, despite this unfortunate reminder, as we walked along in the rising wind, he suddenly blurted out, 'I'm happy – I think I was bored!'. This was one of the few times I heard him say something spontaneously upbeat. It gladdened my heart.

Mariam had once described to me some of her family holidays in Iran: a week or two in a mountain resort, all expenses paid by the oil company where both worked (Danush as an engineer, Mariam as secretary to the manager). By contrast, the caravan park must have appeared rather humble to Nouri, but all he said was that the prefab 'cabins' reminded him of Woomera. (I thought, 'Thus far, unfortunate associations have been evoked on this walk!') I wondered if the inside of my little cabin also reminded him of those demountables in the desert, above which desperate men climbed into razor wire to flay their flesh. But I refrained from asking. At least here, unlike Baxter, there were windows looking out onto greenery and the horizon.

As we sat and chatted in the cabin, once again I was surprised by Nouri's general knowledge, especially given the fact that he had had almost no schooling since he was 10 (he was the only child too emotionally unstable to attend school outside Baxter). Not many 13-year-olds would choose to discuss local and international current affairs, as he did with me, and say things like: 'I like your line of politics – not many Australians think like you.'

As soon as we began to retrace our steps, it started to rain. Not heavy rain, but fine, wind-driven needles in our faces. We half-ran, half-walked, and neither of us minded getting wet (although when we got back Mariam fussed around with a hair dryer to make sure we dried off quickly). It was a relief to see that Nouri could run without apparent effort, as I knew that he'd had virtually no exercise for three years.

Nouri seemed to avoid eye contact, but when he did look at me I noticed that one eye appeared to be slightly 'turned' and he rubbed it frequently. Mariam explained that this eye had been injured when Nouri (aged 12 at the time) was punched by a guard during the forced transfer to Baxter. It had been January 2003, and the family were daring to hope that after the revelations of the HREOC hearings they might finally be allowed out of hell, or at least into some less punitive form of detention. Instead, they told me, they were awoken before dawn, manacled, forbidden to dress, beaten and forced into a van for transport to Baxter. I was shocked to see marks on a child's wrists consistent with the use of handcuffs.

Witnessing her husband and protector retreat from her into his own purgatory must have been agony for Mariam, but watching her beloved son descend into his own crazy, dysfunctional world must have been even more heartbreaking. As mothers, we are compelled to protect our offspring from harm. The closest I've come to experiencing anything like her anguish was one sleepless night when my daughter, Anna, then aged nine, started hallucinating. She 'saw' spiders hatching out from the sleeves of her pyjamas. Already afraid of spiders, the sight of them crawling all over her body struck such terror in her that she screamed all night. To her, the spiders were real. I spent the whole night trying to calm her while her father firmly held the cuffs of her pyjamas to prevent more 'hatchings'. I was terrified that my little girl was losing her sanity.

In our case, the drama ended the next day, when medication for a cold was suspected and discontinued. But Mariam witnessed her young son's metamorphosis over a period of three years – from a happy, loving boy to someone fearful, angry and suicidal. And she was helpless to prevent it. One morning when I phoned Mariam, she described how Nouri had been thrashing around all night, crying out, half-asleep and half-awake, tormented by visions of blood and death. It was only when she got him into the shower at seven o'clock in the morning that she was able to calm him down. It broke my heart that there was no-one there to help her, not even Nouri's father, with his own demons to battle.

Looking back, I think the family's time in that house at the beach might have been one of Mariam's happiest periods in Australia, including the present. For that short time she was able to *hope* – that one day her family might return to their well-adjusted, pre-detention selves. It was early days, and she was able to believe that improvement was not only possible but probable. I, too, felt some optimism about the future and returned home feeling happy about my visit.

My own pain is quite different. It involves a profound loss of faith in the goodness of my own country. Ignorance is one thing, but to know about and condone cruelty is quite another. No Australian politician can plead ignorance of how Australia's refugee policy impacts on vulnerable people, yet many continue to support an obscene system capable of destroying people forever, as it has this family. After all they've been through, they remain on Temporary Protection Visas, with all the ongoing anxiety and insecurity that entails. Supporters of mandatory detention believe: 'These people don't count – it's the deterrent effect that's important'. But 'these people' *do* count, and the price of deterrence is unconscionable.

Postscript In 2006, Nouri underwent eye surgery to correct the alignment of his eye and so rectify the constant double vision he suffered as a result of this incident.

If I had known how much distress – often futile – all this was going to cause me, would *I* have chosen to remain ignorant? Did the three years of my life swallowed by involvement with this ruined refugee family contribute anything to anybody? Certainly I neglected my own family and friends during this time, being almost continually distracted and emotionally absent. Have the hundreds of hours I've spent writing letters and emails and talking to people about the family made a positive difference to the wellbeing of any of them? I don't know. I can only hope that my friendship with Mariam, which continues to this day, brings her some comfort, however small.

I've invited the family to come to Kangaroo Valley for a holiday, describing the natural beauty of the place and assuring them that they will have their own house. I doubt if they will ever come. Nouri says that he never wants to go *anywhere* ever again (he spends school holidays almost entirely indoors, escaping into computer games). Mariam knows I am fond of her and politely responds that a holiday is 'a nice idea', knowing that her son will almost certainly veto it. And Danush, who remains largely housebound, even now, says nothing. I suspect that for this family, a 'holiday' is no longer possible.

'The best of times; the worst of times'

Academic ***Anne Pedersen*** *shares the infectious joy of some newly-released detainees*

I first went to the Perth Detention Centre at the beginning of 2003. I returned there more times than I care to remember. I didn't make a conscious decision as to whether I would get involved personally or not. There was simply no option – once I had been inside, and had heard the stories, to do anything else but be involved would simply have been unthinkable.

It was a pretty awful experience. The centre was small, crowded and unpleasant; the situation of the detainees seemed hopeless. Visitors were not even allowed to use the toilet.

On many occasions I was overwhelmed and appalled by our treatment of asylum seekers. The first person I met there was Wasim, a stateless man, detained for almost five years. He had committed no crime, but was detained indefinitely. Although Wasim was then released, after three further years living in the Perth community he is still not allowed to work, obtain social security or receive medical help – he lives off charity and the help of his wife (an Australian citizen) and friends. For a proud and independent man, not being able to financially support himself or his family is soul-destroying. Watching his mental health deteriorate and being powerless to really help has been heart-wrenching.

It was equally devastating to receive a letter from my friend in Baxter, Wahid, saying, 'I am forgetting what my name is. My number is ***'. I felt I had been transported to the concentration camps of Nazi Germany. I felt sorrow for Wahid, distress, powerlessness, shame at being Australian. At Wahid's request, I visited his friend, Zal, who was transferred to Perth. We sat in that horrible, pokey, hot, little reception area, I showed him photos of my family and friends; the next week, he showed me his photos. We quickly became close friends, and I visited him each Sunday. Zal's trauma in his home country was being continued in Australia. He could only cry when asleep: he 'saw' himself leave his body, rise above his bed and, as if detached, watched himself crying from above the bed. When Zal woke, his pillow would be wet from tears.

There are many, many more of these stories. They were hard to hear, but undoubtedly much harder for the refugees to endure. I sometimes had to remind myself that I had a safe life to return to once the detention centre door closed behind me. I felt that to concentrate on my own feelings of distress was self-indulgent.

The weekend of the 2004 election, I knew in my heart that John Howard would be returned. The thought of the asylum seekers (and their advocates, for that matter) going through another three years of the same just wasn't worth thinking about, so I didn't. Then it became official – John Howard had won. I, like all the other advocates, was due at the detention centre the next day, Sunday. I remember lying in bed, pretty much incapable of getting up, wondering whether this was what happened when people are clinically depressed. Happily for me, I wasn't clinically depressed, and got up around lunchtime (most unusual for me), baked an apple cake, and went off to the detention centre. I can't explain how much I dreaded going – if I felt this bad, how would the detainees feel? What would I say to them? As it turned out, I didn't need to do or say anything. The detainees simply said that they watched the election on the news, said to one another, 'Okay, we're stuffed', and got on with their usual activities. It seemed their expectations were minimal, so they were not particularly disappointed. We all got on with our usual Sunday lunch as though nothing had happened. This was one of many times when I admired the detainees' courage.

Regardless of the horrible stuff, there were and are a number of incredibly positive experiences. Each Sunday for lunch, other advocates and I brought food and drink, and sat at a large table with about eight detainees. Despite frequent unhappy stories (such as visa rejections), we often managed to have a good time. One by one, the detainees were all given visas and released. And this in itself was always extraordinarily positive – for example, a message on my answer-machine saying, 'Hello, this is Zal here, I have visa – please come pick me up'. Again – how do I explain how I felt when I heard that message? I actually can't – the joy, the elation, the relief, and the utter happiness can't be pinned down in words.

On the Sunday after Wasim's release, we all had a big lunch, and I swear he went from being a middle-aged (at age 29), pasty and desperately unhappy man to a young, vibrant and happy man, saying, 'I am as happy as can be'. The day he was released, he literally skipped down the street, which got him some very funny looks. Perth Detention Centre is so small you can't run, even in the exercise yard. So to run was a magical experience for him.

About a year later, Wasim married his long-time friend and fellow refugee, Myriam, whom he first met in detention many years earlier. His wedding was simply wonderful, with many released detainees and supportive friends in attendance. Wasim said beforehand that he wanted the day to be perfect, and it was. I am now a close friend of his family – we have an 'orphans' lunch every week with another refugee friend. (As an aside, Wasim 'came down' pretty quickly after his release – not being able to support yourself for years on end will do that to you. But there have definitely been some good times.)

A final positive example. Another newly released detainee came to live in Perth: Salah'adin, who is part of our 'orphans' family. He had been locked up almost seven years with no likelihood of being released; this was before the 'Liberal Rebels' did their bit [*see Timeline of events*]. He was so deeply depressed in Baxter that he was transferred to Glenside Psychiatric Hospital. To celebrate his arrival, we all went down to the local pub, where there was a band playing. He had never danced before, but gave it a damn good shot. He was bopping around like a little cricket. At one stage he was shaking my arms vigorously above my head in an iron-grip while jumping up and down – so I had to jump up and down like a thumping big cricket. A couple of minutes later, he threw me across the dance floor in the style of the 1940s, although we perhaps were not as elegant as in those old movies. The dance floor was about the size of a postage stamp, and we were both a serious danger to all there. The lead singer said to the audience, 'Well, you are all very, well - *active* - this evening'. I got a rather rude nickname after this incident: 'Crazy Dancer', which I thought wasn't altogether fair. All in all, Salah'adin's joy in his freedom was infectious and truly wonderful. But, like Wasim, his joy did not continue indefinitely. He had been traumatised in his own country and, once in Australia, was locked up longer than some rapists and murderers instead of being given the help he needed. After his release, he needed support to cope with all that had happened. Being on a Return Pending Visa [*see Glossary*] does not help him feel secure and safe. But certainly there were moments of real happiness for Salah'adin and for us, his friends.

Few moments in my life have been as special as these. I learned a great deal from my refugee friends. I learned the meaning of courage – I wonder whether I could have survived the horrors they endured. The readiness with which they accepted me into their lives was remarkable, after the appalling treatment they received from the Australian government. They seemed to differentiate quite clearly between 'the government' and 'Australian people'.

My family gave me both emotional and, at times, financial support. Just as important were my friends who supported me along my journey. Certainly, the nature of my old friendships changed during the period of my refugee advocacy. Some friends supported me completely, and some acquaintances become friends along the way. They listened to my rantings, and I don't imagine that was easy. The whole refugee movement is all-encompassing, and I found it difficult to concentrate on other issues. Especially when I regularly visited the detention centre, it was difficult to talk about superficial topics for extended periods. The temptation was to stand up and shout, 'Hello? Hello? Why are we talking about this trivial thing? There are innocent people out there being locked up for up to seven years and Australia is letting it happen!' At times I was boring, tedious, and downright insufferable. Some old friends found my commitment to the issue too difficult, and those friendships were lost. I also can't forget the help of sympathetic politicians and professionals. Most work was done pro bono, and without these lawyers, psychologists and psychiatrists, where would we be? Nor do I want to overlook so many inspirational and supportive advocates.

I remember when I saw Zal off at Perth Airport – he was off to Sydney to live with friends who'd supported him in detention. Before he caught his flight, we dropped in at Perth Detention Centre (it's actually at the airport) to say goodbye to some other detainees. That was not easy – they were sincerely happy about Zal's release, but there was also stress and pain in their faces, given that their situation was still as it was. After about half an hour in the stiflingly hot reception area, we said goodbye and walked over to the main terminal. Another advocate and I watched Zal walk through Departures carrying his little bag. He turned and smiled at us; his new life was just beginning. As he disappeared through the terminal, I just lost the plot and flooded the airport with tears (this may be a slight exaggeration). Why did he have to go through five years of unspeakable pain in detention before being given a visa? Why were the detainees we just saw still in an intolerable and seemingly unending hell? Mixed in with these feelings were feelings of utter joy that Zal was free and winging his way to Sydney to start his new life.

So, to quote Charles Dickens in *A Tale of Two Cities*, 'It was the best of times; it was the worst of times'. The last few years have been pretty full-on. I am angry that this situation ever came to pass. It simply wasn't necessary – Australia gets so few asylum seekers compared to other countries. It would not have been hard to treat them with respect, compassion and fairness instead of like the very worst type of criminal. On the other hand, I've met some amazing and courageous refugees, many of whom are still close friends.

And I'm sure I wouldn't have gone the distance if it weren't for the fantastic supportive advocates I came in contact with. It needs to be said that (touch wood) none of my friends have been deported. It may be that I wouldn't be quite so philosophical if that were the case. But with the situation as it is, I wouldn't change my involvement in the refugee movement – I have gained far more, and had far more positive experiences, compared with any stresses I encountered.

Remembering

*Postgraduate research student **Diane Gosden** reflects on the refugee advocacy movement and its implications for Australian law*

What I remember most is the suffering. The image of people huddled on the deck of the *Tampa*, not being allowed to land on Australian territory. Later, the children and old people in Villawood – those most vulnerable people in our society, held there like birds in a cage.

The Iraqi man there saying, 'Even Saddam doesn't imprison children!' And the young African man, appalled at such treatment of old people.

The men there who seemed to be going mad, each week worse, deteriorating ... the mothers trying to hold their families together. And those who spoke hardly any English, their fear of everything and everyone, even the visitors. Amidst that, there was a strange dignity. An experience of respect and dignity that came in the interactions of those held and those visiting. It was a quiet thing, and unexpected. It was there like a breath that sat in people's eyes as they shared time together. Was it possible that it might have some role-modelling effect on the guards?

I remember the queues, waiting in the queues to visit. Sometimes it would be one hour, two hours or more – standing outside in the sun or the rain. By the time you were finally processed and emerged into the Visitors Area inside, you had to shake yourself out of the stupor you had gone into. But there was always some other visitor in the queue who was older, who had come further, or had more physical disabilities.

I remember the blackness of being a witness to this happening in Australia, and then the scratching around to do what you could, to find pro-bono lawyers, to read Tribunal files, to appeal to the Minister, to do practical things, and to walk a tightrope of hope with those people you visited.

To move between visiting the immigration detention centres and the Australian life outside was almost schizophrenic. As the court challenges went on, the reality became ever clearer. Australian law allowed for these people who had sought asylum to be held in our immigration detention centres for the rest of their lives, in whatever conditions existed.

Of course, there were the protests, the desperate telling of what was happening. And there were the reports, the inquiries, and the evidence of harm that built up, one case on top of another, but with no change.

And in the midst of that, the deportations. Afterwards, someone might hear from that person just occasionally, and then often not at all. And for those people who were eventually released from detention, some could rebuild lives and some could not.

It seemed that there was no core leadership to combat what was happening and what had been happening for a decade. But at the same time, and perhaps because of that, so many people were doing so much on their own or with a few friends, wherever they were and with whatever they had. The fight was happening outside the political structures of our country, apart from the minor political parties – the Australian Democrats and The Greens – individual Independent MPs and individual members of the major political parties. This meant that the battle had to be fought essentially as a citizens' movement.

In Canberra, on 15 October 2006, I stood with 1000 other people to remember those who died seeking refuge in Australia – people have died in detention, on TPVs, and after being deported. This occasion remembered those who died in the SIEVX disaster, the white poles naming and remembering 'unknown boy', 'unknown girl', 'unknown mother', 'unknown father'. This is the remembering of what it is to seek refuge in the twenty-first century. [*See stories by Sue Hoffmann and Steve Biddulph.*]

There has been a humanitarian wave sweeping through part of the Australian population in opposition to these policies. Humanitarian action can go a certain distance in what it achieves. For justice to be achieved, it needs to be accompanied by its sister, human rights.

I believe, like many others, that there needs to be a profound change in Australia's Constitution to overcome this lack of protection of human rights. This is not only for asylum seekers' and refugees' rights. It is for *human* rights. And this needs to happen in community awareness as well. That's the challenge.

Kids

***Kerry Millard** is an award-winning cartoonist and book illustrator whose work has appeared in many publications, including* The Sydney Morning Herald.

Terrorist comment

***Phil Somerville** is a freelance cartoonist.*

Middle Eastern dissident

***Hinze** (aka David Pope) is a freelance cartoonist.*

Fleeing the Taliban

***Cathy Wilcox** draws for* The Sydney Morning Herald *and* The Age.

Part 2

Dark places

Landscape, isolation, heat. The physical environment and space allocated to asylum seekers and refugees in Australia shapes both their experience and our perception of them. Detention centres in remote areas, forgotten places, engender fears of being forever out of sight and out of mind. In Australia the image of the wild and threatening heart of the land links the asylum seeker with deeply-held fears of the untamed and the dangerous. We are as colonisers, here on borrowed time. Remote penal colonies have a strange familiarity, and in a sense remind us of the price we pay for dissent. Detainees in these facilities describe a harrowing sense of being forgotten and denied social contact. The sense of the endless desert, its emptiness and monotony, is all-consuming. Indefinite detention, being 'nowhere forever' in a form of limbo where there is no other reality but the present moment – this breaks the spirit. The conscious design of the newer detention facilities, a complex panopticon, allows for surveillance and regulation but no sightlines, no horizon, only walls and sky. The breakdown of individual identity and the relentless scrutiny contribute to madness. Detainees speak of a loss of orientation in time and place.

In the quiet suburbs, where some detention centres lie, all roads lead to guarded camps. A former hostel is now a prison. Neighbours hear shouts and cries, catch glimpses of patrols. A trail of visitors brings food. Some days there is a strange, playful atmosphere, like a carnival: the stateless dance to music under the hot sun. What do the neighbours make of this use of our suburban space?

These places have allowed and encouraged blindness to the harsh reality of containment and isolation. Denial, indifference, and disavowal: we do not see.

WILLY-WILLY IN WOOMERA

Actor and playwright ***Diana Greentree*** *joins the Easter 2002 protest at Woomera and witnesses a dramatic break-out*

In astonishment, I watched as 50 bleeding human beings tore through a gap in the razor wire. Refugee activists rushed to shelter them, tearing off T-shirts and exchanging them for the starkly white Afghan garments of the escapees. Some were children. All were terrified, joyous, tearful as they leapt into the dusty desert of freedom.

In the next tent, two young men from Afghanistan, the same age as my son, sit huddled and afraid.

'How can we help them?' a young friend tearfully whispers. 'Can we give them our map? Some water?'

I look out at the treeless desert that is Woomera, at the police who've surrounded our protest camp and who've turned night into day by setting up huge lights. The campsite is ablaze.

'They'd die out there,' we tell our friend. She says they'd rather die than be returned to the detention centre. She sneaks out again.

We can't look at the tent where the two boys wait, hardly daring to breathe. We know we're being watched. A hush falls over the camp, dark figures scurry from tent to tent. Are they escapees? Police? Who is a friend?

Two young men approach us in the dark. 'Have you heard of a woman hiding? Her name is Suriah. We have her two little kids and they're crying for their mother.'

I gulp and reply nervously, 'Suriah? Um … no. No. Haven't heard anything.'

We eye them suspiciously as they go from tent to tent. We begin to wonder if all this is such a good idea. We know the refugees will be found and returned to detention. Will they be punished? Is it worth it? We look at the heavy police presence. We, too, are imprisoned. It's getting cold, and we hear there'll be a police raid on our tents. Not much chance of sleep. The wind is strong and whips red dust into our noses, our eyes, our food. The moon cruelly shines over the desert, and we wonder if people are out there, crawling on their bellies from shrub to shrub.

The early morning is very quiet. I peer fearfully from the tent. To my surprise, the police have gone. Someone has a radio and we hear on the news that the South Australian police have now refused to do the Federal Government's dirty work. A cheer goes up.

Our young friend tells us the Afghan boys have gone. She is without her walking boots. The legal team informs the camp that most of the escapees have been caught. Tears roll down our faces as we learn that the young mother and her two little children have been returned to the detention centre. What is the price of a moment's freedom, we wonder.

So now it's Easter Sunday, and 1000 protesters are chanting and banging saucepans as we head towards the forbidding walls of the centre. The police await us, looking somewhat overdressed in leather chaps, chest guards, gloves and helmets – full riot gear – as they face the singlet-wearing crowd.

We see the refugees now, standing on roofs, waving and shouting to us, reaching for our hands through the razor wire. 'Thankyou, thankyou, Australian people,' the detainees call. Some have tiny children perched on their shoulders and they, too wave and call to us. A policeman wipes away a tear.

The refugees now hold high into the air a huge cross made from grasses, in a touching acknowledgment of our Easter Sunday. I am filled anew with anger and shame. They throw us a huge bunch of flowers, scavenged from who knows where in this barren desert. We stay a long, long time, calling, crying, trying to give support. And again, they call, 'Thankyou, thankyou'. I'm glad I came.

It's early Monday morning and we've been told to expect a final raid. Somehow the police seem less frightening, and we peer out of our tents as we watch them quietly walking in packs of five or six, waving torches round the outsides of our tents.

'Delta Echo, X-ray ... Alpha Victor Delta,' one of the cops says with an air of importance. They record our car regos but, strangely, don't look in the tents.

'Good morning fellas,' I say.

'Morning,' they reply. 'Lovely day.'

Covered in a layer of red dust, we pack up. Where hundreds of tents crouched yesterday like multi-coloured beetles nestling into the sand, only a patch of soft, red dust remains. A willy-willy whirls across the barren stretch that separates us from the detention centre. It picks up some leaves, some shreds of paper and carries its gift through the stark steel walls of the prison.

Six months in Woomera

*Health professional and activist **Mira Wroblewski** recounts the disturbing lessons learnt during her stay in an unusual township*

I travelled to Woomera over Easter 2002 for what I thought was a one-off visit to Woomera Detention Centre. As a child of East European refugees who came to Australia after World War II, I was confused by the contradictory stories in the media and elsewhere about what was happening in immigration detention centres. I had the idea that this weekend would give me some insight, and then I would go back to my 'normal' life. Little did I know!

I had no idea what to expect. However, nothing would have prepared me for what I saw. At about the time I pulled in, detainees from inside the detention centre were dropping over and through the fences, helped by people who had come to protest about their incarceration. The first thing I saw was a number of men running desperately up the dirt road towards our campsite, being pursued by police on foot and on horseback. Some were bodily dragged through the dust to a waiting paddy wagon. Others kept running. I knew nothing about Australia's immigration policy. I knew nothing about detention centres. However, I knew desperation when I saw it, and I knew unreasonable force. Some inner instinct prompted me to join a group of protestors who made a cordon around the paddy wagon, so that those who were caught and being dragged could not be locked up.

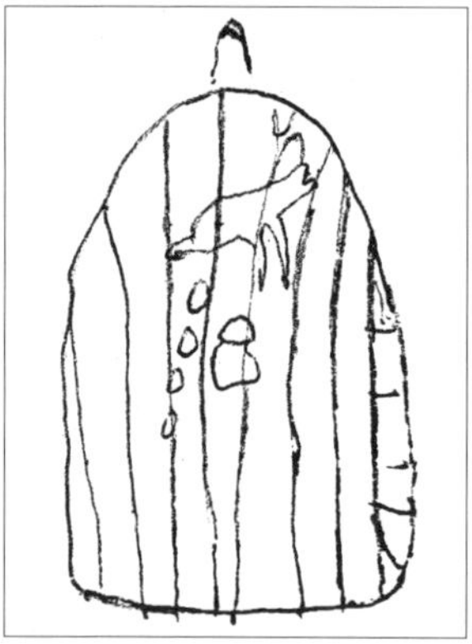

'This is not how I feel, this is how I am' – by a 13-year-old girl in Woomera

Suddenly we were confronted with a wall of police horses. They advanced over us, shoulder to shoulder, one step at a time. It was incredibly frightening. By sheer force, the unfortunate men who had been caught in the dust were bundled into the wagon. We never saw them again.

That night it was hard to find out what had happened. I hadn't moved in political or activist circles before. I had no idea that these communities were (quite rightly) wary of strangers, who may or may not be working for the authorities. I heard that people had escaped from the detention centre. Many had been caught but some were still free. I saw some haunted faces in our camp – men and women. I heard of children, too.

Throughout the night we could hear police vans driving around the camp. Periodically there was the tramping of boot-clad feet between the tents. Rumours went around that we were going to be raided. I lay in my tent wondering what sort of surreal universe I'd been teleported to! In the morning we formed a long group and walked out to the detention centre. This was my first view of Woomera. I saw those fences, and I knew my fears the previous night had been right. You just know when something is wrong. I had no idea what type of people were in there, but knew that no-one deserved to be.

The rest of the weekend went by in a blur of shock, punctuated by images: my first sight of children behind those fences, crying and yelling out to us. The men sitting on the roof, young men, younger than me. They were holding signs that said 'Freedom'. I saw some of them trying to get out, cutting themselves on the razor wire.

Then something happened that changed my life. A woman in a long garment and a head scarf came out of a demountable and came to the fence near us. She began to call out to us. Was it Arabic? Farsi? It didn't matter. We could somehow understand her perfectly. She was calling for help. She was pleading. We could not understand her words, but at some basic human level we understood her. We tried to call something back, hoping she would understand us the way we understood her. Then we saw a man in uniform, fully kitted-out in a way I hadn't seen before, with a helmet, visor, and a large, heavy riot shield. He tried to drag her back from the fence. We started yelling at him to stop.

Most of the people I subsequently visited in Woomera had been there for years without ever having a visitor. They knew no-one outside, and I later heard that many had been told that all Australians hated them. Suddenly this woman saw that not everyone hated her. She stayed at the fence calling out to us. The guard became more and more violent. He began hitting her with his riot shield. She was a smallish woman, shorter than me. We yelled at him to stop as he gradually beat her to the ground with his shield. All of us were crying, even the men. The guard dragged the woman through the dust, into the building – and something inside my head snapped, like the flicking of a switch.

We later heard that on the Saturday night of the protest, people inside the centre had been struck with batons and tear-gassed. People also told me, however, that through the whole night they could hear the drumming and see the lights from our camp. Despite the violence, they were elated. A little girl later told me how she and some of the other kids inside were dancing on the tables to the sounds of the drums.

In the following week, back in my flat in Adelaide, I moved around in a fog. I cried almost constantly. At a debriefing meeting for the protest, I started to learn some of the facts. That instead of receiving help in Australia, these people had been dumped in places like Woomera to rot. I also heard that some people calling themselves the 'Refugee Embassy' had stayed behind in Woomera after the protest. I met these people the following week and decided to go back to Woomera for a while to help them.

Over the next weeks I lived in my tent in a carpark at a truck stop called Pimba, some 10 kilometres out of Woomera. The place was incredibly dusty and noisy: hot during the day and cold at night. I would regularly be woken by the glaring headlights or booming brakes of trucks. It was certainly challenging! I found out during this time that the people running the bus called the Refugee Embassy were a group called the Jesus Christians. To me, they sounded similar to a cult; many of their attitudes and beliefs were also very challenging for me.

The Jesus Christians had lists with names of people locked up in Woomera. I wrote letters to many, and then started visiting them. I would come back after each series of visits and debrief about my day, not realising that one of the men was in the process of writing stories about the detainees. These were eventually published as a booklet called *The Worst of Woomera*, in which people's thinly-disguised stories were easily recognisable. Many of the people who were in that book were extremely upset by it, as they hadn't given permission for their stories to be included. Some of them were so distressed that they asked me and others to try to stop its further publication. Unfortunately this was not possible.

For me, one of the most difficult things in visiting Woomera was the mistrust. As I got to know the people and the backgrounds they came from – the repressive regime in Iran, Afghanistan under the Taliban – it became entirely understandable. However, I was always worried that my lack of knowledge about their cultures would cause me to do and say something wrong, and that I would lose their trust. It was very easy to be banned from visiting, so I had to always appear to be friendly with the guards, even the ones who I knew were abusive to people inside. It was a fine line to tread.

I was banned from visiting for two months. I had arranged to visit one cold morning. The wind through the Visitors Area was pretty unforgiving, and I wondered why I was kept sitting on a bench outside. After about 20 minutes of waiting, suddenly three guards came marching around the corner. There were two quite large men and a stern-looking woman. They asked me to stand, and informed me that my visiting privileges had been revoked and that they had come to escort me out of the centre. They would not give me a reason. I was literally frog-marched out.

The friend I was to visit was told that I hadn't turned up. When I phoned him later in the afternoon, his friend told me that he had to be taken to the medical area and be given sedatives. People inside received so few visitors that they often couldn't sleep from excitement the night before a friend was to visit them. The letdown when visitors were refused entry was terrible. It was common practice for visitors to arrive at the office, having completed the requisite paperwork weeks before and having received permission to visit, only to find that their papers had mysteriously disappeared. This happened regularly, even when people had come from interstate. These people just had to drive away. There was no hope of querying or overturning the decision. This was one way in which scrutiny of what was happening at Woomera was minimised.

It took me two months to find out why I had been banned. Finally I got a reply to my letter, which said that I had been banned 'for the safety and security of the centre'. In the years to come, I saw that this was the standard 'non-answer' for just about everything. Finally the manager spoke to me candidly. He said that a couple of people who'd had their stories published in *The Worst of Woomera* had approached him and said they thought I had colluded in the book. I sent him copies of the many letters and emails I had sent to try to stop the book from being published, and my visiting rights were finally returned.

I remained in Woomera for another six months. I no longer wanted anything to do with the Jesus Christians, and moved into a caravan park on the outskirts of Woomera itself. Woomera is a town administered by the Department of Defence. I found that it was impossible to rent accommodation, as I had done elsewhere in Australia. There was no reason to live in Woomera unless you were employed in the district. Some people told me that ACM, the company running the detention centre, was looking for staff. My other option, equally unappealing, was a job with the only other large local employer: Roxby Downs uranium mine. At this point the proprietor of the caravan park, who'd heard that I was visiting people in detention, made it very clear that 'my type' wasn't welcome in his establishment.

Fortunately, at this time I met Henri, the manager of Woomera Base Hospital. Henri was descended from Polish Jews, and shared my disgust at what was happening. On hearing that I was visiting the refugees, she gave me a job at the hospital as a cleaner. Apart from allowing me to stay in Woomera, this allowed me contact with the asylum seekers, who made up most of the patients there. This was another surreal world where, for instance, two grandmothers were guarded day and night by two ACM guards stationed at the door to their room. They noted every move the women made, including visits to the bathroom.

One of my duties was to make breakfast for the patients every morning. For a lot of my time there, these two women were the only patients in the hospital. We mainly communicated by mime, but I also asked them to teach me a bit of Arabic. One of the phrases I learned was the Arabic for 'peanut butter'. It was impossible to mime, so pretty soon it became part of my Arabic vocabulary. In return they chided me in Arabic for being 'too skinny to find a husband' and tried to give me their food. We became increasingly friendly, and even managed to joke and laugh in a mixture of languages and mime.

My obvious friendliness and interest in the women didn't go unnoticed. The most hostile guard officiously told me that he was noting how long I spent cleaning their room. He said it wasn't part of my job to be friendly, and told me to leave the door open so that he could monitor our conversations. The 'monitoring' continued, particularly when he found out I was visiting the detention centre. This was the beginning of my realisation that in this 'new Australia', people who viewed refugees as human beings were somehow considered dangerous.

Things became gradually more hostile and bizarre. The word at the local pub (frequented by many ACM guards) was that the new cleaner at the hospital visited the refugees and 'spoke their language'. This was certainly an overstatement since my Arabic pretty much consisted of 'hello', 'goodbye' and 'peanut butter'. Henri had also been approached by ACM, querying her employment of 'the woman who speaks Arabic'. Yet another meeting followed. Henri made it clear that she was not impressed with gossip about one of her staff members, that I had never done anything inappropriate within the hospital, and that her employment practices were none of ACM's business.

Despite Henri's support, I was told to 'stop speaking their language'. I began to notice that nursing staff were following me to certain parts of the hospital, particularly when I was cleaning the doctor's office. None of this was any real hardship to me, though the atmosphere was hostile, to say the least. Very few of the townspeople were sympathetic to what was happening to the refugees. Many worked for ACM or were families of ACM staff. A number of nurses at the hospital were married to guards. Others saw the centre as bringing jobs and money to a town that had very little to sustain it. I believe that this hothouse environment must have encouraged the many acts of inhumanity and brutality within the detention centre that we have all heard about. However, I don't believe that this absolves individual responsibility in any way.

During this time I was pulled aside by ACM staff, and once by the doctor, for such 'dangerous behaviour' as:

- putting fresh flowers on the patients' breakfast trays
- buying a Cherry Ripe for a teenage girl who was in hospital for self-harming because of the appalling stress of what was happening to her and her family (this was despite 'reporting' the Cherry Ripe to the guards before I gave it to her), and
- continuing to say 'Good morning' in Arabic to my surrogate grannies.

I had never imagined that basic kindness would be the cause for hostility and paranoia. I was given a variety of reasons: 'If you are nice to them, they will expect it all the time'; 'You shouldn't be upset that they cut themselves, it's a part of their culture'; and the ubiquitous, 'They are violent terrorists, it's in their nature'. At the time I couldn't really understand it. In retrospect I can see how any different point of view no longer allowed abuse to be normalised.

At this stage, I was told that a locum nurse was to share my hospital-supplied house. One night she came home from work very angry. She said that she had been asked to report to ACM about what I was doing at home: who I spoke to on the phone, any visitors I had and so on. She flatly refused, saying that whether or not they agreed with it, I was clearly doing nothing either wrong or illegal. Again and again I was struck by how threatening it was in this system to care about refugees, to treat them like human beings.

Eventually, Henri told me that she was under increasing pressure from ACM to no longer employ me at the hospital. I assumed that having a sympathetic person observe the number of refugees who were brought in with injuries from assaults, self-harm and suicide attempts was thought to be not in the company's best interests. Henri gave a reference for a job at the local hotel, and I went to work there and live in the flat they provided. At this stage I was told that my phone was being tapped. Indeed, I could hear this on both my landline and my mobile.

I met many inspiring people in Woomera. It was also incredibly distressing. I met children with the same aged and dead eyes that I'd only previously seen in UNICEF commercials. I heard children being called by numbers instead of names. I saw people with gouging scars from wounds they had made to take their minds off their inner pain for even a short time. I heard of kids drinking shampoo and cleaning products to try to suicide. I got to know a man who sat all day watching an ants' nest, getting to know all of the individual ants and their social behaviour. It was closer to normal life than anything he was experiencing himself. I met people who had been struck with batons and tear-gassed and locked in solitary confinement. Too many who had tried to suicide.

Many of the women and children in Woomera lived in a house in town euphemistically called 'Woomera Housing'. The house was surrounded by a fence dotted with security cameras. They were crammed in, with little privacy. The women and kids couldn't go anywhere without guards. This was supposed to be the humane face of detention! They could only see husbands, fathers and brothers once a week. Often the men and boys would suffer greatly from the separation, and deteriorated mentally and emotionally.

I would often see women and kids from Housing around the town, though always supervised by guards. I would smile and say hello (or '*Salaam*') at a distance. I was not allowed to speak to them or approach them. The guards were so sure that their behaviour was acceptable that I even saw them humiliate the women and kids in public in town. One time I was shopping in the local supermarket, a tiny place, and I saw a female guard loudly berate an Iranian mum as 'stupid' and 'slow'. She did the same at the checkout as the woman had to decide which groceries she could do without because she had exceeded her budget. This time the guard rolled her eyes for me in that horrible look of complicity that was supposed to bind me to her and her behaviour.

The women in Housing were given a weekly amount of money to shop for their families. It was enough for basics, but took a lot of careful budgeting. For a woman who'd arrived on a boat from Iran, to deal with a new language, new money and unfamiliar types of food, and to add up in her head the price of her groceries as she went, is obviously very difficult. To do that after a perilous boat trip and years in Woomera, while being berated and yelled at by a guard, is something no woman should endure. And the guard was a woman!

Kids from Housing were brought to the town library about once a week. I had been using the Internet in the library. I wasn't allowed to talk to the kids. I could see the older ones looking longingly at my Internet screen. When I asked one of the decent guards whether I could show the kids the Internet, he thought for a moment. Then he replied that he couldn't allow it. However, it really couldn't be helped if the chairs they chose happened to be behind mine while I was on the Internet. This became the norm whenever that guard was there. There are always flowers among the weeds.

Towards the end of my six months in Woomera, I left for a mental health break. It was December 2002. Just after I left, a fire was started inside the centre. The damage and increasing public pressure resulted in the centre's closure. People inside were gradually moved to Baxter IDC in Port Augusta. I felt that my period of intensive visiting had come to a natural end, and I moved back to NSW. I kept in touch with people in Baxter, and continue to keep in touch with those who were released.

Before I left Woomera, I was privileged to see the solar eclipse across the desert and over the detention centre. The air turned cold and the birds stopped singing. I took it as a sign that, even after the darkest period, the light always comes back. I hope it will in Australia.

VILLAWOOD: punishing the innocent

***Moya Turner** describes the inhumanity of immigration detention that she witnessed*

I am now in my seventies. I was a community nurse and welfare worker for 40 years. I received my first recognition from the Queen in 1977, and I have an OAM and other community awards.

In February 2001 I wanted to find out the truth about these 'boat people' who were always in the media, so I decided to visit the detention centre in Villawood. After phone calls to ChilOut [*see Resources*], I began my visits, and since then I have ridden my motorbike to visit people every week. I still feel emotionally drained after each visit.

My first impression of Villawood was the startling amount of razor wire ringing it; maximum-security prisons in NSW have less. If only Australians who oppose the idea of refugees arriving on our shores could have seen these young women and children gripping the fence in despair.

Visitors had to line up for up to two hours, then pass through five separate razor-wire fences as we were being processed. The ACM guards [*see Glossary*] searched us and our belongings, attached bands to our wrists, and placed a stamp on our hands. Once inside, I met some detainees. When I heard each one's description of horrific violence, persecution and torture – including witnessing family members being murdered – in their own country, I understood why they had to escape. They had embarked on dangerous journeys in search of a safe country – journeys I doubt I would have had the courage and stamina to endure.

I have vivid memories of the following incident. On 20 October 2002, during visiting hours at Villawood IDC, I heard screaming from a razor-wired enclosure near where women are imprisoned. I looked over and saw a small Asian woman lying on the ground with seven guards standing over her. Four guards were holding each arm and leg and the three others appeared to be supervising. The guards were literally dragging her along the concrete surface of the enclosure. As they did so, the woman raised her head, continued screaming out words I did not understand and at the same time looked directly into our faces. A Mandarin-speaking detainee near me said the woman was asking us to help her. Given the razor wire separating us from that dreadful scene, there was nothing we onlookers could do.

A detainee then told me the guards do this early in the morning, when there are no visitors to watch them. This was the first time he had seen someone being deported in the afternoon. He also told me that when men are being prepared for deportation, they are handcuffed, while women are forcibly injected in the arm, after which they stop struggling and go quiet. Sure enough, as soon as the Asian woman was dragged into the office, her screaming ceased.

As a palliative care nurse, I have often seen people facing death, but I have never in my life seen another human being with such deep fear, as when my eyes met those of this Chinese woman. She seemed to know that she'd face a terrible fate, perhaps even execution, on her return to China. Her fear will remain in my memory for the rest of my life.

PEOPLE WITH LIVES THAT MATTER

***Konya Roy**, a child psychiatrist, remembers a moving visit to a family in Villawood*

I've come to Villawood IDC with colleagues to do an assessment of one of the families currently detained there. We sit in the closed, seemingly airless, graceless, four-walled room with the high ceilings. A dingy-looking table, broken plastic chairs and artificial lights. Such a blighted place – no sense of life or breath or even organic warmth – all is sterile, man-imposed.

The family sits before us – the mother and father, tired, care-worn faces with eyes speaking of lives once-lived, now humiliated and helpless. They had been through so much to get their children to safety, to bring themselves to a place they hoped would allow them to live in relative peace; unassuming, simple lives.

Their words are softly-spoken, in slightly broken English, but still urgently trying to convey a message, some understanding of the injustice that continued day after day. I hear their words, full of pain, and I am filled with so many thoughts: What has it been like for them? What have they experienced? What have they seen in the world before, and what do they see now?'

I try not to become emotional, as it will affect my ability to do the assessment interview, so I clamp down on anything that leads off dangerously into ... quickened breathing, is it anger or fear? These people, they are sitting here, just a couple of metres away from me – could it have been me sitting in their place, hearing the taunts of the neighbours in their town, threatening them, telling them that if they didn't get out of there, their daughters would be raped and their son would be taken away?

But no, it's not me, I've never experienced that, I've lived a life in Australia of comfort and security, warm, central-heated, shag-pile-carpeted, velour-couched decency, with knowledge and discussions about terrible things that go on in the world, elsewhere, but which can be safely switched off with a remote control, or interrupted with a phone call. That's where I'm from.

I look at their faces, see the etched sadness sometimes replaced by a blank hopelessness – the eyes empty, the mouth slackens, the voice fades out. When I see this, I glance at the children: have they noticed the light suddenly flicker out in their father and mother's faces?

The two daughters and the son are all sitting dutifully, quietly next to their parents. Their clothes are clean, tracksuits, jumpers. The girls have their hair tightly pulled back – one in a ponytail, one in braids. The elder is a teenager, the younger about twelve. I pay more attention. They look like 'good girls', the sort of girls I remember from my schooldays. The ones that would always do their homework on time, and hand in projects that had carefully cut-out photographs from brochures and magazines that their mother had helped to paste into their project books.

No, hang on, these girls were sitting in a lifeless detention centre room with their family, not allowed to go to school outside. Villawood had no projects for them, they had nothing to do.

Later, we went outside to the visitors' compound, where the family sat with some friends who had brought them cordial and orange cream biscuits.

'Please sit, sit, have something to drink, something to eat with us,' the mother urged, sending her son off to find plastic chairs.

We sat down, and I was transported straight back to weekend afternoons in my childhood with Mum and Dad, visiting family friends – 'Cup of tea? No, you must! And have a biscuit …'.

Sitting outside in the grounds of a cold, dehumanising place of deprivation and despair, this family showed us hospitality, grace and warmth – the need to be the people they actually are, people with lives that matter.

Returning to Villawood

Retired schoolteacher ***Lynette Chaikin*** *describes the crushing impact of incarceration*

Something terrible was happening. It was not feasible that a mother who had given up everything and taken enormous risks to give her children a better life would do such a thing. I had to meet these people who were being demonised. I had to apologise to them and welcome them to my country. I had to reassure them their situation would improve.

My first visit to Villawood had been to the old hostel 25 years ago, when many of the Asian 'boat people' were there. It was bustling and crowded, and the new arrivals were free to come and go. The accommodation was basic and cooking forbidden. Not being permitted to cook was cause for complaint – they could not wait to leave. Banquets were often secretly cooked in their rooms – the dining-room food made them ill. Guards and barbed wire did not exist.

Returning to Villawood 25 years later, I was stunned. The first thing was the wire: two rows of it encircling the compound. What a difference! Our old hostel was now a prison.

After I had been visiting for about six weeks, I noticed 'K'. His name was Abdul but everyone called him by his last name. He had been in Villawood for five years. He walked tall and was respected by all the inmates and the visitors. He taught the children soccer and led the prayer. I used to see him regularly. One day he did not come out. For two weeks I put his name on the visitors' list, for two weeks he did not appear. 'He is sleeping,' I was told. 'Now he just sleeps.' When he did eventually appear, I did not recognise him. It was extremely hot yet he wore a sweater and a beret pulled over his eyes. He seemed to be in a sleepwalking trance.

'K,' I said, 'I am going to fight for you. I will go to Canberra.'

The tears streamed from his eyes.

We had a team fighting for him for the next two years. Just after seven years in detention, he was deported. They hired a plane and off he went. Just like that. Of course he was arrested as soon as he arrived back in his country in north Africa. He had told us many times he would be arrested if returned, as he had refused to fight against his brothers in the south. He did not agree with the fighting, and that was why he'd fled the country. The price he paid for his belief in fairness was a wasted seven years in the hell-hole of Villawood. I will never forget him.

Some were luckier! We fought for them and they were released. We had engagement parties in the compound; we danced and swayed to the music, singing with joy as the young couples exchanged their vows. We all brought food for the feast and for a few hours the barbed wire seemed to disappear.

One detainee was determined to make Villawood a better place; create something nice for the children. He made a beautiful garden. The soil was hard and sandy, but he dug and dug. He was rewarded, over the months, with a garden of flourishing plants. It lifted our spirits each time we visited - no doubt the effect on the inmates was also positive [*see Judy McLallen's story*].

I left Sydney for six weeks, and when I returned there was a wall. The garden had been cleared. Not a trace of it left. There was a need for more security, more wire. A new 'mission statement' was placed on the wall. The interests of the shareholders of ACM, which ran the detention centre, were of prime concern. Not a mention of the poor souls trapped in limbo with nothing to do, uncertain of their fate, stuck in a time warp.

Detainees always spoke of the boredom. A few of them had been sent to prison, as they had protested about their plight. 'It was better in prison,' they would say. 'We had a routine and the guards did not come and wake us at night. We slept well. We even went to art classes. It was really good. But here, we have nothing to do. Here, we sleep during the day and we can't sleep at night.'

Visiting Villawood is always difficult. It never gets any easier. At the end of the day we visitors escape through the gates, away from the wire and hardly dare to look back. When we finally turn to wave goodbye, it is always pitiful. Why are they there? For what purpose? Why are we afraid to let them out? Who will they harm?

I do not go to Villawood so often now, it is too heart-wrenching. I do feel guilty. There are many country people who come each week. They drive long distances. The weather is never a problem for them. The visitors come from all walks of life. It is wonderful to meet them, gentle, good people. We all share anger. Why is our country treating people like this? We are outraged. We meet weekly and sit with our new friends, who are going nowhere. This is all we can do to protest. We must share their sorrow and hear about their lives. We also share our own stories and tell them about the other Australia, beyond the wire.

We see the children take on the expressions of their parents. At first they are sad, and then the anger takes over. One small three-year-old banged her head repeatedly against the wall. She could not understand her mother's pain.

Like many of the visitors to Villawood, I feel diminished. As I sit in the compound, surrounded by the wire, watching the security van endlessly circling the buildings, I remember the old Villawood hostel, where people voiced their annoyance about the food. That was their only real problem. They had hope. They knew that tomorrow or next week they would find a job. They had a future.

I look forward to a time when the wire is torn away and the new arrivals can come and go, just as they did before. Even terrible food would be okay. There would be light at the end of the tunnel, a future. They would be free.

Life lessons: what refugees and asylum seekers have taught me

***Sister Aileen Crowe** takes us through the maze of emotions she experienced in her encounters with some inspiring detainees*

Years ago, on a holiday in Broome, I drove past the road that led to the Curtin Detention Centre, but I could not turn in that direction. Frankly, I was too scared. I did not know what I would find and I did not know what 'they' would do to me. I believed that the officers and guards would not allow me to see 'them', let alone talk to 'them', and this was a relief - an excuse not to turn down that path. On another occasion, on a wild, windy day, assisted by a small group of youths and with the grit of the desert sand lodged in our eyes, the university chaplain and I tied coloured ribbons on the wire fencing at the entrance to the Woomera Detention Centre. Along with this enthusiastic group of uni students, we tried to find prayerful thoughts, which were in fact more comforting for us than those for whom they were meant. Somehow sharing our frustrations and our helplessness at the gate of such a horrendous reality had some therapeutic value.

I began to feel more and more outraged. I signed countless petitions and even created petitions for others to circulate and sign. Along with friends, I attended regular protests outside Villawood, where we tried to communicate messages of support - across the barrier of police on horses, past the empty, decaying, former-migrant hostel buildings - to the people we could see in the distance, on the small balconies of their prefabricated bungalows, waving pieces of clothing in response.

I also attended a meeting with members of different churches from suburbs surrounding Villawood, to try and find a way to assist people who were released from the centre and had no relatives or friends to accommodate them. After some months it became clear that temporary accommodation was needed and, working together, we could develop an ongoing service. Volunteers were coordinated, and a 'House of Welcome' was opened in a former butcher shop.

I was invited to Villawood to meet 'the doctor'. I had vaguely heard about him and was somewhat curious. I didn't have the courage or the enthusiasm to go by myself. I didn't know what I would do when I got there, or what I would or could say – I am not good at introducing myself to strangers. 'Bring some food,' my friend said. I didn't know what sort of food people from a different culture would be interested in, so I said I'd bring some drink and some paper cups – on a hot day in the western suburbs, a few cold bottles of Coke should be okay. My friend had lived in Morocco for some years, so she brought tabouli and interesting dips and pita bread.

Armed with our goodies and our IDs, we queued at the gate, unprotected from the heat of the early afternoon sun, and waited until we were allowed in. We filled in the obligatory form and rejoined the queue inside the first two gates, in readiness for entry to the reception desk. The one or two clerks on duty were particularly slow and rude. I diligently produced my driver's licence, which was carefully noted, and nervously handed over my form, with my personal address and telephone number as well as details of the 'friend' I was about to visit. A plastic arm-band similar to that worn by hospital patients was fixed tightly to my wrist. I was then scanned with a 'magic' wand, allowed to collect my goodies and move to the next stage. Unbeknown to me at the time, this was a simple, uncomplicated screening process. In ensuing years, an airport-style screening box was introduced and, later again, the backs of our hands were stamped with indelible ink and checked as we departed through a short, dark passageway. Also, the reception area was relocated and refurbished, and razor wire was installed on all the boundary fences.

Clutching our goodies, we were escorted through another locked gate into an open compound – a small paddock with a tiny shelter in one corner and a rusty children's swing in a distant space. Plastic chairs were scattered around, and clusters of people gathered under the shade of the few trees. Children listlessly clung to their mothers' skirts while men gathered in groups speaking foreign languages as names were loudly called at regular intervals over the public speakers. Not too far from the motionless swing was a small shelter with a couple of guards sitting at a table near a locked gate. On the other side of the fence, one or two men paced up and down, up and down, the whole afternoon. Occasionally the gate would open and a detainee would emerge, hand his or her ID to the gatekeepers, and expectantly survey the area, their face lighting up as they recognised their visitor(s). Hugs and the three customary kisses were followed by the inquisitive opening of gifts and sharing of food. Time passed quickly, and visiting time was up when the officer in charge went from group to group to remind us to begin our goodbyes.

We sat and stared at the locked gate for an uncomfortable length of time, then my friend jumped up and moved quickly towards the doctor, who had come through and surrendered his ID as required. He was a distinguished, dignified gentleman with an engaging smile, and driven by an enormous sense of purpose. His questioning energised him as he drew from me my reasons for wanting to meet. His humour defused any sense of being interrogated. In an empathic way he described what it was like for people to be detained, outlining the stages of depression and psychiatric states that resulted the longer the time spent in detention. Detained as he was, he kept himself physically and mentally well enough to record case studies of other detainees and to analyse their psychiatric conditions as they rapidly deteriorated.

This visit turned out to be a very sober lesson in what it was like to be a refugee or a person seeking asylum. I was in awe of this man, who could rise above the racism, discrimination and injustice of mandatory detention and work for those who were not coping as well as he was. At the same time, I was becoming angry and depressed by what I was hearing and seeing around me, and a sense of helplessness was beginning to overwhelm me. There I was, being comforted by the doctor himself. We politely said our goodbyes after receiving his permission to bring other people along to visit in the coming weeks. As we walked through the locked gate, I glanced back to discover him watching us intensely.

My rage was unleashed when I returned to the office late in the afternoon and sat with some of the staff. Debriefing was a priority, and staff customarily dropped what they were doing in order to be there when needed. I described the experience, and ranted and raved about being part of a society that allowed this to happen to fellow human beings. The following week I was accompanied by a staff member, a bright, attractive, young woman who shared her story with the doctor. The youthful bantering between the two was light and positive. The doctor clearly enjoyed the afternoon visit. She, on the other hand, burst into tears on the way back to the office, and none of us left until 8 p.m., when her anger had subsided. Unbeknown to himself, the doctor became our impromptu teacher, a living witness to the indignity of detaining people who are not criminals, and a defenceless promoter of human rights for very vulnerable human beings.

The doctor lit a fire within, which is not yet extinguished. At times it has roared with vitality and fury, while at others the ashes have been barely warm. As I began to uncover people existing in the community with hardly enough to eat and children not able to go to school or so traumatised from the detention experience that they neither laugh nor cry, my sense of injustice forced me to act on their behalf. I would sit in the presence of six-foot-plus men as they wept because they were not allowed to support their wives and children. In assisting with applications for humanitarian visas, I would insist they tell me everything – the whole truth and nothing but the truth. I heard information I could not put in writing, for fear it would get back to the country of origin and the extended family would suffer. Through their tears, horrific stories would emerge, but sadly the tears are not regarded as 'credible' evidence, and hard facts are often difficult to come by. I accompanied people seeking asylum every time they went to the Compliance office to have their visas renewed, to ensure that they would not be harassed or dumped in detention again. One six-year-old told me of her experience at Compliance one day, when her father was suddenly taken away: 'Aileen, I screamed and screamed and everyone was looking at us, so they had to let Mummy and me go home'.

There have been extremely frustrating and deeply touching moments navigating the complexities of people's lives as they attempt to live a 'normal' life (though devoid of any sense of security). Interesting moments have included the fun of buying a school uniform for an eight-year-old who until then had not been allowed to go to school; the anxiety of meeting with a boss who wanted the employee to clean for two extra hours without a pay increase; the need to give a couple of driving lessons because driving instructors were insisting on 50 lessons, even though the person had an overseas licence; the humbling experience of attending an orientation night for a Year 7 student along with his parents, who were told quietly by the principal that the school fees, uniforms and books were all attended to.

I hit my lowest moment the day one detainee rang while on the fifth or sixth day of a hunger strike. I had supported him closely from the day he entered the detention process. We had regular conversations, sometimes in the middle of the night – about whatever needed to be said. He fostered a wide network of friends across Australia, and because of his appetite for phone cards I nicknamed him 'Mr Telecom'. When I first met him, he was a bright-eyed young man with a marvellous sense of humour and great artistic talent. When he told me he was going on a hunger strike, I desperately tried to persuade him that there had to be other options. He simply said, 'Aileen, this is my right,' and I had to agree that I had no authority to take it from him.

I was at the University of NSW trying to find the auditorium where a conference was beginning, when my mobile rang. It was a miserable, rainy day and, balancing an umbrella, I quickly rummaged through my handbag to locate the phone. Mr Telecom's voice was very weak, and in whispering, broken tones he explained how the pain in his head was far worse than the urge to eat. It was unbearable, listening to this talented young man telling me just what he was experiencing at that moment. Silent tears dribbled down my cheeks and I wished he would terminate this ghastly conversation. After what seemed a long time, we said our goodbyes and I began to sob my heart out. Since I couldn't control myself, I decided the best thing to do was go to the car and pull myself together quietly. An incredible sense of powerlessness overwhelmed me and I sobbed all the way home and most of the day. Here was a man that had been broken by the system – all sense of hope had been drained out of him, and the only way he could maintain control of his own life was to let it go.

The following day, when he asked me how I was, I said I wasn't feeling well at all and explained what had happened the day before. For some reason, I just felt he had to know. He tried to comfort me by telling me not to feel that way. A day passed. The phone rang again. His voice was a little stronger. Mr Telecom had taken a cup of weak tea. I was openly delighted. Curiosity got the better of me and I asked what had happened to bring about the change of heart.

'I couldn't bear the thought that I had upset you so much,' he said.

Day by day he got stronger. A mutual friend and I drove across to Baxter to be at the gate when he was finally released, and chuckled together as he banged the china in the restaurant with his stainless-steel utensils – a sound that he had not heard for more than two years, he said with a twinkle in his eye.

Over time, the Department of Immigration has changed its name, and Ministers have come and gone, as have public servants and Compliance office staff. Detention centres have closed and others have opened or been redeveloped – the rusty swing upgraded to a children's playground. In some instances the razor wire has been installed and, later, dismantled. Migration law has changed so often that even lawyers find it difficult to negotiate. Certain RRT members did not get their contracts renewed, regardless of whether or not decisions were finalised, while others remained for years and years. Of all the RRT hearings I endured, *not one* had a positive outcome. After all the court hearings I have suffered through, I can only conclude that justice is not the ultimate end in proceedings where the competition is around how much evidence can be eliminated before the hearings begin. I have learned that the Ombudsman's Office has great difficulty obtaining records from private, for-profit companies such as GSL [*see Glossary*], and the United Nations High Commission for Refugees has had correspondence sent to the Minister's office mislaid. I have met the relatives of people who have been detained illegally, have known others deported to danger, supported others who found themselves in psychiatric centres, met some who escaped to seek sanctuary in the community, and received phone calls from some living lawfully and happily in New Zealand.

I cannot conclude this fragmented account of some of the people who have led me through a maze of emotions over the past eight years without mentioning the wonderful network of advocates capable of knowing just when I have reached my own limits. At the most difficult times, word would get around and supportive phone calls developed into lengthy debriefs for each other. We offloaded our pain, our frustrations and our sense of powerlessness. We met for a meal to strategise or to celebrate, and gathered after conferences and information nights.

I have met some wonderful people from all walks of life who will, like me, remain committed until the day that detention becomes a short period of time while identity and security checks are processed; when people recognised as refugees can settle immediately because the TPV is abolished; when people on Bridging Visas can work and study so that even if their application fails, they can return to their country of origin with money or new skills to begin life anew; and, when fewer people are actually required to depart because they have been given the opportunity to access more appropriate visas, lessening the enormous responsibility placed on the Minister to make such weighty decisions about the future of vulnerable families.

THE DESERT IN MY COUNTRY

***Naleya Everson**, a volunteer para-legal and migration agent, makes sacrifices and battles nightmares to visit remote Curtin IRPC*

May brings winter early in the mountains. It seems sudden, pushing under my door, but maybe I just missed autumn, it all seems the same in front of the blue screen of the computer. I'm 22, sitting as usual, knees huddled up with a phone on my shoulder in front of the screen, 'Can you please put me through to 1317?', but both of the phones in Curtin Detention Centre are busy. In front of me is a piece of paper with questions scribbled on it. I called a psychologist earlier, somewhere between my two-year-old's dinner, which my mother gave her, and a bedtime story – the first I had read to her in six months.

I asked the psychologist what sort of questions I should ask them – '... bed-wetting, nightmares, suicidal ideation ...'. I'm waiting to interview families in Curtin, thousands of kilometres north of Perth in an army base in the desert, about what is happening to their children.

Finally I get through. Mahmoud, a refugee and voluntary translator who comes to the phone, speaks in whispers. He's afraid of what will happen to him if the Department of Immigration finds out he is helping the families. Some of the families speak on the phone themselves. There's excitement in the voice of a 14-year-old boy who tells me it's the first time he has ever spoken to anyone in Australia outside of detention. He's been there for two years. One a.m. and I get off the phone, I don't feel tired, sort of wound up, there is an unremitting sense of urgency with me constantly. I go over the notes.

'... A man cut himself from his feet to his chest, screaming and shouting as he did it. My three-year-old son kept talking about all the blood and woke up screaming that night. His reaction to these sorts of things is shock. They happen so often that he has grown used to them and goes into a quiet trance-like state when they occur ...'

I only let myself dwell on what it means for a second; if I think too long it becomes unbearable.

Possums clamber across the roof above me. I must be tired because the screen starts to blur. I need to write notifications about the children of 11 families and send them to Child Protection Services. I've come across a copy of the visa regulations, which say that children will be given visas if Child Protection certifies that they should. I know very little, but have an unshakeable belief that the law will not allow children to be abused in this way.

I leave it for the next day and go to bed. Images of the nine-year-old who slashed his wrists and the man who jumped out of a tree are created and re-created in my mind as I lie awake for an hour. Later I wake crying from a nightmare; I was in the camp trying to protect a child, I tried to run and scream but my legs were stiff and my throat empty.

Over the next weeks I try to organise a visit to Curtin. A young childcare worker offers to come with me. She is dedicated, organised and outraged, among the growing group of Australians that have seen what is happening and will do anything. Only a few priests have ever been to Curtin, no-one else. We are determined.

After weeks of gymnastics, the manager gives us short notice for a visiting date, assuming we will not be able to organise ourselves in time. Wrong.

Everything about Curtin seems unreal: the drive through the red desert from Broome, the Air Force warning sign at the entry to the long road leading to the centre. Shrubs line the road as we approach, and the wire comes up suddenly. It's not as big as I expect, not as menacing, no razor wire like Woomera and Villawood, just a couple of fences and some barbed wire. We unload bags of donations from the car; the air is buzzing and shimmering with the heat. My heart thumps. I gather the confidence you need to walk into these places – you need to exude an absolute certainty that you are going to be let in. There is every chance that the manager will try and block us with some dreamed-up protocol.

We are early and, waiting outside a tin demountable, my chest feels tight. A white ute arrives and a burly guard with sunglasses gets out. He lets us in. All the clothes have to be unpacked. The guard checks the collars of baby jumpsuits.

We are taken through to an area with old plastic chairs under a tree. After some time a guard comes with Mahmoud, a tall, clean-shaven, young Iranian man with a scrupulously ironed shirt walking through the dust. We are all nervous: in four years visiting detention centres I have never figured out what I can possibly say to someone locked up in the desert in my country for years. Yet I am relieved that we get in, and happy to meet Mahmoud after months of talking on the phone. He seems happy that we have come, and in disbelief that we are actually there.

We have work to do, being allowed to spend only two days visiting 50 people. Every 15 minutes a new family comes out. Most of them have been there for two years and no-one has ever come to see them before. They think Australians must hate them. They tell us about their lives there, about their children, they cry and the children sit silently. It overwhelmingly reminds me of a hospital: they seem fragile and bruised, with dark circles around their eyes. A guard and a translator sit close to listen in. I feel sick. I explain what we are doing to try and help. I feel heartless saying goodbye after 15 minutes. I come with hope that I can help them, but the weight of the responsibility sinks in, it is each of their lives, every single one of those lives, and they are so far away from any of us. I give up writing notes, mostly because I cannot think any more. I just want to run.

The two days are over. Leaving the centre, I have a feeling I can't put words to, the feeling of it not being real next to the knowledge that it is. Driving away down the highway, I slow down. We have to go back. I almost turn the car around – how can I leave them there?

Cold air, green pines and a very ill two-year-old greet me at home. She has been sick the whole time I have been away. My mother thinks it is the stress of the work I'm doing. I sleep for two days and then keep on working.

After two-and-a-half more years in desert detention centres, Child Protection gave their certifications and most of the families were released on Bridging Visas. Most of the families were also finally recognised as refugees.

I have only one photo of my daughter from the year I went to Curtin. Someone else took it.

Brown envelopes from Nauru

*Community pharmacist **Elaine Smith** tracks her long-distance relationship with a very talented Afghani detainee*

Another brown envelope from Nauru! It must be from Daud (not his real name). His brown envelopes can bring many surprises: gifts of art, enthusiastic letters and news of day-to-day activities in the camp. I have learned about soccer matches, the concerts, women's needlework displays, the chess competition. We concentrate on the good things.

Today I hurry to open the package and find a green embroidered handkerchief. A little note pinned to it reads: *'This is the afghanistans most famese* [sic] *embroidery. It name is "Kamaki" it is a gift from my girlfriend when I came from home to Australia.'*

Now I am not so happy. Why is he sending this to me? Surely this token from his fiancé should be with him always. I know he is under pressure from Australia's Department of Immigration to go home. If he goes home, his fiancé will want to know he has kept it safe these three years. If he is accepted by Australia, then he should have it with him to remind him each day until they can be together.

I feel a bit panicky now. Has something happened? It should not be mine. Has he given up all hope? I feel frightened. I know some people have attempted suicide; others are losing their grasp on reality. Most are despairing and depressed. They have been told that they will never be accepted by Australia and their only choice is to return home.

I know this handkerchief has been soaked in sea water and tears. Daud told me:

'After a very big struggle in Indonesia I reached to Ashmore Reef on my number tenth boat. I sat on 10 boats to reach Australia. I have very big stories of life and death. I am a very big survivor. I was arrested many times in Indonesia and then escaped from the jails. If I reached on my first boat to Australia I think I had not been rejected by your government. This is all because of my luck. I am not a lucky person. One day I will achieve my destiny, struggle will defeat the luck.'

Now he is stuck in Nauru, losing heart. He began with so much energy, enthusiasm and confidence. Can he see no future for himself, no chance to marry and make a safe life for a family?

His previous gifts did not make me feel worried. I remember his first letter so well. He wrote to tell me about the soccer matches in the detention camps on Nauru.

I had begun writing to a number of refugees in the camp. I sent tentative letters to them, feeling very unsure. I knew nothing of Afghanistan, nothing about Nauru. Now I was writing to five Hazara men, and finding that I liked them very much. I wanted to send a message to the people held on that isolated island that they were not despised and abandoned by the whole world. The Hazara group have been cruelly targeted time and again, most recently by the Taliban. I wanted to tell them that we sympathised with their terrible circumstances and we recognised their heroism, their integrity, courage, intelligence and determination.

I knew there were negative images in the Australian media, so I wanted to find a way to show their humanity. White Australians have not experienced witnessing whole villages executed, family members tortured, children taken at gunpoint, utter powerlessness in a place where there is no functioning police force or legal system. These stories only seemed to further alienate the refugees from average Australians, and evoke no compassion or understanding. So I thought the only way to bridge the gap was to illustrate our common humanity. I wanted to relate what I was learning about their love for their families, their thirst for education, their joy in sports, their driving hope for a safe life. My friends were helping each other in the camp, organising sports, teaching each other skills, holding study classes, doing woodwork, making clothes, putting on concerts. I asked my friends to write and tell little anecdotes about their hopes and dreams, to explain their hobbies and passions. The refugees could not understand why I wanted this. Here they were struggling for justice, trying to save the lives of their kids, and I was asking about hobbies and sports!

But Daud heard about my strange request, and in his lengthy and detailed first letter, wrote: *'I received no letter from you but I studied your letter you send to my friend. I am a soccer player. Besides football I have a keen interest in fine arts.'* I began to hear about chess games, art displays, a traditional cooking fair, sports and music. Most of his letter told me about the soccer competition. I learned the names of the teams and the scores from each of the games. Daud's team played in the best game of the competition, but they were defeated and did not go through to the finals. I heard about his trouble with shoes.

This lovely young man, not yet 21, began to tell me his story, send me photos. His words were a window into the camp. I could understand so much more. His shoes were wearing out because the camp was built on a rough, mined-out plateau. The surface was hot, sharp rocks of limestone and coral. This was no tropical paradise. IOM (International Organisation for Migration, the camp managers) gave each person one pair of sneakers for the year.

'Our sports shoes are very thin especially in our rough play ground. It was my tenth shoes with which I entered yesterday in the ground. I got nine sports shoes by exchanging my shirts, pants and other things with other refugees. A few shoes given by my friends who doesn't do sports.'

By this time I was writing to many people. They asked me for shoes, sunglasses, toys for the kids, but mostly for a watch, a picture of the *Tampa* and a camera. They sent back rolls of film for developing. I found I could place each photo, using Daud's map. The photos showed me the metal containers they lived in, the clinic, the running track, the makeshift bathrooms with sheets of plastic for walls, the women's house, where they could go with the babies and girls to be together, away from the hundreds of men and guards. The camp was a fenced-in sports ground.

Then, in the next envelope, was a drawing of the water line-up. I had seen this in photos, too, but not understood it. The guard in Daud's picture says, *'Sorry, water has finished. You have to wait till tomorrow.'*

What was this about? Then I learned that Nauru did not have enough water for its own people, let alone the 1000-plus refugees. Water for staff was shipped in, but for the camp there was a desalination plant that was started up intermittently. There was fresh water for an hour or two, then salt water for a few hours, then nothing. Rain was a gift from God, to wash the salt off the skin. People were driven back from the unflushable toilets by the smell and the insects.

The surprises in the brown envelopes kept coming. I saw the portrait of an old man who can only grieve for his family left behind. Picture after picture arrived, telling me more than all the letters and photos, and Daud explained to me that he had worked as an embroiderer since he was twelve.

'You are an artist,' I wrote to him, and began sending art books, postcards from art galleries, embroidery thread.

'I learnt the embridry [sic] *because I like it. I am not an artist before this camp. Before I just drawing the blue print of embridry. In the camp one of my best friends is start teaching me about art. He has very good skill. So I start painting in Nauru camp. My daily practising and madness about art shows the result, and now he is astonish about me that I learn so quickly. But I just follow the words of the great artist of the world. Michelangelo said on the margin of his pupils drawing, "Draw, Antonio, draw Antonio and lose no time." "Take courage Andreas, Trust in me. You will find joy enough!" I felt that Michelangelo said these words to me and I just drawing and drawing. I think art is life and I want to dedicate all my life for art. I want to prove that I have ability like the great artist, and Inshalah, I will be a big artist.'*

He waited eagerly for letters and parcels from me; I waited eagerly for those brown envelopes with a treasure folded inside. *'I need some pencils, 4B, 5B, 6B. We need some books about art specially figer drawings, full body.' 'I will need some books, a book about history of art. A book about colour mixing, and of course some embridry materials.' 'I need a book about anatomy.'*

I began to receive copies of master art works, drawings, oil paintings, embroidery. The Taliban would not have approved of his whimsical works, let alone the nudes and religious classics.

He told me about the art and embroidery classes he was teaching. He was attending English classes himself, taught by a friend.

'I want to be as expressive with language as art,' he wrote.

He found he really liked working with pastels. He experimented with everything I sent. Then I heard about Daud and his friend painting murals on the Nauru jail walls, pictures showing Nauru dancers and Afghan dancers. He continued to fill me in on the chess competition, the

running race he won. Then, suddenly, I receive a note with a drawing called 'Screaming boy':

'I have written my name for deport. Very few of my students are left in my art class because in the camp the people are very in tension. They are always thinking about their futures. No body are playing soccer in our play ground. I think these all things are because of the tension.'

Refugees are called for weekly meetings. DIMIA has been applying pressure. Daud sent me one of their documents. It states, *'You may not stay in Nauru indefinitely and there is no chance of you going to Australia by staying here longer … The Australian Government is exploring all options for return including involuntary return.'*

Then, on 30 November, he was flown out. I phoned him in Kabul. I did not know what to say; he tried to make a joke. I phoned a few days later, but he was gone, trying to get to his mother. It was a dangerous thing to do, even at that time.

Now he is in Pakistan. I phone again but still do not know what to say. He is working again as an embroiderer.

'I have given up art,' he tells me. His fiancé still waits for him. I have his pictures on my wall and I have the green handkerchief. I tell him I am writing this story. Then, an email:

'hi
how are you hope you are fine.
I read the email wich you send to me, this is ok you can write any things about me no problems for me at all.
you can write about me caz i trust you i love you so much you knew i am always telling my friends that i have a very sweet mother in austrialia her name is elain smith and she loves me so much.
take care of your health be happy always.
your son "Daud"
thanks'

Nauru: counting the human cost

*Writer and researcher **Susan Metcalfe**, who visited Nauru several times, chronicles the hardships and hopes of detainees and locals alike*

When I finally decided to write to a few people in detention, I chose Nauru in the hope that the geographical distance might provide some psychological distance for me. Once I was corresponding with one person, this quickly grew to include many others, and my role ultimately became central to many of the people who were the last to leave over the past few years.

The nightly phone calls often included talk of suicidal thoughts, anxieties, depression, fear, deep uncertainty about the future, hopelessness, grief and more grief. Some were in tears as they tried to speak; they didn't feel they could keep going. They were grateful to so many Australian people for their support, but how many more years would they have to wait for their freedom? Others did not have the English words to explain, but their mental anguish was clear, and I worked to reassure them we would never give up. Most tried hard to make the best of a difficult situation, but it was often the depression of the people around them that was hardest to bear.

It was also clear that the Department of Immigration was tasked to maintain pressure on people to return to their homelands. More than once, some of us received frightened calls from young men with shaking voices who felt sure they would be taken back by force after visits from Immigration. The aftermath always meant days or weeks of calming people down and many found it impossible to ever relax in the face of such heavy-handed intimidation.

On my visits in 2005 I spent time with the remaining 52 people, who sat and told me their desperate stories. Independent visitors from Australia had been rare, and I had already developed close relationships with many of the people over the phone and by email and fax. Some of the young men took me to their rooms and we sat, we cried, we shared their pain of years of uncertainty, living in limbo in Nauru. Over hours, sometimes, men and women talked about their journeys, their lives back in their homelands, their children, their mothers. Some had lived for much of their lives under surveillance in Iraq, some had been tortured, all had experienced some degree of trauma.

I will never forget the embrace of one man whose body shook as he begged me through uncontrolled sobs to help him. There was no possibility that he could safely return to his country, but he had a wife and children he needed to support. He was broken by the years in limbo and felt powerlessness to fulfil obligations to his family. But, most of all, he loved his children. He missed them deeply, and the separation was unbearable for him each and every day.

The despair I have witnessed in people in the camps (I have now made six visits to Nauru in the past two years) has manifested from years of uncertainty, struggle, feeling powerless and from not being heard. Everyone was tired of waiting, of hanging on to hope and battling with the fear that they might be forced to return to the hostilities they had left behind. Some workers in the camp were angels, others unsympathetic. Everyone coped differently with their situation, some self-harming by burning or cutting themselves, some spending much of their time crying. But all of it has been unnecessary and it should never have been allowed to happen.

During my visits to Nauru, I have spoken with many Nauruans about the offshore processing centres. What I discovered most profoundly in my first visit was that Nauruans were as misinformed about the people in the camps as the asylum seekers had been about Nauruan people. There was an intangible but distinct separation between the camps and local life, and neither group had much understanding of the other.

I sat with one Nauruan man who wept as I told him some of the stories of people in the camp. He had known nothing of their suffering or of the length of time people had remained in his country. I told him about vulnerable teenage boys who were away from their families for the first time, sometimes crying alone in their rooms, and how the Australian people they corresponded with had become their replacement families. I told him about the despair of women trying to raise children in a camp environment, about the many people who took medication to sleep or to relieve their anxiety and depression. He shared with me stories about his lifetime of hard work, of his savings now lost by Nauruan governments – his grief was still raw as he spoke about his erosion of faith in his country.

I discovered that the Nauruan people genuinely believed that hosting the camps was a humanitarian act. Many understood that they were offering their traditional hospitality by taking people from the *Tampa* and giving them food and shelter. This is the way of the Nauruans, and I have been fortunate to experience their kindness and warmth on all my visits.

The Statehouse Processing Centre is now perhaps the best-resourced area in the country, with 24-hour power, water and three meals provided each day. In contrast, most Nauruans must endure regular power outages and many struggle to put one meal on the table each day for their usually large families. I have personally felt guilty to be sitting with people eating so much food in the camp, when local Nauruans just down the road are not able to provide adequate food for their children. It is an unfair and unnecessary comparison to have to make, when asylum seekers could so easily be processed on our own soil, in a wealthy country.

At the core of what has made the offshore processing of asylum seekers so unacceptable has been the lack of legal representation and advice, the lack of a right to an independent appeal against decisions, the length of time taken to resolve people's situations, the effects of the uncertainty, which have no cure. Without a fair process, held in another country, innocent people can be denied a future and left in uncertainty for indefinite periods.

As I write, one Iraqi man remains in limbo in Nauru after five years – his future is uncertain. At the same time, a group of Burmese men seeking asylum have just begun their stay on Nauru. No-one knows how long they will remain or how they will cope. On my recent visit to meet them, they showed me only the greatest kindness and hospitality, and I hope that their need for a safe resettlement option will soon be met.

Of those who returned to their homelands in recent years, I am sure that some cases were not fairly processed. It is most likely that if those people had stayed in Nauru, they would have eventually been resettled as refugees in Australia. Since their return, some of those people are doing okay, others are living in precarious situations.

Even those who have come to Australia are struggling with their new lives, particularly those who remain on temporary visas. TPVs were introduced in 1999 as one of the Howard Government's punitive attempts to deter asylum seekers. A person on a temporary visa cannot sponsor their family to Australia and is not guaranteed entry back into the country if they leave. Many women and children remain in difficult circumstances in other countries whilst they wait for their husbands to eventually be granted permanent status. For some men who have already spent years in detention, the separation from their families could last more than a decade.

The stories I have heard from Iraqi people, in particular, are devastating. One recent call was from an Iraqi man on a TPV who had just heard that his young female relative had been raped and murdered by insurgents back home. Others remain concerned about health problems of family members, or the obvious dangers of bombs going off around their friends and relatives each day. When they watch the news on TV they are frightened. When they hear that 30 or 40 people have died in the violence in their country, they do not know if it might be the death of someone they hold dear. Their futures remain uncertain. If the Australian Government chose to help, it could, right now, grant permanent visas to all those in Australia whose status is unresolved.

The asylum seekers I have been involved with over the years simply want to live normal and peaceful lives. They do not want to do battle with the Australian government, they do not want more problems than they already have. The individual human life is the one I am fighting for, for each human being to be treated with respect and dignity.

The generosity of spirit, the kindness and the hospitality of so many asylum seekers and refugees I have met has been the reason I could keep going. My involvement with refugees has also led me to meet some of the most wonderful Australian people, with hearts of gold. Their kindness, their care for refugees and the support they have given me have been extraordinary.

I have paid a heavy personal price – physically, emotionally and financially – for my involvement in advocating and supporting refugees and asylum seekers, but I could not have taken a different path. These people have paid the heaviest price of all, and until the Australian government adopts a less political and more sensitive attitude to the arrival of human beings to our shores, we must all keep speaking out.

I REMEMBER HIS EYES

Child psychiatrist ***Louise Newman*** *visits a remote facility and confronts the despair of a philosopher detained there*

We are in the small plane. It is hot; level, monotonous miles of nothing, waiting for the appearance of the mirage-like glint of a town in the desert and a camp. You are the Government man and sit too close to me, your thigh pressed against mine. You smile, but I don't know why, as we journey to this dark, dark place. You give me policy papers to read and approve. You seem to believe this is somehow alright, necessary, acceptable in the name of some greater good. You put on dark glasses and I cannot read your face any more. Blazing sun blinds me. What are we meant to see?

I am thinking about the last time I came to this place. The pity of it all and how it left me scarred and not the person I was before. I saw too much and could do very little. That time I met a man who could not speak. At home he was a philosopher, a thinker. In the camp he became a protestor and now is broken, parched like the sand. Words hang in the air like ashes. His eyes are empty. He cannot tell me what he knows. I touch his hand as he cries. We arrange for him to go to hospital. The Government man wants him to stay in the camp. The camp can be like a hospital, the Government man says, the cells can be monitored, the man could speak if he wanted to. The Government man is impassive, his eyes are arctic blue, determined. I feel I am wilting before his gaze. The philosopher has been in a solitary cell for weeks. Madness has come upon him like a blessing, and he listens to the far-off voice of his mother.

The lawyers are angry. Letters fly back and forth, circulating around the philosopher, who has no capacity to know what is happening. Finally, late at night, he is transported to hospital. I am numb; no joy in this battle.

We arrive at the camp. You tell us it is improved, new buildings, new staff, new ways. To me, it still seems like a place in nowhere, limbo. We are in a small bus and it is hot, hot, relentless. You show us empty education rooms. We drive past burnt-out shells of rooms which stand untouched and rusting like monuments. You want them removed, but I think they should stay there, statues, covered in wreaths, gradually buried in desert sand. Some future archaeologist will come upon them and wonder what they could mean.

In the kitchen a young woman, pregnant, makes tea. She is black, beautiful, her face marked, her eyes downcast. We walk through. No-one speaks to her. We look at people in small rooms, the only air-conditioning. Most lie still on their beds. You tell us that a sportsground is being made. You seem surprised when I laugh at the idea of a football match in 45-degree heat.

We prepare to leave through the metal gates. I have a thought that we might be trapped, rising panic. Through the wire I see a Sister I know who visits. We embrace, and I cling to her arms, some sense of normality. She says she knows all this can be borne but I tell her that for me, without faith, it is different. I do not have her calm.

Home now, I only see images of the place that I could leave but the philosopher couldn't. The Government man is pleased with our visit. He is a believer. I am empty, and dream of the philosopher. Forsaken, I cry in my sleep.

Visions of Baxter

*Social worker **Bobbi Sawyer**'s visits inside the wire took her to emotional extremes*

This is a story about a butterfly. It was a hot day and I was waiting for Jon Jureidini inside the compound at Baxter. As I stood by the guard's office, I struck up a conversation. I have no idea why – I had done this before and it always led to feelings of disgust and wishing I hadn't bothered. Well, at least I was making an effort to be friendly, although if Jon saw me he'd probably think I'd got a touch of the sun.

I comment about how boring it must be for the children in here. The guard responds angrily and proceeds to rave about how they would have stuff to do it they weren't so lazy, how they have soccer balls, cricket bats, PlayStation, videos and a pool table. I wander away; again, I can't be bothered. I am aware of his voice droning on in the background – 'If they don't like it, they should go back to where they came from'. I sit on the cold cement steps, slip off my shoes, dig my toes into the grass, and drift away.

I hear some children in the background. I turn and see two boys at the window I've just retreated from, waiting patiently for the guard to acknowledge them. He doesn't. They wait, then get cheeky. He scolds them, and they wait and wait. I ask what they want and smile. The guard finally responds to them, and they request some videos. He refuses, telling them to go away and play outside: 'It's a lovely day.'

They look disappointed and walk away. One boy turns back to me. He is small, maybe seven, and from Iran, is my guess. He asks if I'm DIMIA or ACM, I say 'Neither', and search for my badge. They both smile broadly and come and sit with me, their little legs dangling from the steps. We talk about nothing in particular, then I point to a butterfly I can see on the lawn. One of the boys catches it to look at its colours. It's quite beautiful, all blues with a dash of yellow. I encourage him not to squash it in his little hands.

They begin to talk about where it has come from and why it has come to Baxter. They make up absurd reasons: 'For the food', they say, 'For the pool table', and laugh and call things to the guard. He ignores them.

I ask about what they would like to do with it. They think for a while and then say, 'Keep it'. I tell them I have an idea. They pass me the butterfly; it acts scared, standing very still as I cup it in my hands. We walk towards the mesh section of the compound; we can see the Flinders Ranges in the distance and the vast, blue sky.

One of the boys suddenly understands my idea. He says, 'We'll give it freedom', and they start to chant as I hold it up to the small wire squares. The butterfly sits on the wire and then flies off. The boys cheer and say, 'This lady knows about freedom'.

We stand there for a long time watching it fly away. I hope it does not come back.

The little boy reaches out and takes my hand. I feel tears well up in my eyes, and look down to see tears streaming down his face. He smiles through his tears as he looks up at me.

The heart of this story is disintegration – the complete annihilation of the human spirit. This is something I'd never really given too much thought to before Woomera, and then Baxter.

So I'll set the scene. I was called early in the new year by my colleague Jon to review a family – he was on holidays. The boy had engaged in self-harm since the forced transfer of the family from Woomera to Baxter.

I saw the family in their compound. The boy was about 12, the only child of educated, middle-class parents. His mother answered the door and proceeded to scream at me for not helping, and challenged me to look at her son. She was furious with me, the guards, DIMIA, everyone. I sat on the floor next to the bed where the boy was curled up in his blanket, looking quite odd. I had hoped that by sitting on the ground she would sit and this might take the intensity out of the situation. This wasn't the case. She stood over me and screamed in Farsi, she paced, she ranted, she raved, she cried. Eventually, when she could scream no more, she sat down to show me the bruises on her knees and the cuts on top of her feet. There were circles on the top of her feet where small scabs had started to form; her knees were blue. As I looked at her injuries I felt like turning away. She spoke at great length about how she had received them. After refusing to leave Woomera, she and her son were handcuffed and dragged out on their knees by the guards, to be taken to Baxter.

I became aware of her son behind me. He was rocking back and forth, sucking and dribbling, flapping his hands, and then he formed a diamond with his hands. He reminded me of my visits as a child to the Special School, where an autistic child sat on his own, rocking, not communicating, in his own world. I had to pull myself back from these images because this boy wasn't delayed, he wasn't autistic; he was regressed and distressed due to brutal treatment at the hands of the guards. I don't remember if he communicated with me at all that day, but I remember his self-soothing actions as if it were yesterday.

I remember him trying to cover his mother's mouth as she was telling the story, as if the whole thing was too unbearable to hear. He became angry with me for making her upset, I assume. I'm unsure of any assessment I did that day, I just remember the complete horror, and thinking they had to get out of there, no matter what.

She eventually became calmer and communicated with me in an unusual way, speaking slowly, almost whispering, imploring me to do something. I discussed hospital and thought we had almost agreed to it. She then showed me an ID badge of her husband from Woomera. It had a photo, he was a strapping man in his late thirties, tanned and fit. She then asked if I could see him because she was worried. I will always regret saying yes. I'd known her husband was in bed in the adjoining room, and if I had craned my neck I could have seen him, but I didn't.

I stepped into his room. He was lying rigid on top of a single bed; the image seems surreal as I look back. It seemed as though he made no impression on the mattress, almost as if he were floating just above it. He was fully dressed and wore a woollen beanie; it was the middle of summer. I suddenly became aware of how hot and close these rooms were. His arms were by his side as he lay on his back, stiff. He was a strange grey colour and he looked about seventy. He reminded me of my grandfather, who died when I was a child. He was in his sixties then, tall and thin and unable to get up from the couch for all the years I had known him. This was after a stroke at 50 and emphysema in his later years. He was on oxygen and, despite this, continued to chain-smoke. He was a ghastly colour, and sounded scary when he breathed.

I stepped out of the room, initially believing the man might be dead, but later realising he wasn't. I had no idea what to do, and felt scared and horrified. I remember trying not to show my horror to his wife, but I don't think she was fooled. I looked like a scared kid retreating from that room, just as I had when I ran through Grandpa's lounge hoping he wouldn't call out 'Bub' and ask me to give him a hug.

KITES AT BAXTER

***Linda Fienberg**, a teacher of woodwork and sustainable design, remembers an act of solidarity with detainees*

During the summer of 2004–05, I read Khaled Hosseini's *The Kite Runner*. It's a wonderful book about boyhood hopes and fears and adult guilt and silence, about growing up in Afghanistan and fleeing to a new life in Canada – and about the exhilaration and spectacle of kite-flying, an integral part of a boy's life in Kabul.

Most refugees in our detention centres come from kite-flying cultures. The Chinese have been flying kites for well over 2000 years, and tens of thousands of Hindus and Muslims fly kites during their spring festivals each year. Flying kites is part of everyday life for all ages in Pakistan, India, Sri Lanka, Chile, China, Iraq and Iran.

That's why we wanted to fly kites at Baxter, where asylum seekers can be held for five years or more. People from every part of Australia had planned to meet there at Easter 2005 to protest this injustice.

Baxter – a concrete bunker, wire-wrapped, with no real people visible, only uniform lines of robotic, black forms and blank gazes. Unlike Woomera and Port Hedland, Baxter is fortified. High, solid walls prevent one from seeing and being seen. The metres of wall surround small, open exercise yards – no-one inside can see out, only up. The people inside have travelled halfway around the world in search of a heartland and instead found themselves trapped in a box – do they know they're surrounded by an amazing landscape of red and saltbush grey?

This is the ultimate in propaganda wars – *what refugees*? Not one of the 350 detainees can be seen by the media crews as they visit by bus, car and even helicopter (the Channel 7 helicopter, paid for by the Federal Police, strangely sees only us). And nor can they be seen by us, the 350 protestors – one for every person inside – who gather here at Easter to let them know there really are Australians who care and who believe that treating people as human is what being human is about.

So the idea of flying kites at the protest – well, it was perfect. How else to communicate with those inside? We also had balloons, wonderful in their party colours – we hope they brought cheer. But Baxter was no party, and it was important that those trapped inside knew we knew that. Kites were right in many ways: as a form of correspondence, each kite a letter individually written by a person in Sydney, Melbourne or Perth with words or images or just colour; delicately, playfully sent, and in a 'language' many inside would have appreciated.

In preparation for the Easter protest, in March 2005 over 50 people joined workshops to make and paint kites. For many people this was the only way to participate – Baxter is a very long way away. Two busloads drove from Sydney carrying the kites, and many more were made on the way, with much cutting, colouring-in and threading accompanying the songwriting and talking throughout the long journey. The rendezvous point for everyone arriving in buses and cars from Adelaide, Perth,

Melbourne, Brisbane, Sydney and more remote places was 3 kilometres from the gates of Baxter.

Baxter is on land traditionally owned by Aboriginal peoples, especially the Barngala people, who kindly invited us onto the land for this protest. This land, 12 kilometres south-west of Port Augusta, is an amazing place. At the horizon, 360 degrees of serpentine ranges, and in the foreground dot-painted, grey-blue saltbush, growing in the finest red dust - so fine that it is still in my tent two washes and 20 months later. And above there's a dome of blue, blue sky …

… and then, as we look, a kite darts, ducks and sidesteps, trying to fool the guards that it is not on its weaving way to visit the 350 people almost directly below it who can only look up, not out. Fascinated, we - the protesters outside - follow its path as it plays, feathery and tissue-light. The contrast between this fickle-free lightness and the grounded, faceless prison below could not be greater.

But suddenly the kite descends and dives crashing to the ground. We all look to find the kite runner, who's been too captivated by the flight (and her own ability to help give life to tissue and bamboo) to notice the police moving towards her. They grab her and the crushed kite, and in due course she is charged with 'illegal flying of kites in prohibited air space'! Moments later, a line of men and women flying a row of 18 kites is also attacked by police, the kites 'arrested', torn or taken away.

What a sad thing! The kites had been intended to give happiness to those inside Baxter and to show the wider Australian community that we were not violent or difficult people - we were just doing something important and different over the Easter weekend.

Of the hundred kites that had been made, only a small fraction flew that day. Some were saved and will fly again.

Children overboard

***Andrew Weldon**'s work appears regularly in* The Big Issue, The Sydney Morning Herald, The Age *and* The Chaser.

Objective view

***Peter Nicholson** is a cartoonist for* The Australian.

You are cruel

***Alan Moir**, The Sydney Morning Herald Editorial Cartoonist since 1984, has won Editorial Cartoonist of Year six times, and two Walkley Awards for Best Cartoon.*

Ruddock tours Woomera

***Andrew Weldon**'s work appears regularly in* The Big Issue, The Sydney Morning Herald, The Age *and* The Chaser.

Part 3

Deliberate harm

Confronting the banality of evil ... This is not history, but here and now; this is our reality, the reality of our country, our times. The detention centre in the suburbs; the petty cruelty and tyranny of policy and practice that claims not to punish but aims to deter; the sadness of story after story. As these stories accumulate, there is a growing sense of disbelief – 'This cannot be my country, my history', and then a profound disillusionment, a loss of innocence.

No-one who hears these stories can remain the same, knowing that evil is ordinary, very simple and enacted in everyday ways, done in all our names, the reality distorted until we take it as given, justified, even necessary, for some greater goal. Core beliefs and assumptions have been challenged by contact with asylum seekers: the powerlessness of attempting to help those who remain imprisoned; the frustration of being a 'professional' in a system which has little respect for knowledge or skills; the continuous distortion of the truth.

These are the stories of individuals confronting the moral and ethical dilemmas raised by their engagement with government immigration policy; stories of personal struggles when roles and beliefs are called into question – 'Should I speak or remain silent?', 'What can I do?', 'Where does professionalism end and advocacy begin, and is there a difference?', 'Can we operate without compromise within a flawed system?', 'How can these things be done in my name?'

With the refugees

*Former journalist **Madeleine Byrne** discusses the difficulty of remaining neutral in the face of inhumanity*

Standing at the front of the bus as it careered through the yellow canola fields and the red desert of South Australia, I awkwardly introduced myself.

'I am a journalist,' I said.

While this was true, it felt like a certain amount of front. By then I had mostly written on European politics and culture after a foray into rock journalism at age nineteen.

Unblinking eyes stared back at me.

'And, ah, I'm hoping to report on this weekend's events at Woomera.'

Silence. I fumbled: 'There should be some interest ... ah, somewhere.'

My audience – white-haired pensioners in tracksuits and hip activists in black, piercings and peroxide – remained unconvinced, and yet over that weekend they did speak to me. Recordings I made during that first 'convergence' on Woomera in September 2001 included a young priest confessing his shame as we crouched in the back of the minibus, and cries of distress as water cannons pummelled asylum seekers, pushing them into the dirt.

The morning was spent playing Arabic music, making earnest speeches, unfurling a banner saying 'Welcome' and flying kites in the air. Kites were symbolic, organisers said, of freedom, and were banned inside detention centres. Management feared that they would carry messages to those new arrivals being held in isolation, in some cases, for periods stretching to months.

During the meetings, organisers discussed what would happen if police made arrests, and I remember feeling uneasy about this. Making the overnight journey to Woomera to join the 200 or so others from Canberra and Sydney was not a political action for me. By then, Australia's response to 'boat people', the daily reports of self-harm, protest, violence had become news. I was curious to see what was going on.

When tear gas and a water cannon were used for the first time against asylum seekers at Woomera in August 2000, there was an instant media response. As people allegedly tried to escape, a local petrol-station owner, David Kirby, was reported saying the water cannon 'blows them away from the fence and they get up again and come charging in. It seems to be an ongoing battle'. His wife, Beth Kirby, who later became the principal media contact, claimed that the detainees threw 'homemade spears and rocks at the authorities who used a water cannon and tear gas to bring them under control'.

Columns of water pushed human bodies, transforming them into crumpled forms like burnt paper in the wind. Tear gas was used against the crowd – for the second time in Australia's history. Former Immigration Minister Philip Ruddock stated that 'one canister of tear gas' was used to control the crowd.

Nigel Hoffmann was working as an Activities Officer inside Woomera at the time. 'We got word – emails – that there would be trouble,' he later told me, as The National Council of Churches had organised demonstrations, called 'Refugee Sunday'. In response, ACM management organised 'falafel rolls for lunch and Arabic-style chicken for the Saturday night meal (when it) normally was cabbage and meat loaf, rice – really, really cheap food'. Hoffmann organised pony rides for the children, alongside soccer and backgammon. Asylum seekers had coffee for the first time.

'But they had extra security staff on – riots squads,' he recalled. Walking back to his office, Hoffmann saw 'a fully kitted-out riot squad, in helmets, with batons and shin pads – everything, a team of a dozen'. Earlier that morning, CERT teams – tactical response staff employed by ACM – were flown in from prisons and detention centres across Australia. Protests rose and fell throughout the weekend, Hoffmann said, but on Sunday 'after dinner, the CERT team went in, following this policy of separation and extraction they have'. This 'provocative' move, he said, terrified the Middle Eastern detainees. 'So a few of the boys threw some rocks and it just turned into a running battle.' The CERT teams used water cannon on the crowd of men, women and children twice; then fired tear gas into the crowd at about one in the morning, Hoffmann said. 'The riot police just loved this stuff,' he said. They would 'line up and charge in, thumping people. A lot of detainees got hurt pretty badly, but they didn't turn up for treatment.'

None of this is surprising six years on. Many Australians, it appears, are now immune to reports of this kind of violence within the country's immigration detention system. Yet, what I saw in September 2001 shocked me.

Later, when I mentioned this in passing to Lyn Bender, a psychologist who had worked at Woomera, she wondered whether this display of force had a broader purpose [*see Lyn Bender's story*]. Perhaps it operated on two levels, she said; firstly, against the asylum seekers, but also against those of us standing there, unable to act. Undeniably, seeing it altered the course of my life, forcing me to develop a professional and personal identity that has not always been an easy fit.

On the journey back, I remember feeling shell-shocked (and making repeated phone calls to media outlets in an effort to interest them in the story). The tear gas and water cannon, I wanted them to know, had been used with no apparent provocation. On the Monday, the calls continued, but with no success; by then, the story was 'old news'.

Now I recall desperation in my movements. I could hear anxiety in my voice. It is the same urgency that I notice in long-term supporters of detained asylum seekers: an almost compulsive need to be heard. Both the general lack of interest and my response have come to symbolise the rather uneasy relationship of two equally important parts of my life. One print journalist I contacted asked, when assessing my claims, where I was standing. 'Oh, you were with the refugee people, then,' he said.

'With the refugee people' BBC journalist Martin Bell has endorsed a 'journalism of attachment', saying that with some subjects it is impossible for journalists to be 'neutral'. Crimes against humanity require accomplices, he claims, and there is 'not only the hatred that makes it happen, but the *indifference that lets it happen*'. Bell, a foreign affairs correspondent: 'It's not polemical. John Pilger is too polemical for me. What I mean is a journalism which cares as well as knows.' He described a journalism 'that is aware of its responsibilities; and will not stand neutrally between good and evil, right and wrong, the victim and the oppressor'.

And yet, when writing on such a contested subject as Australia's immigration detention system, Bell's fine ideas can often seem little more than that. How is it possible to report fairly on a subject when the two sides are so unbalanced, not only in terms of public sympathy but in the sense of who has a voice?

That year I did get a chance for a one-on-one with the Minister, after stepping in for another journalist. What remains with me now is a memory of his foot bent so that it tapped, perhaps nervously or with boredom, throughout the interview. Offering an occasional smile, in his tortured syntax he detailed a new visa for women suspected of being trafficked as sex slaves.

In contrast, asylum seekers and refugees now in the community rarely speak. Much of their silence over the past decade undeniably reflects badly on local journalists, whose laziness and unwarranted respect for the official story has allowed lies and shameless distortions to remain uncontested. But diffuse fears about speaking publicly, of being 'Bakhtiarised' – of being hounded by the media, in concert with the government, as that hapless family from Afghanistan was – have also reinforced the status quo.

None of this is surprising. Those found to be refugees were released on three-year visas (TPVs) that required the Minister's approval before having any chance of living in Australia on a permanent basis. This, the persecution that forced them to flee, and then their terrifying, mystifying ordeal in detention meant that they trusted no-one.

Getting close requires a negotiation of two often conflicting demands: those of your profession and of your peers, which at times cannot be simply reconciled. One of journalism's noblest characteristics lies in its recognition that fairness (not impartiality) uncovers the truth. Good journalism, while motivated by justice, makes this clear through its openness to the shifting, messy complexity of human motivation and behaviour.

What does this mean in practice, though, when reporting on Australia's mandatory detention system, which has damaged so many lives?

Immediately after leaving SBS TV in 2004, I started work on an investigative piece about staff in immigration detention. Dominating my mind was a simple question, which expressed itself in an image: what thoughts passed through the staff's minds as they walked through the detention centre gates, or put on their uniforms each morning? Through this research, I started to understand how different it was reporting on something you feel strongly about. Previously, I was well informed, but here the politics were shaped by the tragedy of individual lives.

The following April, as part of 'The People's Inquiry into Detention' – Australia's first national non-governmental inquiry into the country's mandatory detention system – I went to Baxter for the first time. Having my wrist stamped, handing over my passport and being frisked when passing through security made it seem like we were entering another world, where everything was new but still strangely familiar.

Inside the Visitors Area, with its joyless, primary-coloured play equipment and the enormous banner stating 'Jesus is Alive', I met with three asylum seekers who had been detained for periods of four to five years. One brought me a book of photographs from his home country so that we might have something to talk about during our first meeting. Within minutes, a guard took it from him (as it had not been cleared through 'Property'). What threat this book of wildlife and nature photographs posed to the security of the immigration detention centre was far from clear.

Absurdities dominate the detention experience. At one end are random acts of violence; at the other, instances of institutional bullying. These kinds of behaviour are expressions of the same impulse.

Going to Baxter was another turning point, as I had become part of the lives of two people detained there and they had become part of mine.

It is late, very late in the evening, as it always is. He rings me on my mobile, as he wants to talk. I slide down the wall, sitting flat against it with my back straight. In the background, I can hear the strange sounds of the detention centre; the sudden clanging of metal, and distorted announcements over a loud speaker. Such noise is a constant reminder of this place's foreignness where noise is impossible to escape. He just wants to talk.

Speaking in the rapid-fire, non-stop style I have come to expect, he talks about his worries about when and if he will be released. His fears about his Australian girlfriend, who no longer visits and has not called for months. I listen, but have little to say. He has been in detention for almost five years.

Two months after my first visit, I went back to Baxter. My friend was told he would be released, only for the decision to be postponed at the last minute. Observed by surveillance cameras and burly guards, my friend made me laugh, telling stories about his time on Cocos Island, which he made sound like a perverse kind of paradise. With his beanie pulled close down to his eyes, he refused to eat any of the pistachio nuts, dates, and other dried fruit I had brought with me. He kept rubbing his legs because of the cold, and repeating fragments from his earlier life.

In some respects, it is easier to write of the brutality than of the daily, monotonous cruelty that ultimately breaks a person's will to go on. In Baxter it is impossible to see anything aside from the sky. Moving about the centre is extremely complex. Coming to the Visitors Area, for instance, from the high-security compounds requires that the asylum seeker pass through a number of locked gates. At each of these, the accompanying guard must wait for permission from the control room before the gate opens. My friend told me that there would be times when he would be kept waiting for 10 minutes or even longer until permission was granted. He would have to wait in the cold and silence, aware that the guards were 'playing' with him, intentionally wasting his precious contact time with the outside world – and nothing could be done. Or, what about the weekly pork barbecues that inevitably excluded the mostly Muslim community; or the final moments when the guards did a head-count of the visitors before they were shunted into the 'airlock', and the first of many security locks was unlatched.

On my first visit to Baxter, I bought a book by an Iranian academic, Azar Nafisi, called *Reading Lolita in Tehran*. In it, I read a quote from the German philosopher, Theodor Adorno: 'The highest form of morality is not to feel at home in one's home'. Many people express dismay at what has happened in this country, and internalise it as a kind of shame, as if it were an aberration of the nation's proud history. But is it? One advantage of getting close is the way it forces you to see the world as it is; defined by great cruelty, but also by hope. Loneliness also comes to inform this awareness as you, too, begin to feel like a stranger in a land both so familiar and known, but also foreign, strange.

Sleeping children

***Dale West**, Director of Centacare Catholic Family Services, decries the brutality of a dawn raid*

At seven o'clock last Saturday morning, uniformed men and women representing the Federal Government burst into our house at Dulwich and arrested six children and their mother. It was clear that the planning for this operation had included a social visit the day before to 'case the joint' and determine who slept where. No thought was given to the re-traumatisation of these children by the surprise attack.

No time to dress properly, no time to pack, no food, no access to toilet, and no explanation. Sixteen months of integration into schools, social networks, and building trust, destroyed in three frantic minutes.

No nappy change for a baby boy snatched from his cot by a stranger, to cry all the way to Port Augusta. No bottle for him, either. No time to change the clothes of the youngest girl, who wet her pants as a fear reaction to being awoken by strangers. Simply forced to sit in the wet until arrival at the Baxter detention environment.

A very different day to the expectation of her St Aloysius teacher taking her to a birthday party.

No time for the oldest girl to place her scarf where it needs to be, as she was led, arms gripped, to one of three waiting motor vehicles.

Three days later, when I was able to visit the family inside the Baxter Detention Centre, the signs of trauma in the children had returned. On high alert, but withdrawn, needing continual reassurance, the little ones are clinging again, trust gone.

Children in our detention system are routinely terrorised. We now know it happens with planning, not by accident. The heart of our international reputation on human rights has been ripped out, like sleeping children from their beds.

My country?

*Mental health professionals **Rae Polden** and **Vanda Uminski** (both pseudonyms) see the effects of the cruelty in our national heart*

Remembering you, we also remember our country. Red hills, burning bushes, salt plains in the north, the silver highway to her far horizons.

We first meet you in a small clutch of families, shepherded by an interpreter and a guard. A small boy is running, running out of control. This is your son. 'You are our only hope,' is your introduction as, hoarse with grief and unshaven, you search our faces, as if to check if we each saw human beings. Soon you are shaken with sobbing, a merchant ruing the day you brought your treasure here.

We are coming home on a red rattler; it winds its long viaduct past the factories. It's a winter sunset. Long unseen upon life's platform, good friends greet us with a kiss. Graham has Aboriginal community friends in the north, he shows us his paintings and artifacts. Mistake Creek – he tells his friends' story of a massacre, what we'd rather forget in this country. So the history revisionists contest it. Silence, as the fire crackles and blazes. It gets cold early.

We've been at the hospital, under the pines and liquidambars that sleepy weekend afternoon, father, mother, a boy and a girl, a playroom specially chosen, ample chairs and spaces strewn with toys. Staff even offered tea, and the children drinks.

You spoke for your family, brisk, staccato, broken English, pleading ('Don't speak, it will be terrible for us all'), never observably stopping for breath, your glance darting round the tranquillity. More than infallibly polite, solicitous about our health, our trip. This first Australian day outside a wire fence, your watchmen had vanished. You heaved a sigh, and a weight had briefly eased across your chest.

We met months before, where scorching winds lift tumbleweed and blow in the faces at razor-wire palisade fencing. Wire sings songs ethereal. 'Trespassers!' broadcast all the notices. A coach is marooned at a roadside map outside the township, far-flung and far-fetched, living for its iron ore and its gulag. At this other Australian shore the sea is shining, out of sight. Fare forward, travellers. Ever so long the journey.

A boiled-eye turnkey minder barks 'No photos'. We idle hours kicking dust as the temperature rises. Water cannons and fire trucks, barely offstage right – ready to hose down all who get too heated. On entry they challenge our footwear – 'No open shoes. Occupational Health and Safety'. We're sent away, we change, 'Only closed shoes here'. Then, searching our kit bags, 'Bloody health nuts' (a couple of muesli bars).

Finally moving, gate to gate within the infernal empire. Past a lone tree and the manager's garden, tended by the inmates, who have no shoes at all. Children pass, chattering, even laughing; guards, not parents, escort them off to school, and we learn that school is on for the first time in months. We enter the hazard of labyrinth to find the main compound. Aimless boys roll tyres on blistering earth. Mattresses are propped against the fence, urine-soaked trousers hung out to dry. We wait, the desert wind lifting our papers, as runners from Management try to contain our subversion. Behind the garden, we sneak a look at the blood-spattered inmates' toilets, with shit-smeared seats. Then the messengers arrive to box us in.

Stoned by a mob, your life threatened, you had led them out and into a trap. Now you weep rivers of your country. You watch your dark-eyed daughter with the birthmark on her cheek hugging her cloth rabbit with its blue-coloured face. She holds her drawing of animals behind wire, in a zoo. It could be you, her, all of you. She leaves without speaking. Your son runs around, then draws endless fire trucks, engines of terror. And then you hold each other around the shoulders.

'The guards are like Afghan soldiers. They shouted and locked us in when wild men burnt our block down. They light their cigarettes, and our daughter jumps. She is terrified of the fires, and of a man who gashes himself. She is mute, she cries, she shakes all the time. She pulls her hair out in clumps. Our beloved girl is weak from not eating, so I must carry her. She can't keep dry, so we wash her sheets often. I have carried her in them to the bathroom. I have even wheeled her there in a barrow. Other children call her crazy, untouchable. They've locked her in rooms. Like others, she's missed school for months.'

Voices tumble over each other. 'None of us sleeps, and we are awake half the night to watch her. My hair has turned grey here, I cannot sleep, I lie in the dark for my headaches. Valium's no good, though they make me take it. They don't believe our story. The judge said it was irrelevant.' At the end, you hold our hands for what seems like forever.

And now, all over again, these months later, we hold your hands, closing the circle as if in beseeching, while the kids take themselves off and it all spills out. It's happening again. How you had warned the guards so many times, but no-one did anything, all indolent or asleep. You went to the dining room and she stayed behind, and you went back and found her hanging, behind the door. And then the reports repeat all the standard clauses. Woe upon them. Who cares for the life of a child, when none do care? They took her sheet and laid her on it. She had no hope for the future. Was that what was going on, that day it happened? You called to her and tried to make her hear you, but she didn't answer. 'Then I found her and screamed. And they laid her in her own sheet, and she was breathing.'

She was back now with her brother, chattering, resurrected, reprieved from the jaws of death. As if nothing had happened. She's won her family's release, on pain of disclosure. No detained children are out of school, there are no blood-spattered toilets, there's no blood on our hands. And there's no general release. The high price of mercy? Mr Ruddock has said so. What else would he have us be silent about in Australia?

The children took us out to the grove at the hospital, with its pine trees, and showed us the playground and the cage with its tiny rabbits. She said, 'That is us'. In farewell, resignation: 'Whatever you can do for us …'.

Birdsong somewhere, immaculate, illuminant, out of reach. The adamant country. Yes, this is our country and these are our people, too.

Pauline Hanson won the election of 2001

***Claire O'Connor**, a barrister who has acted for many detainees, reflects on the racism that underpins immigration law and practice*

As a lawyer employed primarily in legal aid and community environments, facing injustice for the underprivileged or those who have limited access to the courts and to fair outcomes was something I was used to.

However, working for detainees in detention centres in Australia was something I had never had to face before. The systemic discrimination and unfair treatment, the breach of civil and political rights, of international law, and the lack of humanity and care confronted and continues to confront me. While there were many, many good people all over Australia who worked to change this policy, it is important to remember that many others were prepared to use those who were seeking refuge in Australia for political gain.

How could this nation do bad things to good people? I think it is important to call it what it is. Racism has always been just below the surface in this nation. A nation whose Indigenous persons live in Third World conditions, a nation that had a 'White Australia Policy' for decades, a nation that has allowed many white persons escaping South Africa and Zimbabwe to settle here, without question. Australia's current immigration law breaches many international legal covenants and instruments that Australia is party to [*see Glossary, 'declarations and conventions'*].

Those in detention were primarily from the Middle East, and most Australians did not care about Middle Eastern people. And before you say, 'What about 9/11?', it is important to remember that many of the people I saw in detention arrived before September 2001, and many were escaping those very regimes that the West criticises.

Over the years I was involved in acting for detainees in the courts, my particular concern became the deterioration of many of my clients' mental health. Initially the work involved representing people charged with escaping from Woomera and Baxter detention centres. The first client I was concerned about was Abdul, from Iran. He had been imprisoned there, targeted by the government for opposing it. He feared for his life, and escaped to Australia in 2000. He was kept at Curtin, Woomera and Baxter detention centres. He had escaped from Woomera in 2001, and I had been acting for him since then. Julian Burnside QC was running a test case in the High Court to see if we could argue that escaping from a place as horrific as Woomera was not escaping from lawful detention. He lost. I then had contact with Abdul from 2001 until 2004 when I was making submissions for him and had watched his mental state collapse. He had cut himself so many times with razors that his stomach was difficult to suture, and he had to have steri-strips instead (i.e. plastic strips used to hold a wound together). He had swallowed shampoo. He had tried to hang himself. The psychologist went to see him and told me that Abdul was, as I suspected, very ill. I assumed he was getting medical treatment in Baxter. I was surprised to learn that he wasn't.

I then tried to have a psychiatrist see him. He hadn't seen a psychiatrist in Baxter for five months. DIMIA refused. They claimed in the court case that eventuated that they were providing adequate mental health services. I then took a judicial review in the Federal Court. All I was seeking was an order enabling a doctor to see him, no more. Applications to get persons into hospital didn't come until later. Not only did the Commonwealth oppose the application for Abdul, they fought it hard: their legal fees ran to thousands of dollars just to prevent a sick man from seeing a doctor. (There are some lawyers, I am sad to say, who have made many thousands of dollars being briefed by the Commonwealth to oppose refugees in the courts and who seemed to ignore the breaches of human rights that were systemic. I am sure many lovely cars and holidays were purchased by them as a result.)

Eventually, after days of hearing, the Commonwealth agreed that a doctor of their choice, not Abdul's, would be able to see him. Just as well. By then Abdul was taking part in a hunger strike: he had stitched his lips together; he was refusing food. He was hearing voices and was trying to harm himself.

On 23 December 2004 he was taken to Royal Adelaide Hospital, immediately detained under the Mental Health Act (SA), and taken to Glenside Psychiatric Hospital, where he stayed for months and months. He continued to receive treatment even after he was given a Permanent Protection Visa. He is still receiving treatment today.

While I was in court for Abdul, three other detainees contacted me. They were taking part in a rooftop protest at Baxter and were refusing to eat. They, too, wanted medical treatment. After Abdul's case, I decided

I would seek court orders not only demanding that they see a doctor but ensuring they got treatment. Eventually all three were transferred to Glenside Hospital, but not before a trial taking days and days. By this time the failure to deliver mental health treatment in detention centres had become a public issue. Nobody seemed too concerned that three men were suffering chronic mental illness; nobody seemed concerned that Abdul was very ill and was self-harming. Few were concerned that there were many children unwell as a consequence of detention.

What *did* raise the public concern about this? What caused front page news? A blonde Australian resident who failed to get adequate mental health treatment. Yes, Cornelia Rau. There were, and are, lots of Cornelias in immigration detention. I doubt whether I saw one person in there for any length of time who wasn't suffering. But they weren't white, and she was.

People in Baxter, including Abdul and Cornelia, who were exhibiting signs of mental illness, destroying themselves or property, not responding to commands, crying or refusing to eat were kept in the 'Management Unit'. It had no windows; you couldn't see out. It had a mattress on the floor, no reading or writing materials, no radio, TV or any personal effects, a shower and toilet in the corner and, most shocking of all, was subject to closed-circuit TV. Detainees were locked in this Unit for up to 23 hours a day, with no contact with the outside world.

Australia has treated good men and women this way. The detention system has not only failed to treat those who were ill and suffering but has contributed to and caused mental illness. Its greatest legacy will be the impact on the children. Many children, some of them unaccompanied by adults, spent months, years in detention centres. They were seeking refuge in Australia, escaping forced military service, persecution, torture and detention because of political or religious allegiances.

Pauline Hanson and her One Nation party may have been defeated in the 2001 polls, but her ideals and policies won. I remember her saying at one stage that those arriving by boat should be towed away. How horrified we were by her views, but then the government proposed offshore processing.

Many of the finest people I have ever met were those in immigration detention. My experience with detention centres and detainees has left me with the lasting impression that Australia still has a racist attitude. One lawyer asked me, 'How can you represent those Middle Eastern people? They just come here and rape our women and children!' He was a legal aid lawyer! I pointed out to him that in fact it is the white people who have a history of rape and pillage among the peoples of the world.

It is that racist attitude that is at the core of the shame that was and continues to be Australia's immigration system. Make no mistake about it, detention centres would never have been built to house white persons escaping black regimes.

From Immigration Officer to advocate

***Diana Goldrick** charts the growing disenchantment that took her on a remarkable journey*

For approximately four-and-a-half years until I resigned in early 2001 I managed a DIMIA team of Onshore Protection case officers dealing with protection visa applications, deciding who should be recognised as refugees and allowed to stay in Australia.

Before June 1999 there were very few protection visa applicants held in detention. Most applications for protection came from people living in the community. However, from June 1999 onwards, 8316 men, women and children arrived on our shores as 'boat people' - asylum seekers without visas. These people were mainly Afghans fleeing the Taliban, and Iraqis fleeing Saddam Hussein's regime.

In October 1999 the Migration Regulations were tightened in response to the arrival of boat people, who would now only be entitled to apply for a three-year TPV, which did not entitle them to the full range of social security benefits and resettlement services available to those people granted PPVs.

Once these people were put into closed immigration detention centres around the country, the process of finalising their applications began. I was involved in organising case officers from Sydney to fly out to the detention centres and interview them. Most were found to be genuine refugees. However, I heard that conditions in the detention centres, particularly at Woomera, Port Hedland and Curtin, were poor – overcrowding was a major problem, and extreme temperatures and inadequate clothing and footwear worsened the situation. Rumours circulated of brutal guards, the rape of women and the sexual abuse of children.

Part of my job was to monitor case officers' interviews of asylum seekers at the Villawood Detention Centre. After there had been a break-out of detainees, the wire-mesh fences were replaced with high, double razor-wire fences, with a 'no man's land' in between holding large coils of razor wire. I remember standing at the security gate, waiting for a guard to let me in, staring at the razor wire. The hairs on the back of my neck started to stand up. I thought, 'I'm a part of the system that locks up innocent people – do I want to be part of it?'

I recall that in late 2000 the managers in Onshore Protection were directed to make decisions on some 'hard' protection visa applications, to show the case officers how it was done. One applicant I interviewed was a small, thin, 20-year-old Hazara man from Afghanistan. He sat slumped in his chair with his head bowed as he told his story. During a raid on his village about two years before, the Taliban killed his father and bashed and 'shamed' (i.e. sodomised) him because he would not join their army. He had arrived as a boat person and, after several months, had been transferred from Woomera to Villawood because he was suffering depression; the only psychologist employed by the company running the centres was stationed in Sydney. Although I found the young man was a refugee under the United Nation Convention on Refugees, I could only grant him a three-year TPV. I heard from the Red Cross that many of these men, women and children were living in our community in poverty. The new policy began to trouble me.

Again, in 2000, I recall that the then-Secretary of the department came to Sydney to talk to the case officers. Several of them told me they considered this most unusual; it had never happened before. My recollection is that the Secretary warmly congratulated the case officers on their hard work but cautioned them to be very careful processing the asylum seekers in detention because we didn't know who they were. I had heard that the people smugglers who organised their passage from Indonesia had advised them to destroy all their documents. To my mind, these words coming from the Secretary directly to case officers carried a very strong message indeed: be extremely careful in granting protection visas to these people.

I also remember that several months later the then-Secretary returned to Sydney to address the case officers a second time. I spoke to several of them directly after that second meeting. They told me that he recounted to them how the then-Head of the Department of the Prime Minister and Cabinet had told him his department would go bankrupt within a few months if the asylum seekers were not released from detention, as it was costing the government a great deal of money to keep them there. The case officers said the Secretary feared that if the asylum seekers were not released quickly, he would lose his job; he appealed to them to work faster and promised them funding for unlimited overtime. To my mind, these words carried another very powerful message: grant the detainees protection visas quickly or there will be no money to pay your salaries, and we could all be out of work.

At that time there was a great deal of media coverage of 'boat people' arriving in Australia and their plight in the detention centres. I felt that the government wanted the asylum seekers released from detention quickly in order to avoid the ongoing embarrassment of adverse media coverage – not because of lack of funding.

I was shocked at both the callousness and the inconsistency of the government's treatment of asylum seekers. I considered that these people were being used and abused for political ends, so I handed in my resignation.

After I resigned, I spent 18 exciting months at the Centre for Refugee Research, University of New South Wales, working on a learning program for primary and secondary school students about refugees and their journeys to freedom. The project was funded by the Premier's Department and developed in conjunction with the NSW Department of Education.

In 2002 the Australian Refugee Rights Alliance was formed to lobby during two weeks of Pre-Executive Committee Meetings and Executive Committee Meetings of the UNHCR in Geneva. Our 15-member delegation included church and non-government organisation representatives, an academic, a lawyer, and several interns from the University of New South Wales. The UN High Commissioner and his officers provided us with unending support. They held discussions with us, introduced us to many people, and provided us with a meeting room, where we showed videos of the public debate that was taking place around refugee issues in Australia and the conditions in detention centres. We spoke directly to groups of delegates from other countries; many of them were shocked to hear about what was happening to asylum seekers in Australia.

The then-Minister for Immigration sent a message that he wished to meet us. I could not see that meeting the Minister would be of any benefit to us, as we knew only too well what his views were, but the consensus was that we should. When he introduced himself to me, I couldn't bring myself to shake his hand. During his long monologue outlining government policy, he permitted few questions or comments. One of our young interns became emotionally distressed at what he was saying, and sobbed loudly.

The Norwegian Ministry invited us to a lavish reception but, pointedly, did not invite the Australian Government delegation. In Geneva, the *Tampa* incident was still fresh in many people's minds. We lobbied hard, and were successful in persuading the other NGOs to include wording in the official document presented to the Executive Committee Meeting of the UNHCR to deplore the use of mandatory detention of asylum seekers by member states. Again, in 2003, I worked in Geneva as part of the delegation and I continue to be involved in this and other refugee advocacy work.

They say that early experiences shape our lives, so I'll try to record some of the important early experiences that influenced me into resigning from an interesting public service career to become an advocate for refugees. My father volunteered for the Air Force as soon as World War II was declared, and my mother took me as a baby to live with her parents in their flat in Randwick, in the eastern suburbs of Sydney. I knew from an early age that the Allies were fighting cruel enemies that killed innocent people. As I grew up, my grandmother talked to me about 'the bad old days' when working men and women were at the mercy of their bosses, who could make them work till all hours and who chased off union organisers when they came to the factories and shops to collect the workers' union dues.

Deta and Gobi, a young couple living in one of the flats below us with their small son, Johnny, often came up the back stairs into our kitchen to ask for advice or just to have a good chat over a cup of tea. They had escaped from Nazi-occupied Europe by paying a stranger to smuggle them over a border at night. Deta was Catholic and Gobi was Jewish. I remember my grandmother commenting, 'They're two of the lucky ones'.

I started school at St Anthony's Convent, Clovelly, and many more people from post-war Europe came to live in our neighbourhood. Some children called them 'Refos' or 'DPs' (i.e. displaced persons). My mother told me we didn't use such language, and that many of these good people had been through terrible times during the war. Although my mother was only in her twenties, she had very definite views on respect for others and a keen insight into human nature.

When I was 12 we moved away to a new home with a large garden, but I missed the colour and vibrancy of the people back in Randwick and my old life playing on the street. In high school I remember the nuns speaking about social justice issues and stressing that the end never justifies the means.

I see that these early experiences influenced my decision to resign from a system that conflicted with my sense of right and wrong.

THE EXCUSE

Poet* Christopher Wareham *dissects the distorted logic that attempts to justify immorality

7 February 2003

His face stares stony straight.
Cold-steel right eye,
cruel with cunning,
guilty forgotten left
squints outward
He does not blink.
Only those thin lips move,
his voice, flat, colourless:
'I am not to blame,'
he says:
'We are not to blame,'
he says:
'They are to blame,'
he says:
'They are blameworthy,'
he says,
'because they are to blame,'
he says:
'They are to blame
because we blame them,'
he says.
His face stares stony straight,
his lips purse, pale,
over a chin that
does not tremble.

For the 'sins' of the parents: children in detention

Solicitor and migration agent ***Michaela Byers*** *outlines the official abuses she encountered while representing detained children*

I first became interested in immigration law two decades ago, while studying law. Not because it was actually taught at Law School - my connection was personal even then. I had been studying Chinese in Taiwan for a year, and fell in love with the country, language, culture and a young man. I wanted to sponsor my fiancé to Australia on a six-month fiancé visa before we married. When I went to pick up the application forms from the Immigration Department, the clerk refused to give me them, on the grounds that it was up to me to migrate to my fiancé's country, as all good wives do. Though I vigorously disputed her prejudices, she still refused to give me the forms, adding that Australia already had enough Asians.

Twenty years later I'm an immigration lawyer, and the department's culture remains much as it was back then.

In August 2001 I watched a *Four Corners* program about a family in detention and the impact of imprisonment on their six-year-old son [*see Ngareta Rossell's story*]. The child lacked animation and seemed lifeless; he was refusing to eat and speak, and had repeatedly been admitted to Westmead Children's Hospital for treatment, only to be returned to detention, where he got sick again.

Two weeks later I was approached by an advocate and asked to represent the family. I did so. My daughter was about the same age as their son, and I thought how it would be if we were in detention. I would go crazy in one day and my daughter would not be allowed to run free.

Between 2001 and July 2005 I represented, on a pro-bono basis, 53 children detained with their parents in Villawood IDC. Many of the children were born in Australia and later detained. A few had been born in detention and had never been outside the razor wire. I was outraged that Australia would detain children indefinitely because their parents had violated immigration law. And each time I visited Villawood there seemed to be more children imprisoned there. I believed this reflected badly upon Australia as a nation of migrants. On closer examination, I could see that the department was using the imprisonment of children as a form of punishment, to force their parents to abandon all hope of a future in Australia and to decide to leave 'voluntarily'.

Most of the parents had had their applications for asylum rejected, or they were 'over-stayers' from Asia and the Pacific Islands. The department's official line was that it was 'best' that the children remained with their parents, at the same time as it utterly disregarded the wellbeing of the children – some of whom were Australian citizens by birth – and the destructive effect of detention on their development. The parents were blamed for their children's predicament.

Despite many and vociferous calls for an inquiry, the department refused to review family detention. It seemed to me – and this was corroborated by the Palmer Report – that, in the department's view, all its 'prisoners' had relinquished their rights as human beings when they were arrested and detained. (Eventually, in May 2005, Prime Minister Howard buckled under public pressure and promised to review the cases of all children in detention – *see Timeline of events*.) As a result of this attitude to 'illegals', the department failed to investigate the legal status of the families; some families actually held Bridging Visas, and were wrongfully detained for up to 18 months. One parent was wrongfully detained twice and wrongfully deported.

The department decreed that children had to be detained for three months before they could go to school outside the detention centre. For the first three months, then, children were in detention with the adult detainees 24 hours a day, seven days a week, and their education was severely interrupted.

The 'Compliance' sections of the department deserve special comment. Their job is to track down 'illegals', arrest and detain them. A Compliance officer needs to form a 'reasonable suspicion' that a person is an unlawful non-citizen. Before July 2005, when the practice was criticised in the Palmer Report [*see Timeline of events*], Compliance officers arresting and interviewing the suspected 'illegal' were able to make a decision to either grant a Bridging Visa and release the person, or to detain them. So far as I'm aware, no Compliance officer issued a Bridging Visa before May 2005. The 'reasonable suspicion' automatically made detention mandatory.

In this way, the detention centres came to overflow with families and children, regardless of the alternatives that were available to the arresting Compliance officers. In this way, children who were Australian citizens were imprisoned, something entirely illegal.

I know one child with Australian citizenship who was detained with his parent and siblings for three years – a national disgrace! This case above all demonstrates how the department was using the detention of children to punish their parents, rather than using it as a last resort to deal with the illegal members of the family.

On one occasion I heard that Compliance was to visit one of my client families at home. The parents came from Lebanon and had three Australian-born children under the age of six. These children belonged to a group who were challenging the Australian Citizenship Act in the Federal Court to defend their birthright. Nonetheless, the two Compliance officers (one male, one female) came to the house with a large white van. I greeted them at the door and introduced myself. The male officer's jaw dropped. I invited them into my clients' house and asked them to sit down. The male officer then sent the female officer to get the Bridging Visa forms out of the van, and then completed the forms. I had heard of the male officer, as he'd raided a number of my family clients' homes, and I had made a written complaint about him. My clients and I were very happy that I'd managed to foil the department's attempt to arrest and detain them that day.

Another example of Compliance officers' ambition to arrest and detain as many people as possible concerns two young children, 11 and six years old, who were arrested at school. Their mother had been detained at the airport. The Compliance officers forced a woman who worked in the school office to go to the classrooms and bring the children to them. She told me that when she handed the children over she felt like Judas. As a way of assuaging her guilt, this woman helped to organise petitions and protest-letter writing from the school, and visits by children to their imprisoned classmates. The pressure worked: the family was released four months later. Other school staff (including the principal) and children were traumatised by the experience. I received a telephone call from an advocate within half an hour of the children's arrest, as one mother could not console her child about one of her classmates being dragged from the classroom. The Compliance officers in question knew where the children were living, so they could have raided the house outside school hours. Raiding the school was quite gratuitous.

I made a Freedom of Information application for this family's file. It contained emails between Airport Immigration, who had arrested the mother; Compliance in Sydney, who arrested the children at school; and the case officer concerned with detention, each congratulating the other on a job well done. All of the officers involved were women.

A couple of months later, an advocate contacted me to say that the mother and children in question had been advised of their impending deportation. I asked the advocate to provide the youngest child's birth certificate, as she was born in Australia. The school faxed the birth certificate to my office and we filed a Court Application for a Restraining Order. I was out of the office that day, so I sent my employed solicitor and two barristers to court to apply for an Emergency Injunction to prevent the deportation of the youngest child. The advocate arranged for a refugee advocacy group to demonstrate against their deportation at the airport. The court duly granted the injunction at 6 p.m. Since it was pouring rain, my colleague was worried about getting to the airport to serve the injunction on the airline on time, but fortunately the Court Registry volunteered to fax the injunction to the airport, and the deportation was aborted.

However, this was not the end of it. Two months later, departmental officers approached the mother to voluntarily sign a Deportation Order. The mother could not speak, read or write English, so instead of doing the right thing, which is to have an accredited interpreter there, they got the eldest child to interpret. The eldest child did not understand the document, and instead translated the departmental officers' 'explanation' of it, after which the mother signed her own Deportation Order. The eldest child telephoned me very upset about the ordeal. He told me that he thought his mother may have signed a Deportation Order. By taking immediate action, I got the department to abort its second attempt to deport the family - this one in defiance of a court injunction against the removal of the youngest child.

Four months later - after much media scrutiny and Howard's promise of a review of all cases of children held in detention - the department discovered that the family still held Bridging Visas and had to be released. Their detention had been wrongful the whole time!

In July 2004, many families were being transferred from Villawood to Baxter. Most of these families were Chinese, and many did not want to go, as they would be far from family, friends and their legal representatives in Sydney. For some, the prospect of Baxter's isolation was terrifying, and many of the detainees protested. Some of my clients decided to protest on the laundry roof; some even took their children with them. The staff singled out one of my clients, a mother, for demonisation as a troublemaker. The manager of the detention centre reported to the Department of Community Services (DoCS) that this mother's daughter was at risk, and DoCS took the child away for two weeks. She returned with a large, dark bruise on her cheek. Under the Freedom of Information provisions, I've received some of the DoCS file about the departmental complaint, and it reinforces my conviction that the system was used to punish the mother for being a troublemaker, as no purpose was served by taking the child away. She was not at risk. The child has remained with the mother ever since, without incident.

By July 2005, all the children in detention were released on Bridging Visas or into 'residential determination' (i.e. community detention). The department has finalised very few of their cases. More than one year after their release from detention, only one of my child clients now has permanent residency, thanks to quite unique circumstances. All other children's and their parents' status in Australia remains undetermined. The mandatory detention policy and relevant sections of the Migration

Act have not been altered to prevent children being held in detention. So, at any time it chooses, the department can again arrest and detain children.

I remain determined to continue working to end mandatory detention, starting with the prohibition of the detention of children. With each family gaining residency in Australia, I become motivated to see similar redress for the remaining families. A visit to Anne Frank's House in Amsterdam last year re-inspired me to continue with the detention work, though its personal and financial cost is high. It takes away from the time that I have with my own daughter. In four years' time, when she becomes a teenager, she will not want to be seen with me, and some friends and family members don't understand why I go to so much trouble to help 'refos'. The financial cost arises from the pro-bono nature of the work; it's very time-consuming and tiring to deal with the pleas of clients to be released, and those of the advocates, who think I need to push even harder.

Passing the baton

*Her 'addiction to fighting injustice' leads lawyer, journalist and writer **Jacquie Everitt** to take risks to help reform immigration practice*

Some time when your youngest child is still a baby, you see a news clip on the ABC of Khmer women detained at Port Hedland, their faces distorted with anguish, their frail bodies outlined in pointy angles by dresses blown tight around them in a fierce, hot wind. You can see the heavy air filled with salt, gritty sand and heat. Small children are clinging to their mothers' skirts, twists of fabric clenched in their fists.

Little heads are cocked sideways, brown eyes flat and emotionless, staring at the camera from under shaggy black fringes. Their noses run and they wear that look of Asian street children. It is the sign of low-grade infections caused by immune systems which don't work well under stress, sadness and deprivation. You don't assume they are deprived of medical attention and adequate food, you simply know they are dispossessed of the usual things humans need to thrive: freedom, security, social inclusion, hope, and power to make the minute decisions that govern our day-to-day lives.

Was 'trauma' the buzzword then? If so, these people look traumatised. Your memory records a scene of desolation, filmed behind a prison grid topped with razor wire – or was it barbed wire? It was so long ago. They hold rough-painted placards above their heads, in arms sagging with the tiredness of depression. The signs call on the Australian people to help them. You don't remember the exact words, but they say something like, 'Australia, please let us out' and 'We are not criminals'.

It is during the Keating Government's time (1991–96), and you didn't know Australia locks up women and children. You didn't know your country keeps asylum seekers hidden from the eyes of the public on the only ugly piece of land along the whole beautiful Western Australian coastline. Shocked, stunned, appalled. You use all the usual emotive words in your mind, because that is how you feel. They are locked up because they are 'boat people'. In your head you use the pejorative that entered Australian vocabularies when the Vietnamese began arriving a decade earlier, damned because of their method of transport, not because they have committed any crime.

Children in detention is an issue that bubbles and boils with emotion. Australia is jailing children and you don't even know. You are ashamed of this on behalf of your government. The news screen fills with other atrocities and you put those beautiful, fine-boned Khmers out of your mind. This fact shames you now far more than the initial government policy formulated in your name to protect you and your family. You couldn't twist your mind in enough dark corners to imagine how these frail Khmers could be a threat.

You work, parent, study, become a lawyer, are appointed to the board of Save the Children, travel to all kinds of places DFAT warns you not to visit. Soldiers guard you, in the early 1990s, from the Khmer Rouge, outlaws now and still active up north in the homeland of the Khmers you saw on television. You fall deeply in love with Cambodia and its people. Is this guilt? You'll never know, but you meet Cambodians and discover first-hand why they fled, learn why they made epic journeys to Australia, why they needed protection. But now those newsreel Khmers are out of gaol, living among Australians. They don't need you any more. Other people gave up their private lives to help them. You are too late.

In early October 1999, you fly on a small UN plane from Darwin to Dili, East Timor, to work for Timor Aid in the bloody aftermath of the August 30 referendum, when the East Timorese voted for independence from Indonesia. Amidst the shallow graves, the charred bodies, the sweet, sickly stench of death, faeces hardened in torture rooms at the back of the house where you now live, the spattered brains and bullet holes of executions decorating the wall down by Dili dock - you see first-hand what makes a refugee. You go to West Timor to visit the East Timorese in the camps in Indonesia.

You meet the militia, who seem to be guards. They are big, solid, much taller than the tiny East Timorese. They look different. They swagger and sneer at the people around them. Their eyes are bloodshot, they wear combat fatigues. They have guns. The guns unnerve you. These camps are not locked, the people there are frightened. They are mostly women and children. Why would anyone need a gun? The faces of the East Timorese are dispirited and dull with loss. They dare not speak.

You tread carefully. You have no passport, you are there on a UN identity card because you have a humanitarian job to do. You look at their blankness and feel sorrow for them. Some have lost family, all have lost their homes, their belongings and are too afraid of private terrors to return. The big men do all the talking, and you swear you can smell the fear as the big people twist their faces in false smiles and send the East Timorese away, scurrying and hangdog, like timid animals.

You return to Australia on a RAAF Hercules. You are sick and exhausted. East Timor was hard in those first few months. You know what you want to do now you are home: use the law qualifications you juggled your life to acquire. You volunteer at a specialist legal centre to work with refugees. They give you a paid job. You go to Villawood, computer slung around your neck and forms in your carry case. You are accompanying another lawyer, to learn how it's done.

You try not to show any alarm at the grimness of the uniformed guards, the fences, the sheer ugliness of seeing children in gaol in your own beautiful city. The shock is worse than you expected. The place is horrible, the people as lifeless as those you saw in the camps in West Timor. The first man you meet in the tiny lawyer's room offends you in a way you were not expecting. He is middle-aged, speaks English, is educated. His voice is soft, but he says very little. Then it hits you. He has the face of the East Timorese in the camps. You see his trauma. He can't answer questions, his eyes dart around. He doesn't want you there, wants you to go. He is afraid of you and your colleague. He is frightened of this camp. He says he could never tell you the things that have happened to him. You are profoundly offended that this man is locked up like a prisoner when he is so obviously mentally distressed. The doctors in East Timor call it 'PE', Pain Everywhere. It is pain that cannot be pinned down, which moves and agonises, is sometimes physical, sometimes a pain of anguish. It makes its owner wake in fear in the night, tense and alert, an insomniac until early light, when he falls into a fitful sleep.

This is how it starts, your addiction to fighting injustice. It escalates, oozes through your being, takes over your heart. You soon resign from your job. There is a stipulation that you cannot speak out on what you see. How, then, can you help? You make the first steps towards assuaging your guilt and the shame of your country. It becomes cerebral. Your heart guides, but your brain does the work. You cannot stand the wrongs that your country's politicians have turned into laws. Your friends drop by the wayside – you're way too evangelical for them.

The saddest moment is the day you lose your dearest friend, who has been your soulmate for so very long, who grew into adulthood with you, who is honourable, whose heart is every bit as good and decent as you hope yours is. You feel the reserve when you speak with her now.

You mention a *Lateline* story on the ABC the night before. You ask if she saw it. It is still the most confronting piece of film footage you have ever seen. It shows a group of Hazara Afghans in Curtin Detention Centre, keening over the apparent 'death' of one of their countrymen. It shows misery stripped so bare, you find it too painful to watch. You understand, now, the meaning of raw emotion. The mourning of these men is from so deep inside them, you physically feel with them the injustice of the ages that has dogged their race. You see the guards, so bewildered, inept and poorly trained that all they can do is hand out tissues to the sobbing, rocking men. You watch the digitised minutes tick by on the corner of the film. No manager comes to take charge and bring peace and solace to this scene; no counsellors to soothe and rationalise. One man, the natural leader, himself shattered, tries to calm and console his compatriots.

This film came into your hands in a brown paper package from 'a supporter'. You have watched it uncut many times. It seems to be footage filmed by an official inside the camp to record 'incidents', to be used to cover their backs in the event of legal action or for other such reasons. It is potential evidence. You don't know how it reached you, but are secretly proud that someone trusted you, believed you would ensure it was used wisely. It played in all the corners of the world – the death of compassion, Australia's shame in pictures. It won a Walkley Award (Australia's premier journalism awards).

You think your friend will understand how you feel and why you did it. You feel your work is useful, and are seeking affirmation from someone from your youth, whose opinion you value, the girl who grew to adulthood with you and shared your ideals. You wait for her to say, 'Good stuff, Jacq', as you and she have said to each other so many times. She doesn't say it. She is very controlled. Your exchange is polite. You are bewildered. You are already on the back foot and fumbling. You don't want this friendship broken, but can't let it pass, either.

At the end she says: 'Jacq, now that we've had this out, I want to tell you how wrong I believe you are. I agree with the government. We don't want these queue-jumpers here'.

You don't see the debate as being anything to do with queues. You know there are no queues for the people arriving at this time, but that is not the issue. It is about human rights and international conventions. It is about the Australian fair go, basic decency, and believing Middle Eastern children are as fragile and precious as our own. You falter: 'But what about the children? You can't think they should be in a prison camp? These children are emotionally stunted. They're not developing.' You realise your words are confrontational, but can't hold them back.

You hear her deep, slow intake of breath. She breathes out: 'Their parents are to blame. They should never have brought them.' You hear Immigration Minister Ruddock speaking – you have heard him use those words yourself. She continues, 'I respect your right to do what you think is correct, but I believe you are wrong'. Frustration creeps into her voice. 'Look, I don't have to see these people. Maybe if I did, I'd think differently, but I don't have to and I don't want to. You have chosen to go into the detention centres. I have not.'

'So this is about freedom of choice?' you say. 'You choose the luxury of shutting your eyes despite knowing what is going on? Your guilt is as big as mine, because you have the intellect to disentangle decency from abuse. What you do or don't do about it is a matter for your conscience.' You say the words, and lose a friend.

So many people seem to have sold their compassion and morality for a government policy. You think of the epidemic of this raging through your country and note that politicians are the first to fall ill. In your mind, you call it 'the Ruddocks', after the person who gave it voice and spread the first germs.

A wise friend reminds you, 'It is difficult being the child of an advocate, there is so little left over for your family.' You have never labelled yourself 'an advocate', but ... perhaps. You realise her words are true. Your younger ones are jealous: all your time is spent with people they don't know. Your older children understand why you do it, but concern themselves with their own lives, calling less on you and more on their father. He takes over everyone's day-to-day care, including yours. The phone moulds itself to your ear. You're forever making the tedious trip to Villawood, flying to Woomera, Port Hedland or Baxter, driving around the countryside to meetings, speaking at universities, in people's living rooms, on people's farms, in all kinds of unlikely places, because there are so many kind, generous Australians who feel as you do.

This is all you and your new friends can think about. Detention centres have become places of torture, not just for the inmates but for you and your friends, who suffer in second-hand ways as you observe the detainees breaking, their health disintegrating, their souls in despair. Your emotions are attached to them, their hopelessness; you are pulled with them. Once on this advocacy trail, you can't get off. Is this an addiction, and when were you hooked?

Perhaps it was the day you stood under the shelter at Villawood, the pouring rain hammering on the tin roof, and watched rivulets running through the bare mud around the cement slab while you huddled in the cold with a refugee family. Was it the day you smiled down at the beautiful baby girl with golden curls and green eyes in her stroller, then looked up into her brother's staring, mindless, dead eyes, his thin body drooping like a puppet in his father's arms? Or that day you met the six-year-old boy (Shayan Badraie) whom you feared would die? This was the day when you knew you couldn't turn back. You made a pledge to his parents, standing there, that day. You said: 'I promise, no matter how long it takes, you'll get out of here'. You had no right to make that vow. You had no way of keeping it, but you knew you would. That was the day when a law-abiding citizen realised that bad laws should be fought, not accepted. Intellectually, you already knew that; you had learnt it, you had won the Jurisprudence Prize at university. Later you prepared a complaint to the Human Rights Commission for the father of the stick-thin boy with the lifeless eyes, a claim that his son's human rights had been violated by the Australian Government.

The president of the HREOC found in the child's favour, recommending that he be paid compensation for pain and suffering, and that Minister Ruddock write a letter of apology. The Minister declined to do either, and you felt ashamed all over again. This time your shame was for the Minister, the man whose pity died with his power. You would have admired him had he been gracious in defeat. 'Sorry' doesn't justify a wrong committed, but it would have helped the parents and their child.

You used to be a journalist, and you write a story for the *Sydney Morning Herald*, called 'Suffer the Children', about this boy. You call a friend and ask her to come with you to Villawood, explaining that you intend to take in a video camera for those inside to have a voice. You need support, a witness in case you are arrested. You shake as you walk in through the electronic arch. You imagine it is programmed to beep, squeal and light up if it detects metal. It goes berserk.

'Go through,' says the uniformed guard. 'We know you.'

No you don't, you think, *I'm only now meeting myself*.

The camera rolls later that night in an ugly room while you are home in bed. The parents speak of his medical deterioration, his dull eyes stare at the camera and he lies limp across his father's knee. The ABC's *Four Corners* uses that film, wins an award, presented by the Human Rights Commission. You watch in revulsion the next evening as the Minister vilifies the family with innuendo, half-truths and lies. He spills their private secrets, details of their refugee claim, to the people of Australia on television. These details are guaranteed 'confidential'. This family has never discussed their refugee issues publicly, not even with you. You watch in fury and disgust as tabloid columnists Piers Ackerman and Andrew Bolt, with leaked confidential documents, reproduce lies. You have the facts, the evidence, stamped and verified by the Government of Iran, kept safe in your study.

You feel sick as his mother tells how the sick boy was torn from her arms and sent to a foster home for 'protection'. You weep to see a loving family split asunder and reach for words to console his parents. Are there any? You watch as the foster arrangements break down. The child is damaged, he is difficult to care for, requires constant attention, and still has the terrors that keep him from sleeping.

You feel proud of the Australian legal fraternity and the three judges in the Federal Court of Appeal: the battle to establish their refugee status is won. You are proud that eventually, in 2006, the boy receives compensation for his injuries, that a law firm recognises the injustice and takes on the immense burden of fighting his case in the NSW Supreme Court. You feel proud that your country has decent and good barristers whose personal ethics refuse to allow injustice to stand. You feel pleased that, as a lawyer, you played some part.

You repeat the camera trick in Port Hedland. Channel Nine's *A Current Affair* uses this film. This time the officials have had enough of you. You are banned from entering any detention centre in Australia ever again, considered too dangerous. Silks and human rights lawyers offer to fight your case but you refuse. You are not beaten, just very tired, and need a break. The family whose child was so ill is now outside the wire. They are alone, you want to help.

You reflect: the years have been good. They have tested and uplifted. You have pushed yourself to limits you didn't know you had. You were angry, sad and elated, in no particular order. There were losses and wins. You feared that something you did might impact negatively on the refugees, who would bear the brunt of your actions. Experience has shown you that the power of those in charge is absolute.

Your adversary was the Commonwealth Government, legitimately voted in. The shame for the refugee policy is mitigated somewhat by pride that you live in a country which protects your right to fight and rail against the government. You may despise a policy and work to undo it, but you will not be gaoled or tortured. You feel proud that yours is a democratic country. You will not have to flee and seek the protection of another nation. The refugees are here because they did not have this luxury, this right. Your shame exists, but others are fighting the battle you have put aside. That is the nature of advocacy. It is a baton to be passed; a baton to be picked up when it's your turn again.

THE PROFESSIONAL VISITS

***John Gates**, a social worker who visited Baxter regularly, shares his feelings of guilt, disgust and futility*

I remember how impotent I felt
I was supposed to come with some answers, a balm
A professional assessment, here's a learned way forward
But the situation made a sick joke of my, of all healing professions
There were no solutions without release
Yes no solutions, no solutions
So I didn't offer any and that helped
I just listened and that was the humanity they needed

As they talked I would feel the pressure all over my body
I'd feel heavy and quickly become flat. My head was splitting
There was no way out. Stop this for them and for me.

I would hear their urgency, their appeals to me
Are we dogs? No we treat them much better
But there was some comfort to me the professional in this
They're okay there's some defiance left
Okay for their depression rating but what of their questions of justice and fairness in this country I call mine.
What's my professional answer to that?

At other times there was uplifted acceptance. You know, Mandela stuff
I would feel it a privilege to witness and listen in awe
How can a human heart bear so much and still love?

When I heard their devastated acceptance I was scared
This wasn't depression as we professionals usually know it
It was tortuously being crushed by a weight
A weight I couldn't lift off them
They would say it was alright they knew I couldn't lift it but listening helped anyway. I hoped it wasn't said for my sake

Sometimes they wouldn't talk at all because it had gone too far
I was especially scared then
Scared of what? That they'd blow up, melt down
Mostly scared that they could never find their way back to the spaces you and I occupy
Scared also by the fact that in that space the hunger strikes and suicide made sense to me
You could call it a case of counter transference I don't think so

The room would often seem to come in on us during meetings and time was slow
Many times I just waited for it to finish, no better plan in mind
The nylon carpet and thin walls of the hut were unpleasant
It was a relief when the families left their session especially the last of the day

I kind of enjoyed the walk out, a kind of ritual
Out of the interview rooms across the path with the dripper-fed Australian natives,
a nice touch if it wasn't so absurd. Over to the guard house, through the entrance then walk along the corridor passing the first fence, the electric beam and the second fence.
A war camp in peace time

The routine body search and the beautiful clang on stepping out of the last door
Then feeling the space open up and wanting to shake my head or run around like a school kid released at recess
Words exchanged with colleagues about how bad or crazy it is and then into the car
The relief, almost joy to be driving away
Halfway to Port Augusta the guilt of being able to leave it behind

The listening, the feeling of uselessness, of powerlessness in the face of a situation has never been greater. The stomach is where it is felt most

I write this so I know it was real. I want to think it was not and it's easy to conspire with such delusions
I witnessed our vicious bare teeth
Aren't all the errorisms just another reflection of such teeth
I know that our privilege sits on turning our backs on brothers and sisters
But I plead to my country don't ask me to do this again

IT IS NOT COURAGE

Child psychiatrist Jon Jureidini describes his response to systemic abuse in immigration detention

When I saw Woomera for the first time, it was at its best. The UN inspection had taken place the day before, and trees had been planted and some of the razor wire removed. It was a beautiful day in the desert, but the detention centre was the worst place I had been; worse than other ugly, violent places like jails and psychiatric back-wards that I had visited. Dark-skinned children, sad-eyed women, young men sprung tight with energy and frustration paced behind the wire. These people didn't belong here, referring to themselves by numbers.

I had come to Woomera to see some children my colleagues were worried about. My first patient was an antagonistic 14-year-old Iranian boy, referred because of self-cutting and unruly behaviour which had concerned his parents and the staff. He told me, after 15 minutes of impatience and irritation with my stumbling attempt at assessment: 'You, psychiatrist, can do nothing to help me. I am locked up, my family is locked up, *that* is my problem'.

He was right. This lesson saved him (and my subsequent patients in Woomera and Baxter) a lot of unhelpful time struggling through conventional psychiatric intervention.

A man I have not met before invites me into his room at Baxter to meet his wife. Baxter was described as an 'improvement' on Woomera – en-suites, computers, playing fields. For this man, his wife and three children there were two rooms, each a 3-metre cube, with a bunk bed and just enough space to enter. I have never been in this room before; it is dark and I am disoriented. It doesn't feel right for a room to be so dark in late morning in the desert. As my eyes adjust, I see the man stooping over a bunk, a woman's face, eyes closed but finally opening at his insistence. She looks around, frightened, and within seconds she is keening, half-scream and half-moan. It builds and continues unrelentingly. Her husband tries to quiet her, looks to me, appealing, a little challenging. I ask a few banal questions, make a few statements that strive to be empathic, but fail. The moaning scream continues. I can't stay in here any longer – for my own sake, and for hers. I don't want to compound the harm that has been done to this woman who has not spoken for two years, not walked for two months, who crawls to the toilet, is carried to the shower, screams when anyone but her husband approaches her, keeping even her children away. I leave and she screams on.

A psychiatrist must learn to tolerate uncertainty. This is not an issue when I work in immigration detention. People say, 'You are brave to speak out'. It does not feel like courage, but rather an inevitable response to sitting with abused children and their parents. Perhaps speaking out acts as an antidote to the helplessness and impotence of working with detainees: it is not courage to take a stand; more a reflex response to the stimulus of cruelty.

AUSTRALIA'S YOUNGEST POLITICAL PRISONER

***Rosalind Powrie**, a child and adolescent psychiatrist, recalls the absurdity of a baby caught up in a punitive system*

August 2004: I am riding my bike along the quiet, leafy street. I look up and see the large, Federation-style white house of the family. On each wooden pillar there are three balloons of different colours. Three pedal strokes and I have passed the house. In the time this takes, I am scooped up in a sudden whirl of excitement. Balloons means a birthday. What month is it? What day? It's N's birthday, I shout in my head. I think back to the day last year when he was born.

August 2003: I am standing at the desk of the antenatal ward. There is no name written in her space on the whiteboard. She is a 'security patient', meaning no-one is supposed to know she is here. I move away from the bustling desk area and head down the corridor. The air smells of new babies. I approach her room and find two ACM guards sitting outside the door – one of them, a woman, offers a tense smile. Her look tells me I have to identify myself, even though I work here. I feel the indignation rising up my spine – it makes me want to spit.

The mother is propped up in bed with a beautiful baby with long, black hair lying loosely across her belly. She is not holding him close – it looks to me like he has rolled away from her and she hasn't the strength to hold him any more. I am greeting her, she smiles wanly. I catch sight of a figure in the corner of the room by the window – an old man dressed in his traditional loose trousers and long over-shirt, all a pale blue-grey, like the sky outside.

'Hello,' I say. 'Congratulations on the birth of your son. He is beautiful.' I am shocked at his aged appearance. It's not just his grey hair and the grey speckled through his stubbled face. It is his eyes, they are mournful and lost – they are also pleading. His English is broken but he graciously acknowledges me. I sit down next to the bed.

I am beginning to feel uncomfortable with what I am asking – it feels so cold and standardised and institutional. I want to say some words which can give hope, but instead I just ask, 'How are you feeling today?', so inane and stupid. Her eyes lower and she shrugs her shoulders – I know that look from the others I have met, victims of the slow death of time torture, of waiting with no answers, no relief, burdened by guilt, sacrificed for some rhetoric called 'the greater good' and 'Border Protection'. I have seen that same shrug many times over the years with survivors of torture and trauma. The shrug that tells me, 'How do you think I feel? Don't you know, can't you see – are you blind?'

I hesitate, my feet are shuffling … where to go now? I dare to prompt something else in this unending agony of moments. 'Tell me …,' I say, 'tell me how you are feeling about your baby.'

She does not hesitate: 'I feel he is our miracle baby – I feel so happy for this, but I feel sad. He is Australia's youngest political prisoner, I am scared for his life.'

I am silent in agreement. This is true: in this state-of-the-art hospital with sympathetic and attentive midwives, I watch Australia's youngest political prisoner's eyes flutter. His body squirms, and his mother puts him to her breast. I don't know what to say or do again. I turn away and meet the father's eyes – he answers my question. The interpreter standing opposite me is crying silently. Stay in control – my role demands it, but I am lost. I hear the father's voice softly saying something to the interpreter: 'The guard asked me if my baby had a number yet'. He continues to talk but I am hanging onto those words. Numbers, not names; the baby is a number.

January 2005: He would be 16 months old now. Over the January holidays my thoughts often return to this family, who I will never see again. The faces of the young children in my office grappling with a plan for their lives, out of control. I didn't want to see it coming, too hard, too cruel. They are gone now, taken under secret cover of nightfall – in the dead of night. There were a few TV cameras to capture their bewilderment and betrayal through the small portals of the plane's window. Mother, robotic and emptied of love, carrying a tiny unborn life – the one child who has never known the anguish of a perfect world and its horrors. I ring just 24 hours before this, not knowing when it would be – mother's voice is flat, like the dead-straight line of a cardiac monitor. I hear children crying in the background as her words tumble out, detached. She gives me a report – what else could I expect? I say I am sorry. I am more angry than I have ever been about anything, but this is no use now. I want her to know her importance, but the machinery of power has crushed any of that long ago – with no mercy, no acknowledgement of who she is, and her life-giving relations.

Gone – our conversations, the black humour, the complaints and despair.

Gone – watching the baby grow.

Gone.

Gone – everything, up into the black sky.

THE LUCKY ONES

*Psychotherapist **Patricia O'Rourke** celebrates the comfort of human connection in a sea of misery*

I remember the peach tree, the abundance of it in that small, square carpark that made it difficult to move the unfamiliar van in, out, in, out, edging my way down the narrow alley and out onto the roaring streets.

I remember the crazy van driving itself at 100 kilometres an hour down roads I didn't know, past shops I'd never seen, into places I'd never been. I remember trying to find a tree for shade for the stinking thing so that I wouldn't immediately boil over with physical heat as well as emotional burn.

I remember them all sitting in the small, hot room. The lucky ones. The ones that had stood politely in the queues, filled in forms, waited their turn. The males were all face, blank … except one who, being a bit slow, had a slack smile and an anxious flick of his eye.

But mostly I remember you, your tears oozing from your eyes and running down your face. Silently at first, and then that sound as your heart broke into feeling. You rocked and cried and keened.

The men sat helpless, your daughter moved, I think, and somehow touched you. Did she hold your hand? Or place her arm around your shoulders? Thank God for daughters, eh?

I remember sitting, a stunned mullet. I had never been with anything like this. The rawness of it flooding out – even all those children, all those women. Something else was here. Was it the family? The bewilderment? The complete finality of it all? There was no going back.

I remember thinking then that all I could do was be who I am and be there. Not run away or block my ears or say something that could only be inane or trite or incomprehensible in the midst of it all. I could be there and look and stay.

I remember meeting you in the waiting room. Were there others there? I remember going over, and you rose up and held out your hand. I took it in mine and put my other hand on top. You took your arm and placed it on mine and pulled your face to mine and kissed first one, then the other cheek, and then again.

Blank.

THE ASYLUM SEEKERS

Poet and PEN member ***Judith Rodriguez*** *writes of our shared culpability in the heartless treatment of asylum seekers*

Bearing your loss
however you can
to our fearful ports
NO PLACE
        my abasement
Your cry in my hearing
your children your children
the salt waste
these depths these deaths
        my abasement
Your feet in my shallows
your hands at my shore
my guns at your face
inquisition
        NO PLACE
Your plea in my ear
your need in my sight
rights and denial
undoing of lives
        NO PLACE
My guards in your path
your grief in my soul
the pledges broken
time passing time passing
        my abasement

The final solution

***Ron Tandberg**, winner of 10 Walkley Awards, works with* The Age.

Visa categories

***Hinze** (aka David Pope) is a freelance cartoonist.*

See no evil

Andrew Weldon*'s work appears regularly in* The Big Issue, The Sydney Morning Herald, The Age *and* The Chaser.

Why so sad?

Peter Nicholson *is a cartoonist for* The Australian.

Part 4

Necessary acts

Acts of support, acts of love, political acts, individual actions. Action and advocacy have come to define a broad community movement. People from diverse backgrounds and places have been drawn together and moved to act by the stories of asylum seekers.

The universal desire to protect and care for children, a desire to protect against the cruelty of indefinite and arbitrary detention of child asylum seekers, and the plight of unaccompanied children has moved to action even those unsure about the rights of detained adults to care and protection.

Those who have engaged in this political process have taken risks and have been changed. To challenge the organisation of the immigration system, community groups have developed campaigns and approaches which speak from the heart. This emotional investment galvanises action and makes for an intensity of involvement that is, at times, overwhelming. Commitment of such time and energy becomes a commitment of self.

It is hard to maintain involvement in the face of disappointment and frustration. Sweet moments of 'victory', the delight on the face of a child released from detention – these moments sustain organised movements and bind individuals together, and have allowed us to continue.

Social activism begins with defining choices and individual acts. To act with others, to share disbelief, pain and struggle, changes lives. We are all changed.

The birth and growth of ChilOut

*Management consultant **Junie Ong** chronicles the early days of the breakthrough advocacy organisation she co-founded*

It all started for us the night of 13 August 2001. My husband Tom and I and our 13-month-old son were having a quiet weekend in the Southern Highlands. Tom was watching *Four Corners* on TV when he suddenly called out to me to come and watch. He was insistent: *'You have to see this.'* It was an 'interview' with Mohammed Badraie, father of six-year-old Shayan, captured shakily on a hand-held video camera in stealth, his wife Zahra and baby daughter Shubnam close by [*see Jacquie Everitt's story*].

We didn't realise it then, but our lives were about to be turned upside down. We watched him beg for help, tears rolling down his face as he cradled a catatonic little boy in his lap. It was a parent's despair, such that we could not look away. And the biggest shock of all, that this was happening at Villawood Detention Centre, in Sydney, in Australia. We thought Australia could not possibly be host to such a nightmare scenario.

How can we begin to describe what we felt as we sat, silent and transfixed? Horror, repugnance, outrage … My head was spinning with a million unanswered questions. How can this happen? Whose work was this? Is this true? Isn't this kind of treatment of fellow human beings against the law? Many of these questions were quite naïve. I was about to learn exactly how naïve I was.

A sleepless night ensued. I sat in bed with a list of friends' names and phone numbers, including the people who appeared on the *Four Corners* program, waiting for a reasonable time in the morning to call them. The reasonable time came at 7 a.m. I knew that if I got up to make a cup of tea and allow the morning routine to envelope me, the moment would be gone.

Working through my list, rousing still-sleeping friends, the anger and the passion took over. These feelings fuelled me, kept me going through every response, warm or cool. What was I trying to achieve? I didn't know, all I knew was that no decent human being could be aware of this abomination and not want to act. I had a lot to learn. I am, however, a good learner.

In hindsight, I think my ignorance of the whole situation with the current wave of refugees was a good thing. A few friends who said they were aware of what was happening were not as shocked or outraged as I was, even though they expressed sympathy for the refugees and anger at government policies. For me it was simple: 'Well, if we know, and we care, this is abhorrent. Come on, let's do something!'

This became my first real, all-powerful experience of how 'the anger and the passion' can sweep all before it. But it wasn't just about the emotion. I had a need to have the million questions answered. I knew that to do something meaningful I had to have information, the right information.

Tom was on the Internet and the phone to the ABC, tracking down all those who appeared on the program and gathering any other useful information he could through that source. The tireless and endlessly patient Jacquie Everitt was the first refugee advocate I made phone contact with. An hour later, more outraged than before, I had a list of names and numbers of people 'in the know' about the refugee situation in Australia – groups, lawyers, psychiatrists, clergy, refugees released from detention. I was away.

Over the first two years of the citizens' action group that came to be known as ChilOut (the name coined by Tom), endless nappy changes were made with the phone in the crook between my head and shoulder, talking with legal eagles, advocates, doctors, journalists, politicians, actors, broadcasters and clergy. Did they know at the time that those ever-present noises in the background when we spoke on the phone were the sounds of a household trying to run its normal course? This, while juggling the enormity of the realisation that the beloved country was being led down a dark and frightening path we steadfastly did not want to go on – with the bath running, a toddler being put to bed, dinner on the stove, preparation for work the next day, Tom flagging me on, more calls waiting.

The intrusive presence of the phone and emails in our lives was like nothing we could have prepared for. At its height, we were fielding endless phone calls and 40–50 emails each night after a day of work and family commitments, the two of us sometimes clocking an extra 30–40 ChilOut hours each week.

And of course there were those visits to Villawood. Those all-important visits. We advocates and the refugees themselves understood only too well why they had to be locked away in the desert, on distant islands. The despair born of isolation and hopelessness is impossible to understand without experiencing it ourselves. They were locked away, excised from those who could help, who might have helped. The knowledge that when we look into the eyes of another human being and we see their pain and suffering, we hear their stories, we sense the yearning for loved ones left behind and lost, we see their desperation, we touch their hands, we hold them close – there is no going back to the life that was before. This knowledge centred me and held me steady; I came back to it again and again.

My first visit to Villawood with Leonie Gardner, who came to coordinate the visitors' program for ChilOut with such energy and commitment, is etched into my consciousness. Our first meeting was with an amazing refugee activist on the inside of Villawood, a man from Afghanistan, nature's gentleman. We brought biscuits, chocolates, flowers and flowering plants. I can never forget the look in the eyes of this man as he stared at these perfect little yellow flowers in a pot and the way he gently stroked the petals as we talked. Two hours later, we found ourselves outside the razor wire on our way home. But we couldn't go. We stood in total silence for a while, words failed us (this is saying a lot for those who know us).

In the months that ensued, Tom and I slept the sleep of the exhausted, our financial affairs foundered, our home-office-cum-ChilOut-engine-room looked like a snake-pit, our social life disappeared, certain friendships became strained, stress became the order of the day. At the same time, in the whirl of sometimes frantic and always relentless activity, we forged friendships and discovered a camaraderie we did not know could exist in fighting the good fight with like-minded others, the sheer highs of small wins, the meeting of setbacks with determination. Our toddler came to know the Villawood visiting area like the backyard we did not have time to fix. Playing with refugee children behind razor wire and attending ChilOut and other activist meetings became part of his routine. Strapped in his car seat, each time we drove into the carpark and his eyes fell on the razor wire, he called out the name of a friend in detention. He seemed to know at age two that this whole thing was wrong!

The gifts of helping are profound, it is true. We are grateful to those refugee friends who have touched and taught us in a way we did not know was possible. And we know that we did not act purely out of altruism. We were also fighting selfishly for ourselves, the values we wanted our children to hold dear, for the kind of Australia they would one day inherit.

Tom and I found time to eventually get married, just as we were handing over the reins to our friend, Dianne Hiles, ever steady and steadfast as she goes.

The ChilOut story continued

*IT Project Manager **Dianne Hiles** takes up the story - and the passion - where Junie Ong left off*

My own daughter was four when ChilOut began its campaign to get children released from detention centres. When she was six, her drawings were 'normal': grass and flowers on the bottom, blue sky on the top, with the sun (always wearing sunglasses) in the corner

– nothing like the obscenity below that we allowed to come out of Shayan's tormented mind.

As well as Shayan's story, one that affected me especially deeply was that of a two-and-a-half-year-old boy, Bawan. After a hunger strike at Villawood was broken up by a riot squad, this child was swooped up with his father, subjected to an attempt to put plastic cuffs on his tiny legs, and flown on an early-morning flight to Port Hedland for 13 days in an isolation cell. Father and toddler were allowed two toilet visits per day; the little one had to relieve himself on a bundle of clothes at other times. The father had no means of occupying his son other than by talking to him.

This drawing by six-year-old Iranian boy Shayan Badraie [*see the stories by Ngareta Rossell and Jacquie Everitt*] became ChilOut's early logo. It shows Shayan and his sister crying, with their parents. The van at bottom right is the ambulance that would take Shayan to and from Westmead Children's Hospital, when he needed to be re-hydrated because he would not eat or drink properly. At top left is a guard with a baton; at bottom left is a detainee, bleeding where he has cut his wrist. All along the top is the razor wire that sits across the fences at Villawood.

I simply could not believe we were treating children like this, in my adopted country. This was not the Australia I had chosen to come and live in. Why was an asylum seeker being placed in solitary confinement (never mind his child)? He wasn't a criminal. For many years I had been active in Amnesty International, and was on the China Team monitoring and criticising human rights abuses there. But we couldn't complain about another country's performance when our own was so seriously wanting.

Here is how we outlined ChilOut's original mission:

1. We are campaigning to get all children, together with their primary carers and accompanying families, out of immigration detention centres and into existing community support structures. This includes all unaccompanied children. Our motivation is humanitarian and non-political.
2. We are opposed to the mandatory detention of asylum seekers and are particularly concerned about conditions under which children are detained, the length of their detention and the high-security, prison-like centres in which they are held. Physical, emotional and developmental damage caused by continued detention is well documented. Some children are on antidepressants, many have been on hunger strikes and been caught in the middle of riots and fires. Children have self-harmed, e.g. sewing lips together, cutting arms, drinking shampoo, hanging themselves. Many suffer from Immigration Detention Stress Syndrome, as documented in *Lancet*, the prestigious British medical journal. Release from detention is our primary aim. Our secondary aim is to make lives in detention more tolerable through outside contact, learning, play and entertainment.
3. We also seek to correct inaccurate media coverage of asylum seekers and counter widespread misinformation. Pejorative terms such as 'illegal immigrants' and 'queue-jumpers' are used in the media and help justify harsh government policies. In our view, once acquainted with the facts of detention, Australians of good conscience will react as we do – with indignation, compassion and action.

We started selling T-shirts, utilising the design [*see next page*] already drawn up by South Australian advocates, and then books. The first, *Asylum*, written by journalist Heather Tyler, contained accounts of individual asylum seekers and detailed some of the horrific situations from which they had fled. We held rallies and did everything we could to raise awareness of the inhumane treatment of children and the inappropriate conditions in which they were being held. We aimed to portray ourselves as a group of middle-class, middle-aged, outraged parents and concerned citizens campaigning for the release of all children and their caregivers from immigration detention centres. Every week, Junie [*Ong - see her story*] used to write the 'Call to Action' (CTA) newsletter, and our email list became a potent lobbying force.

ChilOut came to media prominence when Dr Duncan Wallace, a Naval Reserve psychiatrist (who served in Operation Relex, which sought to maintain our border security by turning back the boats to Indonesia), was prevented from addressing one of our early information nights. We had quickly set up a website, and a range of people signed up to be volunteers or to receive information. One of our most successful initiatives was the Visitors Program, which gave 'ordinary' Australians the opportunity to queue for hours outside Villawood, undergo the rigorous security procedures and get to know the unfortunates detained therein.

After tolerating months of anonymous telephone calls, with gruesome personal threats and abuse, Junie decided to call it a day at the end of 2002. We were thrilled that just prior to her departure, she and ChilOut were voted number one in the NGO sector in the *Australian Financial Review*'s Power 2002 Listing. This was even more of a fillip when we learned it was other NGOs that had done the voting. Junie's vision, commitment and managerial knowhow undoubtedly laid the foundations for ChilOut, on which the group has continued to build.

She handed me the baton of leading ChilOut, and I inherited a team that worked wonderfully, harmoniously well. Perhaps my most enduring memory of the whole campaign is the production of the CTAs. They were intended to inform and motivate, and I hope they also communicated my ongoing sense of indignation that we as a community were failing our human rights obligations so woefully.

I bought the original of this Moir cartoon for a not-insignificant sum at a Linda Jaivin refugee support fundraiser. Somehow it seemed it should belong to a ChilOut-eer (I was relieved when this was pointed out to the person bidding against me!).

In December 2005, ChilOut was honoured to receive the HREOC Community Organisation Award for Human Rights. The citation read: *'The judges credited ChilOut for their relentless campaign and their contribution in pressuring the Federal Government to remove children from immigration detention. The group of "middle-Australian mums and dads" that formed in 2001 after seeing the plight of a six-year-old Iranian boy in immigration detention has demonstrated the remarkable power of committed individuals to achieve change. They showed the faces of the children behind razor wire and brought the suffering of those children into Australian living rooms – confronting us all with the reality of children in detention.*

'ChilOut supported people inside immigration detention through visitors' programs and worked tirelessly to increase public awareness on the plight of refugees, asylum seekers and their children. Their campaign had a clear goal, and this award recognises the efforts of the many people involved. ChilOut's reward was getting children out of detention, and this award is a celebration and recognition of their efforts.'

While it often seems that, as a society, we are following a very dark agenda, it is encouraging to know there are so many people prepared to stand up for decency, compassion and humanity. We were indeed fortunate to find thousands of Australians of good conscience.

IF THERE IS SOMETHING RIGHT

***Ed Mund** (a pseudonym) wrote this poem to his local MP, who would not support proposals to reform detention laws*

If there is something right
The evidence is the absence of complaint
Or, if sought, the assertion that 'I'm fine, thanks'
Or, if sought thoroughly, perhaps that 'I have what I need'
Or, if observed discreetly, that a person is happy
If there is something wrong
What kind of evidence do you believe?
Letters from the sufferer or
Letters from their advocate or
Pictures from the sufferer or
Pictures from their advocate or
The tears of the sufferer or
The sweat of their advocate or
The blood of the sufferer or
The corpse of the sufferer or
A message from God?
Or
Is it when the story's told on TV news or
Is it when the newspaper tells the story twice or
Is it only when the statistical probability is certain –
That you believe your belief is wrong?

Bearing witness: when they came for the refugees, they came for us all

***Pamela Curr**, a longtime advocate and lobbyist, chronicles the erosion of human rights and common decency*

It was back in 1999, after a group of us began weekly Sunday vigils at Maribyrnong Detention Centre (MIDC), that I first realised that human rights in Australia were not for everyone. A Palestinian-Australian man contacted me, convinced that there was a man from Palestine being held secretly in MIDC. When he called, staff denied the man was there. He asked me to ring and, much to my surprise, the guards acknowledged that the man was indeed in an isolation room there. At the time I was coordinator of the Fair Wear Campaign, working in the same building as the Moderator of the Uniting Church, Pam Kerr. We shared the joke over the occasional confusion with our names: I later found out that they thought I was the Moderator of the Uniting Church!

This man was depressed and suicidal after five months in isolation. I could not believe there was no care for such an obviously sick and depressed man. He was not even allowed to be with other detainees. My sense of outrage increased as the weeks went on with no results despite continual calls, letters and lobbying. Even when the man ate a fluorescent light-bulb, the stonewalling continued.

At 3 o'clock one morning, unable to sleep and feeling totally powerless, I took a can of house paint and a brush and set off to take out my rage on a large wall in Lygon Street. With no experience as a graffiti artist, I wrote 'FREE MOHAMMAD' in a shaky and irregular hand. I then went home to bed. Later that day I saw that my message had been changed to read 'AND FREE JESUS TOO', a salutary lesson in mixed messages.

It took months to get Mohammad released. Mental illness meant as little then as it does now, despite the so-called lessons learnt from the Cornelia Rau debacle [*see Timeline of events*]. It seems that the department will act only if suicide looks inevitable, so ingrained is their indifference.

The first of my many visits inside MIDC was in 2000, when I accompanied an Iraqi mother and daughter just released from Woomera who were desperate to see friends lost en route from Indonesia. These were early days, and I still had much to learn about the malice of the refugee policy. With no formal settlement services, it was left to churches, local councils and concerned individuals to frantically cobble together houses and support for people on their first nights free in Australia, after months travelling and then in detention.

I drove the family to a house where another Iraqi mother and her son were living. There were mattresses on the floor and little else, not even enough plates or cups. We laughed as they told the story of 'Mr and Mrs Visa', who once a week walked around the camp trailed by children, going from donga to donga. They handed the occupants a piece of paper and told them they had 15 minutes to get to the gate and onto the bus. No time for goodbyes.

Looking back, I realise how my feelings about my country have changed. Until this time I had been proud to be a sixth-generation Australian. I felt a warmth towards my fellows. Naively, I really believed Australia was a place where the common good underpinned our governance and community infrastructure. I also believed that the law protected our human rights. I was soundly disabused of this notion when the High Court upheld the government's position that they had the right to indefinitely detain asylum seekers. The other terrible shock was the decision that saw the immigration law overrule the Family Court's right to make decisions in the interests of children in detention. Seeing the ways that good and decent lawyers' arguments for human rights were cast aside has shaken my belief in this country.

Another shock has been the misrepresentation and dishonesty about asylum seekers in the press and by politicians. This came back to me recently, on the fifth anniversary of the 'Children Overboard' debacle [*see Timeline of events*]. I heard first-hand from a number of families and children who were on the boat about an event that was never reported. Their requests to be heard at the Senate Inquiry at the time were denied. As is often the case, asylum seekers are denied a voice when matters concerning them are debated. A letter sent by the Iraqis from Manus Island was tabled and not even reported on.

So it is that the story of seven-year-old Mohammad was never told. As the boat was foundering, this little boy was vomiting and distressed. His father and mother had three children to care for, and the boat was going down. The captain had refused to take the children on board and everyone was told they must go into the water. Shortly before they had to jump, Mohammad's father gave him an adult seasickness tablet. When the time came the family jumped with their children. Later, when everyone had been rescued and was safely on deck, amidst the chaos of people changing out of wet clothing and looking after the many children, a father was crying out 'Mohammad, Mohammad' in great distress. He was ignored until a man who spoke English told the captain that the boy was missing. The captain said that this could not be the case because the head-count was correct – the boy must be on deck somewhere. Soon after, a sailor called out that there was a light blinking, bobbing in the waves. A boat was despatched, and there they found little Mohammad, in his life jacket with its blinking light, sound asleep on his back. A miracle – he could so easily have drowned. But no miracle that Australians would ever hear about. This boy and his family are now in New Zealand. When I suggested that we tell this story, my Iraqi friends said, 'What for? No-one cares about what happened to us'.

I feel angry when I consider how often Australians are instructed to take responsibility. This message is pressed on the most vulnerable and least able by politicians and government departments. Yet, unbelievably, no member of government or public servant was held responsible for the terrible decisions, brutality, dishonesty and lies that have characterised the behaviour of the Immigration Department. After the release of the Palmer Report in July 2005, we were told that 'the culture' was to blame. No person was responsible for ignoring the plight of Cornelia Rau, nor for overlooking the many signs that she was mentally ill. I was bitterly angry at the way all those who knew and had ignored her plight evaded responsibility. I had begged, pleaded, coerced and demanded for seven weeks that she be released, and no-one was responsible. No person was held responsible for deporting an Australian citizen, Vivian Solon, and then of hiding this terrible fact even though she had children living in Australia and significant health problems. As for Ministerial responsibility, this seems to be a quaint custom from a bygone age.

On the other hand, being involved with the movement has given me the privilege of experiencing the best of human beings, of kindness and courage from refugees and their supporters. As advocates, we are able to support detainees in detention, because we are notified by other detainees when there is trouble in the camps. When someone is sick or suicidal, it is detainees who ensure they receive help. When a deportation is under way, it is the information from other detainees which helps us track the movements, and has assisted us to stop a 'removal'. As the years have worn on, the communication links on both sides of the fence have grown to a sophisticated level, advocates with their computers and detainees with their mobile phones. It was detainees who alerted me to Cornelia Rau's desperate plight in late November 2004 and who kept me informed even when Cornelia was placed in isolation. Without them, we would not have known she was still there.

In May 2004 at Baxter, a young man had abdominal pain and was told that he could not see a doctor. After five days, detainees held a sit-in outside his room, telling guards that they would not move until the man was taken to 'Medical'. The guards' response was to call in a CERT. ACM guards in full riot-squad gear charged into the compound to deal with the 'trouble', but this was cut short when they saw how sick the man was. He was immediately taken to Medical and then to the hospital at Port Augusta. Later that night he was evacuated to Royal Adelaide Hospital by the Flying Doctor Service. When I spoke to the surgeon, he told me that the man had a burst appendix, with pints of pus in his abdomen, and that he could have died. There is no doubt that the detainees saved this man's life by their action that night.

Even in their distress, the capacity of detainees to recognise when one of their fellow detainees has greater need is inspiring. Many of the long-term detainees have come from situations of torture and persecution.

This mitigates against rather than for them. Because of their fear on arrival, many withheld information which would have strengthened their cases. How does a young man tell an angry, disbelieving immigration officer that he was raped during interrogation in his home country; and, having withheld this, how much else can he not bear to reveal to an officer who demonstrates disbelief to every statement he makes? I have known people in detention with the physical marks of acid burns, smashed and deep scars, scars apparent to the naked eye. Once it was that evidence of torture was *prima facie* evidence of the need for refugee protection.

Of all the dilemmas I faced through this terrible journey into Australia's moral abyss, the one I find hardest to explain is how one human being can look at another human being and ignore their pain. It begs for an analysis of self. Could *I* respond in this way if circumstances were different? Why do so few guards and officers question the treatment of the people they spend every day with? How is it that they cannot put themselves in the others' shoes? How is it that those educated, privileged, comfortable immigration bureaucrats could implement such treatment of women, children, men and families? How did they face their own families after a day spent this way? How do politicians justify their decisions to imprison children and lock up people without charge on the grounds of deterrence?

We have choices. We can join the sea of indifference and cruelty, or we can stand up and be counted. For me it was never a hard decision. My father had a rawhide whip which his father had brought back from Africa. He told us that this whip was a reminder of 'man's inhumanity to man'. I knew these words by heart as a four-year-old, before I even knew what they meant.

The advocacy movement is diverse, comprising people from every political, faith, gender and age group. In the early days, many said, 'Why don't you unite under one umbrella?' Looking back, I think many of us realised that we could spend five years fighting over how to work together or we could just get on with it. And we did. Sometimes we disagreed, but we never stopped.

In retrospect, we needed everybody. The activists and hell-raisers worked in the face of media silence. Everybody knew about Woomera after the Easter Protest. I remember driving through the desert to Woomera and getting a call from the BBC in London asking about it. We needed the advocates who rang and wrote to refugees, reminding them the government did not speak for all Australians. Night after night, the one or two phones ran hot as advocates did their best to comfort and encourage. Inspiring people like the late Betty Dixon who, in her 70s, travelled backwards and forwards to Port Hedland, Woomera and Baxter visiting, writing, lobbying and driving politicians crazy with concern for 'her boys'. On their release, her home was a haven for all. There were so many Bettys. We needed the doctors, lawyers and psychologists who have donated their time and professional skills freely to giving the refugees a chance. There are those who sit at their computers, making sure that every advocate and activist knows when someone leaves detention, or calling for help in emergencies and keeping the wheels of dissent turning. People like Jack Smit of Project Safecom [*see Resources*], tucked away in rural Narrogin, who has built an archive of information about this terrible period in our history and who can extract a quote, a name or a case at a moment's notice. When we add the actions, protests, arts exhibitions, plays, concerts and installations, we see a broad community of dissenters who decided for themselves that they would make welcome the people who came to this country seeking refuge.

Once I had an organised life with a tidy house and garden. Now I have a life filled with warm friendships and a richness of human contact that I would not swap for anything.

Another country

*Writer **Rosie Scott** outlines the process and the meaning of publishing an anthology of detainees' writing*

The very first detention camp story I heard shocked me into action. It was an incident in Port Hedland where guards taunted a group of Muslim women and children – holding food out in front of them and snatching it away at the last minute. It was mild compared to the horror stories we've all become accustomed to – a group of sadistic men amusing themselves on a slow day by giving women a hard time. But I could not get the story out of my mind. It horrified me and proved to be the tip of an iceberg.

Like most Australians, I knew little of the Howard Government policy on asylum seekers. Suddenly it seemed vital to get these stories into the media. A full-page ad beginning, 'We are outraged and ashamed of this country's contemptible treatment of asylum seekers …' was one way to do it. Four PEN members [*see Resources*], working with many organisations and individuals, raised $60,000 in four weeks in 2001, enough money for the ad and a sizeable donation to the Refugee Council. More than 2000 people signed the double-page spread in *The Australian*, including many well-known Australians. It was heartening to see how many people wanted to express their strong opposition to the treatment of asylum seekers.

But the awful, unbelievable stories kept coming. Like most people I know who have become involved, I became rather obsessed about the detainees' plight, an Ancient Mariner at dinner parties.

It seemed to me that Australian PEN was in a good position to help. In 2002 Tom Keneally, Annette Hughes and I formed the Writers in Detention Committee. We knew writers unjustly imprisoned were living in harsh conditions, always with the threat of deportation and possible execution hanging over them. We decided to publish an anthology of their writing, which became *Another Country*. We wanted to make these writers' voices heard, for their self-respect and affirmation as writers, and because we wanted Australian readers to find out first-hand what was really happening; and, most importantly, we wanted to be able to advocate successfully for their release.

Tom set up a meeting with Dr Aamer Sultan, a former detainee who won a Human Rights award in Villawood and contributed a poignant story to *Another Country*. Sitting in a Sydney café, he explained that detainees had been so damaged and traumatised in the camps that rejection of their work could be the final straw. We realised this was going to be no simple literary anthology. For many, these words and stories were a matter of life and death. Aamer's words proved to be prophetic.

I started by sending out emails to all the women refugee advocates I knew. Their response was magnificent. The stories and poems started with a trickle and then began flooding in. For me, each story and poem was a little explosion of trauma. I felt horror and pity at the conditions they described, and was also moved by the writers' courage and the power of their words. It was mainly women refugee advocates who typed the writers' work, had it translated and convinced them to send it to me. Ngareta Rossell, right from the beginning, was an incredible support.

In the end, it took a year using the networks to get in touch with writers in the immigration detention camps, collect their work and make it ready for publication. There were many problems along the way, including, at one point, a threat of legal action.

We couldn't have succeeded without the network of dedicated, committed, practical and compassionate women who still devote hundreds of hours to helping asylum seekers. They visit and tussle with the ghastly demoralising processes of applying for visas, as well as the hundreds of other little details necessary for their survival. They are unsung heroes, and I feel privileged to know them. Many committed men are doing it too, of course, but in my case nearly every poem and story received for the anthology involved a female advocate. The camps destroy the detainees' spirits – and these women and men set about restoring them. It is one of the most successful grassroots political movements in Australian history.

The quality of writing we received was beyond our wildest hopes. We received vivid and compelling messages as if from some unnamed country on our borders where despair, depression and suicide were the norm – but where courage, talent, resilience and kindness also appeared.

I remember sitting in the bleak yard at Villawood with Hassan Sabbagh and asking him to write about the miraculous garden he created in the camp by digging the bare earth with a spoon; meeting Cheikh Kone for the first time in a Glebe café and being struck by his energy and optimism after three years in Port Hedland, and then reading the story of his dreadful journey to Australia. I read Mohsen Zand's powerful poems before meeting him, when we were both on a panel at the NSW Writers Centre, and holding his hand, which was freezing because he was so nervous. My last image of Baxter was seeing Sarath Amarasinghe and the other men in the visitors' room standing motionless, staring after us sadly as we left. Ardeshir Ghoulipour and Tony Zandavar stayed at my house and told terrible stories about the horrors they had endured. I remember sitting on Bondi Beach after my first visit to Villawood with Tom, still so shaken that this familiar scene seemed unreal. This was when the title for the anthology came to me – it was as if I had just returned from another country.

Melbourne, Sydney and Canberra PEN became involved, and we helped the other refugee advocates by using PEN's name in our letter-writing, lobbying, organising several public demonstrations and fund-raising. The constant stream of letters I wrote to Minister Vanstone regarding urgent cases elicited only four formal acknowledgments in four years.

For all of us involved in *Another Country* it has been a roller-coaster ride – with all the joys, worries, sorrows and responsibility of working for people unjustly imprisoned, desperate and depressed after years of incarceration, knowing that they could be deported back to the dangers they fled, as the Edmund Rice Centre's report *Deported to Danger* shows so clearly.

For me it was like travelling without a map – in Kafkaesque territory without landmarks or road signs, and a continual feeling of threat on the horizon. Immigration law is classic totalitarian stuff - labyrinthine, agonisingly slow and often cruel and senseless and, because of this arbitrariness and lack of guidelines, extremely difficult to navigate. This period in Australian history, when the Howard Government enforced the imprisonment of thousands of innocent people in brutal camps, will go down as one of our darkest.

During all periods of suffering, there are extraordinary stories of heroism, grief, despair, love and barbarism, humour, courage and cruelty. Many of these are as yet known only to the refugee advocates and the detainees themselves. This is why writers, organisations like PEN, and books like *Another Country*, *Deported to Danger*, *Bearing Witness*, *Dark Victory* and *A Certain Maritime Incident* have an important contribution to make [*see Resources*]. We have to tell these stories, to keep a compelling and accurate record of what really happened. We have to ensure that in generations to come, this shameful policy does not become yet another secret history known only to a few. By writing about these events we ensure that those who carried out the policy, including Howard, have their responsibility clearly documented, their startling lack of compassion demonstrated beyond doubt.

Another Country went into its third edition, generated capacity events in Melbourne and Sydney with luminaries like Claudia Karvan, Bryan Brown, Christine Rau, Rachel Ward, David Malouf and Tom Keneally and nearly all the contributors present at different times. One hundred people gathered from all over Australia in the desert outside the Baxter detention camp for one of the most unique book launches in Australian literary history.

It helped to earn Australian PEN the Community Human Rights Award of 2004; and various international organisations, like the UN, the International Coalition on Detention, and International PEN have used it for distribution, reference and the formation of Writers in Detention committees in other countries. It is in educational and public libraries, and has been awarded an Amnesty essay prize. A 10-minute ABC arts segment featured it, and many articles and reviews were written, generating so much publicity about refugee issues both national and international. Most importantly, I believe it contributed to the release of *all* of our contributors.

I will finish by telling one of the many stories of the anthology. I first heard of Tony Zandavar, one of the contributors to *Another Country*, when Annise Gaffney wrote to me in May 2003. Annise and Tony have given me permission to retell this story.

'Enclosed is a poem by a gentle, intelligent Iranian man now into his fifth year of detention. He is no longer capable of this or any other type of writing as he is now paralysed by his depression and struggles to communicate in any way.'

Later she wrote again: *'He is a wonderful guy and it breaks my heart to have been witness to his deterioration over the past couple of years as his hope for any kind of future has been stripped away. He lives with the constant terror of deportation and forced return to the danger from which he escaped ... If he could safely return home he would have done so long ago. As well as struggling to cope with his own misery he is forced to watch his friends slowly unravelling around him. For almost five years now he has lived in these dreadful circumstances, witnessing suicide attempts – slashed wrists, hanging – and the ongoing acts of self-harm by people driven to the brink by despair and hopelessness ...*

'When I told him his poem had been selected but that a little bit of rephrasing would be necessary he told me he would try to write a couple of others. As I have explained, his deterioration makes it almost impossible for him to concentrate, and his writing is now very confused and fragmentary, but I am honouring his wishes and sending them to you anyway because I know what a mammoth undertaking it was for him to write them.'

She wrote again after her son visited Tony: *'He said being in the presence of someone suffering such a profound hopelessness and to be unable honestly to offer hope of a solution was one of the more distressing experiences of his life.'* She continued, *'Your interest in his work has resurrected a little spark of hope and provided a small purpose in otherwise empty days. I know Tony has continued to write a little more and I know that is entirely due to your encouragement.'*

A crowd of dedicated advocates had been working on Tony's case for years, including his future wife. The Writers in Detention Committee and Sydney PEN raised money for a lawyer through donations and a benefit concert. We phoned and wrote to him, publishing and reading his poems at many venues. He has rare gifts as a poet.

It wasn't until September 2004 that he texted me: *'Hi Rosie, I'm free now and heading 2 Adelaide by bus hope to see you soon Tony.'*

Tony is now happily married with a young son and living in Tasmania. We attended his wedding to Ruth, which he described as 'the happiest day of my life'. Like many other detainees, Tony's courage is a testament to the resilience of the human spirit, and we all feel privileged to know him. The happy ending to his story is what advocates want for all the desperate people who come to Australia seeking asylum, the modest goal they all work so hard for - to allow refugees the chance of a contented family life far from war and persecution, where they can bring up their children safely and in peace.

LOVE is stronger than FEAR: the SIEVX memorial

Psychologist and author ***Steve Biddulph*** *takes us inside a controversial and necessary project*

'Like birds on the water.' That's how one rescuer described the dead bodies of over 300 parents and children spread across several kilometres of ocean when the sun rose on 20 October 2001. It was an horrific sight, the lowest point in an already dark time of our modern history. It needed to be remembered, and its lessons burned into our national consciousness.

The 20-metre fishing boat, the SIEVX – as it came to be known – had been crammed with refugee families. Armed Indonesian police had supervised its loading; one man who became frightened and tried to take his family off the boat was pistol-whipped and made to stay aboard. The boat never had a chance: it sank the next afternoon in terrible weather and, despite being in the middle of the largest ocean surveillance ever carried out by Australia, Operation Relex [*see Glossary*], no rescue came until 20 hours later, when fishermen came across a few dozen remaining survivors.

But the SIEVX hadn't been ignored. Survivors talked about two military ships that came in the night, shining bright spotlights towards them. People had swum towards the ships, calling out and blowing the whistles on their lifejackets. The military boats had set a Zodiac (a small, inflatable speedboat) on the water, presumably searching for something or someone. But as groups of people swam towards them, the ships turned off their searchlights and sailed away.

It's clear that the ships were not Australian. Our nearest vessel, the HMAS *Arunta*, was many hours away. But what was our responsibility? We had created the context for SIEVX to occur: women and children were on that boat in overwhelming numbers because their husbands were trapped by changes to our visa laws. The normal rights of family reunion under international law were denied them. Having come on ahead, these fathers could not, as expected, return to or bring their wives and children to join them. Left without support, the women and children were easy prey for people smugglers.

A group based in the Uniting Church in Bellingen, NSW felt that a memorial to these lost lives was vital to our country's redemption from these terrible events. We felt that the country's values were being put to the test – that we were 'in trouble with God'. SIEVX was what happened when politics was allowed to mix with humanitarian needs, and we had to use that turning point to begin reasserting more caring and responsible national values.

With funds donated by members of our own team, we employed as a project officer Beth Gibbings, a highly qualified person with experience in community arts, a long background in activism, and a gentle and collaborative way of working. Beth worked for over three years, paid part-time but working full-time, to hold the project together and bring it to reality. What we eventually achieved is largely attributable to her. A committee formed with Rev. Rod Horsfield at Launceston's Pilgrim Uniting Church became the stalwarts for the next two years of the project.

My own involvement had been gradual. As a family psychologist and author, I had been shocked and disturbed at the maltreatment of families in detention, and tormented about what to do for the best. The more I learned, the worse it became. The needlessly harsh conditions, first in Woomera, where 400 people shared two toilets, where parents had to carry the excrement from their children, who were too frightened to go there after dark. Where bright lights shone on people all night, where they were woken several times a night for utterly needless head counts. These were concentration camps in the true sense – camps to punish civilians who had committed no crime.

New arrivals were also being mistreated. I heard that a young mother who had been kept with others on a stationary refugee boat off Port Hedland with her little children for 10 days in temperatures over 40 degrees by the Navy, suffered a sudden rise in her blood pressure. For four months, refugee support visitors desperately tried to get her proper medical help while she was in detention, but none was given. She died of a stroke, aged only 26. Her husband and two young children were deported back to Iraq, their journey tragic and in vain.

Like tens of thousands of others across the country, I could not sleep for thinking about this. If we did nothing, we were equally responsible. Our local Rural Australians for Refugees groups tried to help in every peaceable way, from sending clothes to people freezing in the desert camps, to phone cards so they could reassure people back home they were still alive, and books so children could learn and not succumb to crushing boredom; to funding lawyers, and letter-writing to work against suicide and despair in young men and orphaned teenagers who felt so desperately alone. A national resistance sprang up, of whom the typical person was just like me: grey-haired, well-behaved, outraged and mobilised at the trashing of our national ethos of care.

SIEVX, for me, was the watershed. The more I learned about the voyage, the people on it and their stories, the more motivated I was to tell all Australians in a creative and positive way – *this must never happen again*.

We decided to begin our memorial-making by holding a 'national schools collaboration', writing to every secondary school in Australia, asking them to work with students in art classes to create a design for a memorial that would be fitting and powerful. We made a short, factual documentary telling the story of one family that was on the voyage, and sent copies to schools that enrolled. Memorials are normally quite dull, and we wanted something so original and creative that it attracted attention and conveyed the force of the tragedy as seen through young people's eyes.

Dr Sue Anne Ware of the RMIT School of Landscape, a specialist in memorial-building, helped us to develop our dimly-formed notion that memorials weren't all about marble and cement, but that the 'meaning', or sense of connection that developed in creating a memorial was what mattered. We were aiming to remember something that many people did not even know about. We had faith, though, that if they knew, they would care. And in this we were wonderfully vindicated.

Hundreds of glorious designs poured in from schools across the country. Art teachers and their students had risen to the challenge. Some designs were intensely confronting – hands reaching from the water were a common theme, as were bars, barbed wire, grieving figures, bodies afloat. Young people were clearly angered and distressed that SIEVX had happened, and also that the authorities had tried to downplay it.

One design stood out, and was acclaimed, in the four exhibitions we held in national capitals to mark the anniversaries of the SIEVX sinking. It was by Mitchell Donaldson, a 14-year-old Brisbane schoolboy, and comprised a procession of poles, forming the shape and dimensions of the boat. We had chosen a quiet spot on the Canberra lakeshore as the site of the memorial, and this design fitted it well. However, Mitchell specified a pole for every person who had died.

The human mind cannot comprehend numbers above a certain level. We can see a dozen, then we go to big, abstract groupings – a hundred, a thousand. What was horrific about SIEVX was the sheer scale of death and, at the same time, our inability – as a country, or individually – to see the dead as individual people. If we were ever to treat refugees properly, we had to see them as individuals.

For us, as Christians (and, in fact, had we been Buddhists or Muslims, it would have been the same), the sacredness of each individual life was what mattered. When we did the design sums, it was patently clear: 353 poles would stretch for almost 300 metres. The scale of the memorial would be immense. And yet it would be simple, human, humble at the same time. A procession of souls, leaving the edge of the lake and snaking across the hillside among the magpies and gum trees of Weston Park.

The logistics of making this come true were quite challenging. We helped the schools involved to source timber in the most remote corners of Australia. We worked with SIEVX survivors and bereaved husbands, many of whom only came together through our events, to ensure the project was healing and appropriate to their needs.

We were shockingly mishandled by the federal body, the National Capital Authority (NCA), who claimed we had applied for a permanent memorial when in fact we had applied in writing for only a three-week standing of the poles, for the fifth anniversary in October 2006. We had been consulting with staff at the Authority for over three years, and to this day we cannot understand how they failed to properly read our application. The word 'temporary' was in the title of the application and on every page. Removal details were clearly specified. We wrote, pointing out that they had refused the application on grounds which applied only to permanent structures, but received no answer. A meeting to discuss the problem with the NCA was cancelled at the last minute, after we had already travelled to Canberra to keep the appointment. Then, weeks later, and only 10 days before the ceremony, the NCA directed us instead to apply to the Australian Capital Territory (ACT) Government for permission, before returning to them again. There was no explanation or apology for the previous error. In fact, the ACT Government and Chief Minister Jon Stanhope and the City Parks Department of the ACT were hugely supportive, but 10 days was too short a time to restart the process a second time, let alone complete the groundworks - a fact the NCA must have been aware of.

In the end, we benefited from sympathy and outrage among the public and the media. Six hundred volunteers arrived from all over the country to hold up the poles in place, where we were not allowed to plant them. Another 1400 looked on in something approaching awe as the poles were simultaneously raised to the haunting voices of a Tongan choir. Beautiful artwork - arguably some of the best student art this country has ever produced - decorated each individual pole. Churches, Rotary clubs, community groups, even a Tasmanian street joined together to make poles. It was a powerful expression of love for people they had never met. Our sense of faith in Australia was buoyed enormously. [*See Sue Hoffmann's story*]

We will re-apply for a six-week on-site standing of the poles in 2007. We know that we will one day make the memorial permanent. But we are happy for this to develop gradually. We want Australia to decide it does want this memorial. We want to take Australia to a more caring place through this and all the other efforts made by refugee activists and community groups, a vast network of resistance to the powers of fear and greed that, for a time, held sway over Australia.

Through involvement in this and many other larger efforts to turn the tide on refugee issues, we became clearer about what was only dimly felt to begin with. A secure and happy world comes from sharing: not from clinging defensively, like a scared Gollum, to one's 'precious', but by looking for opportunities to help a suffering world. In short, love is stronger than fear.

Injustice that will not let me go

***Frederika Steen**, retired Immigration Officer, finds hope amidst the struggle to support refugees in the community*

I am a Dutch-born immigrant child, raised in Tasmania, a teacher, public servant and volunteer worker. Values of truthfulness, compassion and justice are intrinsic in our family history and experience: a mother who was a nurse; a freedom fighter father who survived the Resistance years in Nazi-occupied Holland. My family, when on the run, was given safe haven by total strangers, a Christian family on whose farm I was born, in hiding. Then emigration, with six other families, to a new life in peaceful Tasmania, about as far away as possible. Even a six-year-old migrant feels loss and grief, and remembers what it is to lose the familiar, the warmth of grandparents, cousins and friends.

Involvement in social justice therefore reflects who I am. I had a brief teaching career in four under-resourced high schools, then nearly 30 years in the Federal Education Department and, from 1984, in Immigration. Community service has been important for me – in Dutch language schools, multicultural education and broadcasting, membership of TAFE and Multicultural Advisory Councils, and community refugee settlement. From the early 1980s I was involved in the Indo-Chinese Refugee Association. It was the start of a continuing friendship with Marion Le, a migration agent. I had been working as Chief Migration Officer in the Australian embassies in Bonn and Berlin, and in early 2001 a redundancy package offered freedom. My retirement dream was to spend time with elderly Dutch migrants and work for Aboriginal reconciliation. Instead, my calling turned out to be supporting the most disadvantaged refugees Australian society has ever seen: those on Temporary Protection Visas.

As a volunteer in the small community-funded Romero Centre in Brisbane, I was directly confronted with the situation of refugees on temporary visas, who looked to us for assistance the government would not give.

Stand-out events mark the passing of recent years, and no image of this time is more iconic than that of the Norwegian merchant vessel *Tampa* on the horizon, rescuer of 438 asylum seekers. Disbelief, disgust and shame when our government refused to let them land. Twenty-four months later, we had a frenzy of national media at the Romero Centre, when some of them finally set foot on our shores. A few of our '*Tampa* boys' commemorated the fifth anniversary of their rescue with letters of thanks to Arne Rinnan, Captain of the *Tampa* and our hero.

There was no joy at Christmas in 2003, the middle of a month's hunger strike by 45 desperate Afghan men on Nauru. It fell to amateurs on home computers to bring this tragedy to world media attention. Elaine Smith [*see her story*] was the hub of a network of people who phoned, faxed, emailed and wrote letters to detainees on Nauru for years. Hassan Ghulam, an Australian Hazara, was their nominated representative, with whom the government would not speak or negotiate. With donated phone cards, and emails when the electricity was on, the hunger strikers kept Elaine and Hassan informed. We issued almost daily bulletins. No Nauru visas were issued to lawyers, journalists or other potential 'trouble-makers', thus preventing independent scrutiny of the 'Pacific Solution'.

It was a relief when Australia accepted the UNHCR's review of rejected claims from those rescued by the *Tampa* on the grounds that circumstances in their country of origin had changed. After the hunger strike, hundreds of cases rejected by Australia were reviewed. In the community, we knew from our own monitoring of international sources that conditions had become less safe in Iraq and Afghanistan. Asylum seekers on Nauru had no such access to information, and about 400 were harassed and misled into returning to danger. Some have continued to email Australian friends after they fled from Kabul across the border to an illegal existence, again, in Pakistan or Iraq. This is unfinished business. The injustice done to them is unforgivable.

People around Australia supported the superhuman efforts of Marion Le and her helpers to represent the claims of asylum seekers on Nauru. Australian charities underwrote this remarkable feat, aiming to bring about an end to the Pacific Solution. Families were released first, and some of the hunger strikers were among those accepted and welcomed to Brisbane in July 2005. The last group of 25 landed in Melbourne on Melbourne Cup Day, 2005. Left behind were two forlorn Iraqi men who had somehow fallen foul of national security, were not told how or why, and were denied natural justice [*see Timeline of events, December 2006*]. For the very first time, Immigration provided counselling, accommodation, orientation, medical treatment and support to refugees on Temporary Visas. Great, we said, but what about the hundreds who came before, what about them?

The sustained criticism and growing evidence of the damaging effects of long-term detention on people began to bite. Even the Nauruans became uneasy and genuinely concerned about the human rights implications of indefinite detention of people who have not been charged with or convicted of a crime. The Senate Inquiry in May 2006 [*see Timeline of events*] into the proposed Migration Amendment (Designated Unauthorised Arrivals) Bill 2006 drew an astounding number of adverse submissions. Senators on both sides of the argument were confronted with legal, moral and political arguments against the legislation. It was an enormous public effort, especially from activists already exhausted by years of lobbying. When the Bill was withdrawn from Senate discussion at the very last minute in August 2006, just before it could be defeated, it was a victory laced with unease, and rightly so. Detention on Nauru soon resumed, with seven Burmese asylum seekers forcibly taken there just a month later. But this time the Nauru Government imposed time limits on visas issued to Australia's detainees.

Nearly all of the 1999–2001 'boat people' have eventually been granted permanent residence and are taking out Australian citizenship. This made a nonsense of TPVs. The few Coalition politicians who negotiated immigration reforms in June 2005 won our respect, but the reforms were political, not principled: keeping children in detention was no longer a 'good look' for the government.

I am still deeply angry about asylum seekers being forcibly returned to countries they had fled, about the government's exploitation of generous Australians who care for asylum seekers in 'community detention'; and family men still on three- and five-year temporary visas after four lost years on Nauru. But most sickening is the fact that the pillars of this inhumane policy remain in place. This includes the manipulation of international boundaries to enforce offshore processing, indefinite mandatory detention, and lives in limbo on TPVs for legitimate refugees. Only abolishing the legislation will fix what is so wrong.

From my very first experience of busloads arriving at the Romero Centre – tired, frightened and disoriented – I was hooked. Some only had a garbage bag for their personal possessions. Their needs were so great and so basic, for they had no English, no resources, no preparation and no contacts in Brisbane. I was outraged that the government could dump genuine refugees in this way – how else can you describe the abandonment of needy people given only one night's accommodation, registration with Centrelink, Medicare, a bank, and a small amount of money? I heard that federally-funded agencies normally involved in refugee settlement were threatened with de-funding if they helped refugees on TPVs. This compromised fine people in government and in the helping agencies. The policies made victims of many people, not only refugees.

I take pride in the compassionate Australian community response to strangers in need. The Romero Centre commenced in March 2000 in an inner-city house provided by the Sisters of Mercy, some months after the first arrivals from detention centres. About 2300 have passed through the centre, most of whom were Shia Muslims fleeing religious persecution in Saddam Hussein's Iraq or the Taliban in Afghanistan. A small proportion stayed in Queensland. They have become our friends: they invite us to their functions and weddings, spend weekends and holidays with the hospitable 'Buderim Buddies', and develop mutual supports like the Tiger Eleven soccer team and the Hazara Ethnic Society. Community support made all the difference to the unaccompanied minors, who successfully completed schooling and became outstanding ambassadors for their people.

Our seven years of service to 'second-class' refugees falls into three phases. The 'on arrival' stage was hectic. Instant help was needed to get people onto buses to family and friends interstate or into accommodation locally. There were stuff-ups to fix. A sibling group, including traumatised teenage girls, was bussed from Port Hedland to Brisbane, when their dead father's brother was waiting for them in Perth. The St Vincent de Paul Society put them on a plane. A young mother with three little children barely survived 28 hours by bus from Woomera to Brisbane. She was going to her husband in regional Victoria, so she had to get back on a bus for another 16 hours that evening, via Sydney, then catch another bus the following afternoon to arrive at her destination at 2.30 on the morning after. Another young mother, also from Woomera and eight months pregnant, arrived in Brisbane, but journeyed back to Adelaide the next day. That is where her sister lived, who would attend the birth of her baby. We respected the pull of family and became scathing of the carelessness of immigration officials who despatched people as if they were things, with so little care.

Emergency medical and dental cases were taken by volunteers for treatment, pulling all the strings available. Medical records had to be demanded from Woomera for the doctors treating an illiterate woman in severe pain who could not sit and could not give her medical history. Was she fit to travel when she left Port Hedland? A young father asked for counselling for his children, who screamed at night. He had held them high as the water rose in their sinking boat. Those with headaches, who could not sleep, were referred to the torture and trauma clinic. We saw the scars of some who had self-harmed, and we heard stories of violence and physical and mental abuse by Australians employed in the centres. Children being politicised by detention was very hard to take. An articulate 12-year-old who attempted suicide three times in the toxic environment of Woomera implored us to get his friends out. A toddler marched up and down chanting, in the only English he had, 'DIMA. FREEDOM'.

The second phase was the hell on earth of uncertainty. Under the terrifying threat of deportation, refugees lived a life in limbo for three or more years on TPVs. Real refugees were deliberately denied help and used as a deterrence. Every day we saw the torment of men cruelly separated from their loved ones, and the despair of unaccompanied minors denied family reunion. Some intelligent young men went to work in abattoirs and on farms because money, not education, was the priority if you were to be deported. They were denied access to the Adult Migrant English Program. Such suffering, and so unnecessary, that I wonder how people so mistreated are not more angry. 'We are used to suffering,' they say. Acts of human kindness have healed some wounds. Perhaps the sons and daughters of the alienated first generation will express the anger.

The compulsory re-interviewing of refugees in 2004 after the expiry of their TPVs seemed like double jeopardy. With close collaboration between lawyers, agents, teachers and friends, a safety net of independent witnesses was made available to every refugee who wanted it. Some of us kept copious notes during interviews (in effect, interrogations) that re-traumatised people. Cynicism had long eroded any trust in a fair process. It distressed me to visit a young man in hospital after an attempted suicide directly related to his 'interview'. The interviewers were insensitive as to why a refugee was granted refugee status in the first place. Vicarious trauma has changed and damaged many advocates, too, as a result of journeying with people who experience such trauma and discrimination first-hand.

In 2005 we entered a third phase, with the granting of permanent residency and an entitlement to Australian citizenship after two years. Our first priority was an emotional trip to find and meet families living illegally in a neighbouring country and lodging applications for family reunion. The subsequent arrival of wives and children marked the beginning of this new settlement process, and also revealed the inadequacy of settlement services. The cohort of refugees on TPVs for years need rehabilitation and recovery from detention and a life in limbo. Extra support for families now reunited after years of deprivation and separation is needed. Its absence may jeopardise their successful integration, and there is no second chance.

More than five years of intense involvement in refugee advocacy has been a labour of love. It has revealed the best and the worst in people. I have journeyed with modern-day saints, religious and secular, and forged friendships with people who share my abhorrence of injustice and cruelty. I wish I could name them all here, because we pulled together as a team. However, we have so far failed to remove legislation that trashes human rights and threatens our democracy, and we still have no Bill of Rights. I cannot forget that many refugees remain separated from loved ones on TPVs from Nauru, West Papua and Burma – it is such injustice that will not let me go.

THE VITAL INGREDIENT

*Visual artist and writer **Julie Shiels** describes her innovative and effective approach to celebrating cultural diversity*

There is nothing more moving than a personal story. A story can touch a heart and change a mind. But some stories come at a price.

My first experience with refugees was in 1979, when I volunteered to teach English to a Chilean family that had escaped the Pinochet regime. We never really talked about what had happened to them, and now I'm glad I didn't ask.

Years later I developed a project with Foundation House for Survivors of Torture and Trauma. One of the case workers described to me the process of documenting an applicant's story. Her job was to record the human rights abuses. She talked about how, in this process, she became an interrogator and how her clients were returned to that dreadful space of having to tell or suffer the consequences.

In 1995 I confronted similar issues while developing a theatre project with the Timorese community. The play, originally called 'Bridging the Gap', was about the relationships between Chinese, Portuguese and Indigenous communities in East Timor, but it coincided with the arrival of a boat carrying asylum seekers from East Timor and was soon transformed into a story about these people's experiences. In the process, some of the members of the theatre group started to unwind the stories of their own lives, but this re-telling stirred up pain. It was through this experience that I became aware of the perils and the responsibility that goes with opening a person's wounds.

In 1999, the so-called 'fourth wave of boat people' began arriving on Australia's shores. At first, we didn't know what they looked like, we didn't know their stories. They were whisked away to privately-run detention centres, where the government would not allow journalists or anyone else to visit them. It was easy to dismiss these nameless, faceless people as 'illegals'. It was only after they sewed their lips shut with a needle and thread that we finally began to listen.

Debate raged about who these new arrivals were and why they had come. I was troubled that some of my refugee friends, who had themselves faced the hardened heart of an uncompassionate Australia in earlier times, were now taking a similar line towards the new boat arrivals from their safe haven of permanent residency. They asked why the newcomers did not stand in line. 'We waited in camps,' said some. 'We went through the legal process,' said others. 'They are taking the place of my sister. Are they who they say they are? Are they worthy of our compassion?'

I wanted to find a way to reframe the debate, to make work that spoke not only to mainstream Australia but also refugee groups from other eras. The government was running a fear campaign about porous borders, and Anglo-Saxon Australians were not the only ones to respond by closing their hearts.

But I also wanted to find a way to tell the stories of refugees without forcing people to once again justify their flight to Australia by revisiting traumatic experiences, and without entrenching suffering as the only marker of the refugee's identity and being. I was sure that there must be other stories to tell, stories that were both humorous and triumphant.

I decided to focus on food – a subject so universal that it could link the experience of the Chilean and Vietnamese refugees of the 1970 and '80s with Iraqis, Iranians and Afghanis who arrived on boats more recently, as well as every other refugee group in between. More than that, it was a topic that could engage an audience who had never been displaced from their homes, because food is a language that transcends time and cultural origins. Food is something that people can talk about with confidence and with ease, enabling them to tell stories that are beyond the suffering. It enables them to describe their life experience without necessarily revisiting the sites of past pain and trauma. I hoped that with this work, we as a society would understand more about the experiences of those who have sought asylum in Australia over the last 30 years and find points of shared experience.

The result was a writing and photographic project, with recipes and story telling at its core. I worked with nine different refugee communities who had arrived in Australia at different times and in different ways. I was able to bring together all of these communities because I had worked with them in varying ways over a 20-year period. We cooked dinners together and for one another, shared food, swapped stories and traded recipes. The project culminated in an exhibition that combined a photo-montage, a recipe and 'the vital ingredient' – a story about an important meal and an associated event. The show was exhibited at the Victorian Immigration Museum from December 2003 to October 2004 and was seen by an estimated 100,000 people. We had brought together witty, tender and sometimes painful stories that reveal much about the refugee experience in all its diversity – from fear and flight from the homeland to the hopes and challenges of re-settling in a new land. The book, *Cooking Stories*, is still on sale in the Museum shop.

Whenever I work with communities, I try to make myself dispensable, to cede responsibility and build a skills base so the work has its own momentum. Many of the people involved with *Cooking Stories* continue to work with their own communities, and in some cases with other communities – one Chilean woman, for example, volunteers as a worker with women from the Horn of Africa. The regular dinners continue, with the Timorese community hosting a monthly feast and cultural 'knees-up', and others who were part of the *Cooking Stories* project have continued the work in other ways. Every now and again I get a phone call or run into one of the participants, and we have a catch-up on how their life is progressing.

Sometimes I have pangs of regret and a tinge of guilt that the focus of my work has changed. Then I think of the line that Paul Kelly and Indigenous writer Kev Carmody penned: 'From little things big things grow'. In this case, it was a big project spawning many small initiatives and endeavours that continue independently. So another way of looking at it is that I did myself out of a job, and that was one of my key aims.

The story of the Bridge for Asylum Seekers Foundation

***Virginia Walker**, a retired public servant, responds to the many needs of asylum seekers on Bridging Visas*

I have always had an interest in assisting people from other countries. In June 2002, a friend who wrote support letters to detained asylum seekers asked me to do the same. I began writing to a 35-year-old Iranian Christian convert ('Mr A') in Curtin Detention Centre whose court case had failed, and later phoning him when he was transferred to Port Hedland. As he was intent on improving his understanding of the English language and Australian customs, I answered his questions about pronunciation, word use, and slang expressions, and even explained that whistling at pretty women was not an appropriate custom to maintain in Australia.

I started corresponding with several Iranians, Afghanis and a Palestinian family in Port Hedland. Each time I rang, another person came to the phone with a request for help, and my circle of people in despair enlarged. Having found out about s417s and s48Bs [*see Glossary*], I began to write supporting letters to the Minister, as well as sending phone cards and parcels of sweets, dates and clothes to asylum seekers regularly, and particularly at Ramadan and Christmas.

Just after Christmas 2002, I made my first visit to Villawood IDC. I hated the razor wire and the indignity of lining up for hours in the hot sun or rain without shelter or water, the lack of seats. Knowing the Corrections system, I felt the then-ACM officers treated visitors like the families of inmates in that system. But we were visiting asylum seekers. Whatever the conditions for visitors, they were much worse for the detainees, and it was very important to go to Villawood to listen to their stories and determine how to help. Many were stateless and in ever-present fear for their lives should they be returned to their country of birth. There were so many restrictions and little to divert them from becoming bored, lonely and miserable. Many were unable to get proper sleep, as other detainees kept them awake – often screaming in fear or in pain.

At the time of my first visits to Villawood, an advocate asked if I knew of somewhere in Sydney where a Kuwaiti Bedoon man ('Mr B') could stay. He was living in Perth, having been recently released from Port Hedland. Mr B had previously been in Villawood and he needed to discuss his legal case and his prospects of staying here with his Sydney-based lawyer. I agreed that he should stay with me in Glebe, as I had a spare room in my quiet apartment.

Mr B had been released on a *habeas corpus* order [*see Glossary*]. Conditions of his release were that he was not allowed to participate in paid or unpaid employment, was not entitled to Centrelink benefits or Medicare, or to study rights or transport concessions. He was required to report to the Department of Immigration office every weekday and at the Parramatta Police Station on Saturdays and Sundays. The only money he had was what a charity in Perth was giving him.

I was also asked to help a Bangladeshi man ('Mr C'), who was to be released from Villawood the next day and did not have anywhere to stay. I found temporary accommodation for Mr C but, unbeknown to me, a condition of his release was to stay with his 'guarantor', who had provided a bond of $5000. Although he could speak English reasonably well, he did not understand this or the other strict conditions – similar to Mr B's – and I had no knowledge about Bridging Visa Es at the time. How was he going to live? I gave him some money, but I was on a superannuation pension that would not stretch to keeping somebody for a lengthy time. Mr C believed he could obtain work and repay his friends. His friends told him in no uncertain terms that he could not work and that he would be returned to Villawood and probably deported, and his friend would lose the $5000 bond, if he worked.

Although another Bangladeshi whom Mr C knew said he would give Mr C a bed and some financial support, this was not satisfactory since he still had no money of his own and no way of obtaining any legally.

A friend and I approached Tanya Plibersek MP, the Federal Member for the electorate of Sydney, who was my local representative at the time, to ask what she thought we could do for this man. At a meeting with her, Mr C explained his predicament. We wanted to raise money for asylum seekers in this parlous position. Ms Plibersek's advice was to set up a group similar to the East Timor charity and to contact the person who had set this up, Sister Susan Connelly, for advice. However, Sister Connelly was away at the time, so we had to go ahead without her wise counsel. In the meantime, my friend offered a spare room to Mr C (she and her mother provided for him until such time as he left Australia in November 2003).

My friend and I held a meeting at my apartment, at which we determined to establish a Foundation that would assist people on *habeas corpus* orders and Bridging Visa Es. Representatives of the Uniting Church in Balmain, operating as Balmain for Refugees, suggested we talk to the Uniting Church about coming under their umbrella. Thus, through a handful of sympathetic friends, 'Bridge for Asylum Seekers Foundation' (BASF) was born. Bridge for Asylum Seekers Foundation was so named to denote a bridge between living on a Bridging Visa in the community and freedom for a new life. The aim of its Management Committee has been to raise the money to provide a basic living allowance to those families and individuals in the Australian community on Bridging Visa Es and *habeas corpus* orders.

Uniting Care NSW/ACT took us under their wing, so we had tax deductibility privileges. Uniting Financial Services provided us with a bank account, stationery and support. On 11 June 2003, BASF was officially launched at NSW Parliament House, supported by a broad coalition of churches, human rights groups, union members, political representatives, and individuals. We are still helping asylum seekers who came to us in June 2003. It is always heartening when we receive news of people being accepted as refugees, who can now start a new life for themselves in Australia.

I had to cease visiting and attending court hearings from late February until June 2006 following operations for knee replacements.

I was in rehabilitation and unable to walk or climb stairs, so I had to move to a ground-floor apartment, where I am now happily settled. Many of the asylum seekers I have helped, helped me with the move, shopping, unpacking and carrying things for me. A week does not go by where I do not see or hear from somebody I have previously helped.

Our work does not only mean that we raise money, we continue our other roles as well. Members of the Management Committee and I still visit Villawood armed with phone cards, cigarettes, soft drinks, fruit, nuts, nibblies and goodies. We also provide support for asylum seekers at court hearings. These include attendance at the Refugee Review Tribunal, the Migration Review Tribunal, the Federal Magistrate's Court, the full Federal Court and even the High Court when it is sitting in Sydney on a case in which we have an interest.

We have raised over $750,000 since June 2003. Nonetheless, because we assist over 100 people at any given time, we are always in a parlous position.

During the past three-and-a-half years, I have been privileged to work with Burmese, Acehnese, Iranians, Iraqis, Kuwaiti Bedoons, Afghanis, Algerians, Sudanese, Somalis, South Americans, Moroccans and Palestinians, to name a few of the people I have assisted through the Foundation and personally. I am not paid for the work, but it gives me immense satisfaction. Through it I have met and worked – and continue to work – with some wonderful people. My old friends and acquaintances have provided a great deal of support to me, as well as to the Foundation, and for this I am particularly grateful.

TWO STORIES

Family support worker Nola Naaman illustrates the fluctuating emotions that arise in her work with refugees

I started out as a mentor, providing transport or access to refugee clients. That was it, simple but not so sweet. The more I met children and youths who were detained, the more I saw agony in their eyes, I saw entrapment, I saw sorrow that I never saw in my own nephews' or nieces' eyes. Of course I wouldn't see it in their eyes because they have freedom of movement, freedom of speech.

I was told by a gentleman on the other end of the phone, 'All you have to do is pick Mandana up from the hotel [where her family is in community detention] and drop her off at the primary school'.

'Yep, that's fine,' I replied. That sounds easy, I thought, as I drove in the morning peak-hour traffic.

I got there, I parked the car, went to her room and picked up a little eight-year-old girl with black hair, dark eyes, dark skin. She smelt of fresh, hot bread. She had that aroma around her every day for two years.

That afternoon I got another phone call from the same gentleman: 'Nola, you need to take Mandana to the hospital to visit her mother'. No explanation, nothing to prepare myself. I parked the car, took her hand, and made a few jokes, just so I could see a smile on her worried little girl's face. It worked, and she looked at ease, though for some reason it made me feel good and bad at the same time.

Walking down the corridor, she recognised the ACM officers standing outside the door. She ran to her mother's room. I was standing at the door, looking around and saying to myself, 'I'm in a Psychiatric Ward'. It was dull, dirty and colourless. Staff and patients looked lifeless and hopeless. *Poor girl, what is she going through, having to see this?*

When interviewing a family at Baxter, I could feel their agony and their need to escape that hell-hole. Even though this couple had given up hope, I could sense their pride, dignity, patience and belief in God.

They were granted a Bridging Visa. They were not entitled to Centrelink, Medicare or job opportunities. They had support from Circle of Friends. Two months later they were still unsure whether to unpack their luggage. 'No,' she said with tears running down her cheek, 'I won't unpack them. They could return us to Baxter or deport us. No, I leave the bags packed.'

What do I say to that, how do I answer? My reply was nothing but a half-smile and a heavy heart. I had to be strong; they need strong support around them, and I can't cry, I can't cry. Wait until … when? I wait.

A few weeks down the track, they received a phone call from their lawyer: 'You have received your Permanent Visa'. Speaking to the mother on the phone, I could feel her happiness. I could feel that what she really wanted to do was scream for joy. I could feel it because I wanted to do it myself. And that's when I cried.

We enrolled them with Centrelink and Medicare, we opened bank accounts. I could for once sense calmness from this family. I could sense a smile from the boy that came from within. I could sense pride from the father. I could sense keenness from the girl. I could sense light-heartedness from the mother. I, too, felt a sense of accomplishment in helping this family cope with detention, cope with anxiety and survive on a Bridging Visa. It was an accomplishment to see that heavy load lifted off the shoulders of each individual and left to float in the air.

A walk in *agape*

Retired banker ***John Fry*** *discusses the role of his Christian faith in advocating for asylum seekers*

The past five years, as I've walked the walk with new arrivals to our shores, represent an incredible high point in my 73 years on this planet. Looking back, I'm amazed at how my Lord was preparing throughout my life for my entry into Villawood. I do not exaggerate! In saying so, I need to share a little of my personal history.

I was born in Perth. I had loving parents - morally correct people, conservative in politics and outlook generally. Mum was the dominant parent, and a bit repressive. I vividly recall her instilling in me her dogmatic - and not always Biblically-based - pronouncements on Christianity, and her dire warnings of 'invasion by the Asian hordes'. I treasured her love, but it took many years to deal with her less-than-helpful prejudices. I say this with sadness, yet some understanding. She was a product of her age.

Margot and I wed in 1958 and enjoyed a wonderful marriage until her untimely death in 1994. We moved to Sydney in 1959 because of my transfer there as a career banker. I've always been a strong family man, with four children and presently 10 grandchildren.

I'm a strongly committed Christian, and have always left my path in life open to the Lord. He has led me in all sorts of directions, often towards the marginalised segments of society - the underprivileged, despised and rejected folk.

In the early 1980s I experienced what I can only describe as a profound spiritual encounter, which led to a complete reappraisal of my values and priorities. This, in turn, led to my early retirement from banking. Since then, I've been fully engaged in various forms of Christian ministry - in NSW penal institutions, including introducing into Australia the highly effective, US-originated 'KAIROS' Christian prison ministry program; in primary and high schools; and in a mission that shares the Christian faith, where possible and appropriate, with Muslims.

Over the past 10 years I've remained actively involved in ministry to Muslims and, crucially, I became increasingly aware that my heart and my mind were not connected. I came to realise I harboured a racist attitude, albeit covertly. Six years ago this started to crumble, aided and abetted by the following events:

- In July 2001, we were studying The Acts of the Apostles, Chapter 10, in my local Bible study meeting – in particular, Peter's encounter with Cornelius, a new, non-Jewish Christian convert. In this passage, Peter showed obedience to God by journeying to Cornelius's home, but also demonstrated, as a Jew, a somewhat superior attitude towards the humble and welcoming Cornelius. Instantly I felt an association with Peter in my own attitude to 'foreigners' in general. Thus, I received a divine reprimand.
- The *Tampa* horror. How could my country do such a thing! It changed forever my life's course and my allegiances.
- The 9/11 catastrophe and its aftermath, from which it was abundantly clear that the 'doctrine of hate' was alive and well, and would continue to escalate. This was my final wake-up call.

It is easy, and in one sense accurate, to challenge the role of leadership at world, national, political and business levels, in allowing the ever-increasing inhumanity of man-to-man to fester. Yet, I also believe that all of this directly reflects the imperfections in the nature of *all* human beings, including me. The battle we need to fight, and try to win, is at a spiritual level: in the hearts and minds of people everywhere.

I pondered where I should go next and, after much prayer, soul-searching and trial and error, I phoned my close friends Stewart and Helen Binns, who had by then been long-time visitors to Villawood IDC. A couple of days later, in November 2001, I experienced the sheer joy and exhilaration of my first visit to Villawood. I did not know what to expect; nor could I hope to! At the back of my mind was my 15 years worth of visits to penal institutions.

Strange though it may sound, my initial response to Villawood was a sense of belonging, such was the warmth of my reception. Indeed, I was overwhelmed by the detainees' generosity of spirit, graciousness, and readiness to share their personal stories. I knew at the outset this was the start of an exciting journey. I felt my covert racial prejudices starting to evaporate as the gap between my brain and my heart receded.

I began a pattern of regular weekly – and sometimes more frequent – visits. Early on I met Amir, a detainee from Iran who had just become a Christian. We quickly became firm friends, and remain so. Over the years, Amir's natural leadership qualities have been used to wonderful effect in providing practical support and encouragement to literally hundreds of detainees in Villawood and other detention centres. Since his release, Amir has been on the staff of St. Paul's Anglican Church, Carlingford, where he and Miss Hui Rong Lin were married in July 2006. Hui Rong, who fled China, was placed in Villawood in February 2004. During the ensuing years, Hui Rong and I formed an adopted Australian father–daughter relationship – a special privilege for me.

Unbeknown to me (unobservant as I am) my dear friends Amir and Hui Rong formed a lifelong relationship right under my nose. My darling adopted daughter made sure I was one of the very first people to be informed that she, from a Buddhist background, and Amir were to be married. I was also privileged to attend two wedding services inside Villawood. The first was between Masood (Iran) and Kitty (Malaysia), the second between Javad (Iran) and Helen, an Australian-born visitor. Love knows no boundaries.

It's natural for me, with my lengthy experience of both forms of incarceration, to compare Villawood with penal institutions. For the most part, I was able to 'walk away' at the end of a day's visits to an 'ordinary' prison without undue stress. Villawood is totally different in that I became emotionally involved to a far greater extent. Why, I ask myself?

First and foremost, refugees and asylum seekers are innocent of any crime, unlike all but a small percentage of those in penal institutions. Criminals face a defined prison term, they can do some paid work, and they have a canteen, cooking facilities, a range of study programs and, in most cases, the ongoing support of family and/or friends. And visiting conditions are more 'user friendly'.

I have visited Woomera only once, and it was undoubtedly one of the saddest and most profoundly disturbing days of my life. I had the privilege of accompanying Father Tom Beever, Pastor of the Roxby Downs Community Church, on one of his weekly visits. As we drove over that long, straight, desert road and approached the detention centre, I was overcome by its starkness and aloneness – mirroring, I thought, the feelings of those trapped inside.

I remained with Father Tom as he visited the detainees, mainly Iranians, in their living quarters. I was shattered by what I saw, and I shared their all-pervading feelings of despair, hopelessness and depression. I wept, and spluttered my heartfelt apologies, as a profoundly ashamed Australian, to one beautiful and deeply troubled young Iranian couple. Before returning to Roxby Downs, we visited the so-called 'Housing Project', which accommodated some wives and children of men still in detention. This separation only exacerbated the overall misery.

I came away even firmer in my resolve to continue to do all I could, even as one small voice, to advocate system reform.

I have been involved in advocacy at various levels and in many different ways, but always peacefully and with respect for authority! Almost from my first visit to Villawood, my activities have included:

- Visits to the then-Immigration Minister, Philip Ruddock.
- Inaugural membership of a peaceful activist group, Friends of Refugees North West (based in Philip's electorate). This group has mounted many successful public meetings, taken part in peaceful street demonstrations, conducted fundraising for holders of Bridging Visa Es, canvassed politicians, and so on.
- Numerous submissions to political leaders on individual visa cases as well as on broader policy issues.

I came to know many folk from the Middle East, and as our friendship deepened I realised more clearly their courage and determination to escape the tyranny of their homelands, and their burning desire – often at great personal cost and hardship – to seek a better life for themselves and their children. I'd like to think I'd have the guts and the get-up-and-go to do likewise.

So far as I'm aware, Australia is the only country where a refugee may legally face a lifetime of temporary protection. With no permanent status, how can a refugee have hope, start to rebuild their life, or be reunited with close family members abroad? Overall system reforms, and the resolution of individual applications, happen all too slowly.

As for the future, I remain strongly committed to my ongoing friendship with, and practical support for, new arrivals to our shores who, for many and varied reasons, are unable to secure prior, offshore approval. Unlike my dear, long-departed mum, I have no fear of 'the Asian hordes', although I have always reaffirmed the need for due diligence in the checking processes, albeit in a humane and timely manner, and not involving long-term mandatory detention. That is my prime motivation for what I try to do for my fellow beings 'from every nation, from all tribes and peoples and tongues' (Book of Revelation, Chapter 7, Verse 9).

As with state penal inmates, I have found a spiritual yearning in most immigration detainees. Of course, this spirituality takes many forms. I respect that some people, for all sorts of reasons, have taken a different spiritual path to mine. We are living in an increasingly broken and divided world; a world desperately in need of reconciliation, love and compassion for one another. We need a little bit of kindness at all levels of society – and, yes, even towards the strangers arriving on our shores.

COMPELLED to act

*Psychologist **Lyn Bender** explains how employment in Woomera IRPC made her break ranks and become a whistleblower*

Trauma can reduce the capacity to articulate and name feelings and events connected to an overwhelming experience. Language and memory are disrupted. It is hard to be accurate about sequences and linear time, or to find words to describe feelings. Instead, vivid pictures, snapshots, sounds, smells, particles of conversations and tactile images flash into the mind and invade the body, like a movie trailer. That is how I remember Woomera.

It is still difficult for me to coherently convey the story of my time at Woomera IRPC; the hotel that was so hard to get into – and even harder to leave.

In late February 2002 I responded to an ad for psychologists to work in remote detention centres. Within two weeks, I was at the Olympic Dam Airport near Roxby Downs uranium mine, waiting for my lift to Woomera. I had signed up on a six-week contract that included a confidentiality agreement.

The South Australian desert has an eerie beauty. Flat, sandy stretches and saltbush, shimmering heat and long, dusty, winding roads as far as the eye can see. After a sudden shower, a carpet of brilliant flowers may bloom. But this part of South Australia had sinister connotations for me: nuclear testing, Maralinga, uranium mining, rocket launching, military bases. And now high-security detention. Not my favourite things.

On the long drive to Woomera, the detention guard who had come to collect me smiled in a way that implied, 'You have no idea what you are in for'. We chatted uneasily.

'So what is the Centre like?'

'You'll find out ... You're from Melbourne, eh? Well, you city shrinks don't know what you are in for.'

He was not kidding. My first sight of Woomera was the Welcome sign. The deep, cynical irony of the giant word 'WELCOME' still sticks in my mind.

Five weeks later, I was giving a sometimes tearful interview in a house in the Woomera township for the ABC Radio National program 'Street Stories'. Six weeks later, I was well on the road in my journey as an advocate for the refugees. What had occurred in between? I had not intended to 'blow the whistle' when I first applied for the position, although I had strong sympathies for refugees. Perhaps I was influenced by my own background, as a child of parents who had fled the Nazi Holocaust. I fitted the job criteria, with experience in suicide prevention, loss and grief trauma, and cross-cultural counselling. I also had a keenly developed passion for social justice and a desire to support the marginalised.

I went to Woomera full of hope. In some ways I moved in parallel with the refugees. I expected a base level of integrity to be observed, at least in the health services. I expected respect for my professional capacity. I presumed the detainees would be treated ethically. Within two weeks, I realised that I would be compelled to advocate for the detainees.

On that first day, in 40-degree heat, I walked past graves the detainees had dug in protest at their incarceration. That was a truly shocking sight. Their signs read, 'Give us freedom or let us die'. Children played in the dust beside their dehydrated fathers lying in their hand-dug graves.

Day after day I sat with weeping men, women and children. I listened to their stories of despair and hope. I have images in my mind of pain, and also warmth. Being welcomed by an Iranian family, into their humble 'home' (a donga) and served tea and biscuits and apples.

Images that stay with me: beautiful, little dark-eyed girls who gave me small tokens and gifts; an eight-year-old girl in the compound, just before the Easter riot, standing in confusion as people threw rocks and shouted. Meanwhile, staff remained closeted in the medical centre. Men crying, screaming and writhing as the guards dragged them into the isolation cells. My attempts to make the officers and management understand that these were traumatised people who were being further traumatised. Kneeling beside a wailing woman and placing one hand on her shoulder while using my other hand as a buffer between her head and the wall as she bashed herself against it. My heart beating fast as, late at night, I wrote forbidden reports advocating the detainees' release. Walking the corridors carrying a weeping, clinging four-year-old girl whose mother had escaped during the Easter riots. 'I knew they would capture me, but I only wanted to taste freedom, to run and run,' the mother later confessed to the interpreter.

I can still picture the guards, cumbersome and bloated in their riot gear, herding a diminutive female figure away from the fence as she tried to touch the protestors and marchers on the other side. They threw flowers to the detainees, who later cried to me, 'They said "Welcome", they gave us flowers'.

'Okay. You can have half an hour to talk to the officers,' was the Centre manager's response to my suggestion that the guards needed training. We stood facing the compound and the 'tent city' that the Iraqis had erected as their permanent protest. 'Let it stay,' I pleaded. 'It maintains some calm. They feel as if they have a place that they have made and that they can have some way of managing. It is the shed where they can get away from home.' That last was my desperate appeal to Aussie blokedom. To no avail: the tents were dismantled.

In the mess hall there was a print-out about understanding and managing traumatic stress. Who had pinned it there, I wondered. Was it a joke or a pathetic, plaintive cry from a fellow traveller?

There was rage as well. The officers had milled around me in the mess hall, drawn to a conversation that had begun at my table.

'Why did they bring their children here? Would you bring your children here?'

'I don't know what I might do in their situation. Maybe they believed that they had no choice.'

'What do you know, you psychologists? You come for six weeks and then you leave. You can be nice to them. We are stuck here.'

When the UN delegation was due to arrive to inspect the camp, there was a flurry of activity. Seedlings and flowers were planted. Now the officers were 'permitted' to play cricket with the children, in the compound that was most visible. Now visitors would see and hear the sights and sounds of happy children playing.

After I was disciplined by the manager for upsetting the troops, it became clear that I was not fitting in. I was asked to leave a few days before my contract was due to end. This was fortunate as, having nailed my colours to the mast in that 30-minute radio interview, I had broken my confidentiality agreement.

I gave my last formal counselling session at midnight on the night before I was to leave. He had arrived as an unaccompanied minor over a year ago. His detention was indefinite. He was now seventeen. 'I want to kill myself,' he said wearily to me. 'You are my eleventh psychologist. What can you do?'

I do not consciously plan strategies or goals far in advance. I tend to formulate ideas and consider my views and then grasp opportunities as they arise. But the refugee cause had got a hold of me. I was hooked.

During my time at Woomera, I had been spotted by activists. In that first week, I was invited to dinner at the Woomera Legal Centre. A feast was prepared by an Iraqi former detainee. In conversation with the lawyers, who volunteered their skill and time to the detainees, I was in disbelief and shock. I laughed a little crazily and said I felt like I was in a Kafka novel. They must have wondered what use I would be.

The Woomera Church was active in supporting the refugees, and I soon found myself working with those who were in sympathy with the refugees. My colleagues were the lawyers, who would email me asking me to assess and support a client who had expressed suicidal intent. They requested reports, in a bid to get the emotionally disturbed detainees released. I had been disappointed by some of my own profession, who had not seemed to cotton on to the idea that our incarceration of asylum seekers constituted a violation of international human rights.

Late at night I would return to my flat in the township and watch the news for indications of how the rest of Australia viewed Woomera. The commentary by some politicians enraged me. I was living a life that in some ways mirrored the existence of the refugees: searching for confirmation that we had not been forgotten.

The townspeople had mixed feelings about the newcomers: business was booming due to the influx of prison staff and their need for supplies, but they were mistrustful of the refugees. On my day off, I lay on the grass at the sparkling swimming pool and overheard conversations. 'They [the asylum seekers' children] are only allowed to come here after hours. They are quite dirty in their habits. They make a mess of the change rooms.' Such talk had a familiar ring. Laps of the pool, emailing my family, and friends from the local library sustained me. I would have long conversations with colleagues standing uneasily in the public phone box in the centre of the town. This kept my spirits up.

By the time I departed, in mid-April 2002, I was ready to sing like a canary. I had first-hand knowledge, connections, conviction, intent, and I was outraged. But it was deeper than that. I had woken in the night in a cold sweat of fear. I was a participant in an immoral venture. After the defeat of Hitler, people scrambled to disassociate themselves from guilt about the concentration camps. 'We didn't know, we tried to help,what could we do?' What would I say in my defence? Who would believe me? As a paid employee, I was profiting from Woomera. I had no choice. I was compelled to act.

The round of television, radio and public appearances was exhilarating, though nerve-wracking. There were echoes for me of the Vietnam protest days and my participation in the Franklin River Blockade. These had confirmed my belief in the power of conscientious action. I also believe in the importance of raising awareness. In my practice as a psychologist, I am bound not to disclose confidential information. It is time to speak, however, when to remain silent allows injustice to flourish.

I had farewelled the detainees and promised to tell their story. As I walked around the compounds on that last day, they magnanimously wished me well and confirmed that they wanted the Australian people to know of their plight. They still believed in the capacity of the Australian people for compassion.

Four years later, on a warm spring day sitting beside the Prahran pool in suburban Melbourne, my friend Susie asks me, 'Why did you go there? Didn't you know?' No, I didn't. I had undertaken suicide prevention work in Port Phillip Prison. I don't like working in that environment, but the prison management genuinely wanted my skill and expertise. We educated the prisoners to support each other. The work was effective.

At Woomera, for the first time, I had found myself in a thoroughly unethical role. They only wanted me to rubber-stamp their procedures. It was untenable. With every interview or action in support of asylum seekers, I felt that I was discharging my moral obligation to humanity. That may sound grandiose but that was how it felt. As a humanist and atheist Jew, it's the best I can come up with.

I now work in private practice and part-time as a Professional Advisor at the Australian Psychological Society. There are times when psychologists bring ethical dilemmas to me for discussion. Occasionally demands are made of them by employers that are in contravention of the APS Ethical Code. It is easy for me to respond. 'Since Nuremburg, "I was just following orders" is no excuse.'

Faces of you

***Jessica Perini**, a freelance editor and writer, describes the events that consolidated her commitment to advocacy*

It seems we have sat and listened to media and politicians' stories of asylum seekers forever. We have seen asylum seekers being swept aside, misrepresented and demonised.

I write these words for you, dear asylum seeker, so that your face can be seen, your name heard. I will write your story so that others may know the truth.

I stepped out into the sunlight. Then the reality hit me. I was here, Australia, late 2001. The clouds rolled in and a night-like darkness descended. This felt like the last ray of sunlight, like somehow I might never again see it. And I didn't, not for a long time after that.

On this day a small fishing vessel with many asylum seekers aboard foundered on its journey to Australia from Indonesia.

As the trawler sank, the then-Minister for Immigration announced to the world that 'a number of children had been thrown overboard', implying that people would sacrifice their own children in order to be saved. This claim, made on the heels of the announcement of a federal election was, to many of us, preposterous. To others, it was a means to an end.

Government Ministers repeated the claim, over and over, even five years later, birthing the myth that asylum seekers were not real people. What person, what human in their right mind could throw their own child overboard? Despite a world of evidence and a select committee of inquiry eventually proving the contrary, the myth persisted. To me, it marked a turning point, a juncture at which human beings were to be portrayed as creatures who didn't even love their own children. It was a wrong I was devoted to righting, even if it meant being unpopular, drawing criticism or even hatred. I launched myself into the truth, and in the process discovered more lies than one could imagine. Humanity had been buried alive and was gasping for air.

Just a short time earlier, when the *Tampa* had rescued refugees off the coast of Australia, I'd watched in disbelief as soldiers stormed the Norwegian vessel. Women, men and children, most likely dazed by their near-drowning, were then forced onto an island made of bird droppings. The Pacific Solution was born.

I discovered through Rural Australians for Refugees that you could write to those imprisoned on island nations, so I did. That's how I heard about Ali. This young man and other asylum seekers were transferred to Christmas Island in 2002 and told that, under the new migration legislation, they had no right to protection visas. Their claims of refugee status were rejected. Eight months later, they were finally told they could apply for protection visas, so they lodged their applications straight away. The Immigration Department summarily rejected their applications. They were soon housed in Baxter.

As Ali and others were moved to Baxter, I started to see the most distressing reports coming from detention centres. When women, men and children started sewing their lips together and dehydrating under the harsh Woomera sun, I felt that something had to be done. I couldn't just write letters and offer my consolation; it wasn't enough. I scanned the papers for something, anything. Misinformation abounded. I joined ChilOut, and day by day their emails kept me informed. Stories that read like war-time Germany abounded: families being woken in the middle of the night and taken to the airport, women being handcuffed during labour. *Is this still Australia?* I asked myself. All the facts were in front of me: names, phone numbers, signed affidavits. But the newspapers weren't publishing even half the stories I read in these emails. By coincidence, or perhaps divine intervention, a publisher contacted me and asked if I wanted to write a book about refugees in Australia. After a night of turbulent dreams, I said yes.

I started to call the numbers on those emails, and word spread. When refugee advocates heard I was writing a book, they spoke to me at length about their visits to detention facilities. They were stretched, and some seemed almost bursting with the burden of all the stories they knew.

One story in particular will never fade. A 10-year-old girl named Lilly had spent four years of her life in immigration detention. One day a refugee advocate visiting the centre happened upon Lilly in the yard. 'Where are your parents?' the advocate asked. The little girl replied that they no longer came outside. After some time, Lilly asked, 'Are there any flowers in Australia?'

When the advocate told me about this, my first impulse was to send this child the biggest bunch of Australian natives I could afford. But I knew that after a few days they would brown and die. Lilly didn't need a bunch of flowers, she needed help to *see* the flowers; help to see everything on the other side of the fence.

Lilly celebrated her eleventh birthday, her fourth in detention. For the first two birthdays she was detained in Woomera. At the tender age of eight she would have seen riot police, water cannons and people jumping on wire fences. I try to remember what I was doing at the age of eight. Probably playing with Barbies or swimming in my neighbour's pool. I don't actually think I knew what a water cannon was until the age of 30, when I saw one on TV at Woomera. Woomera, so close to Maralinga, where they tested atomic weapons. What a place to put a child. Wouldn't you think that by the age of eight she had seen enough desert, enough war, enough weaponry to last her a lifetime? Over the last four years she had seen people, including her own family, slowly degenerate before her eyes, as all hope slowly ebbed away.

I started to write letters to every newspaper I knew of; I bombarded them with emails, I sent postcards to politicians. I got calls from *A Current Affair* and *Hack* (the Triple J current affairs program), but often the stories fizzled into nothing – I could give them no names, I could show them no faces. My friends feared deportation. They feared reprisal from the very department charged with their care.

Then a ray of light, for just a few moments, shone through the clouds. The Family Court ruled that it was illegal to keep children in detention. Sadly, shockingly, abusive calls flooded the Family Court. Imagine abusing a court for criticising the indefinite detention of minors! It's hard to understand why anyone would want to keep a child behind bars, but some do want this, and are willing to write letters and sign their names to them. ChilOut encouraged its members to write to the Family Court about their concerns, and these people thanked the court for its humane decision. The government appealed the decision.

On the eve of the next election, in 2004, I was filled with hope. I raced to a ChilOut meeting packed with other hopeful people. Our cars brandished 'Not Happy John' stickers, testimony to tactics discussed in a café over salad. The High Court was on the agenda, the Commonwealth Government in our sights. Two days before the election, the High Court ruled that it was legal under Australian domestic law to keep children in detention. *Legal.* International law didn't come into the equation. Humanity didn't rate a mention. A 12-year-old once asked me, 'Why can't I take my camera into the detention centre, take a photo and then make passports for all the children?'

My eyes flooded with tears. I knew it was so simple, a child could understand it. But the problem was not with children, it was with adults. How can we reach people? I came up with a campaign called '20,000 Flowers of Hope'. At that time, ChilOut had 2000 members. If each of those people gave out 10 flowers on election day, we could reach 20,000 people. That is why I (and many others from that meeting) spent the day before the election handing out roses to hundreds of happy, smiling people. 'Free rose?' I'd ask, and many astounded people said 'Yes!' No doubt they wondered what the catch was. But there was no catch, only a message stating that the rose represented a 10-year-old child by the name of Adam, who had spent four-and-a-half years in immigration detention. The message simply asked that on election day people not let Adam wilt and die like the flower inevitably would.

The Howard Government won that election, too; that night I could still feel the sting of thorns in my hands. The flowers died and refugee advocates got very tired. By 2005 we had been fighting for an exhausting four years, with seemingly little progress. The Pacific Solution was still operational. Ali and his friends were still locked up in Baxter, slowly losing what senses they had left. Their remaining strength ebbed away as they refused to eat. What could we do? Write letters? Console them?

Tell them things would be okay? Our exhaustion was nothing next to their abject despair.

In July 2005, ChilOut made a last-ditch effort to free the children. In Martin Place in Sydney, each child's face flashed on a screen, staring at city workers. Leonie, three years old, detained all her life. Alex, six years old, detained three years. Jake, 10, detained for 41 months. The roll-call went on. And then a breakthrough: the face of every single child in detention was published on the front pages of Australian papers. Finally, outrage spread across the nation. When people saw the faces, the cherubic cheeks, the little fingers, the wide eyes, they finally realised: *these are children*.

In July 2005, children were finally released from indefinite detention behind the razor wire. The Migration Act was amended to effectively say that children should only be detained as a last resort.

I have told you some of the stories I have witnessed. Some are a mix of fiction and fact, for the simple reason that people still fear reprisal, still worry that they will be deported, that what little they have been granted may be taken away. But like the children whose faces were shown to Australia, I believe that things won't change until the story is told. These are just everyday people doing everyday things. There are some tales I don't wish to recall because they are too painful. Equally, some things fortify me: the strength of the human spirit, the ability to smile in the face of injustice and the lies of men. You cannot suppress these people and expect them to wither, disappear or be stowed away quietly on an island made of dung. There will always be those who stand and bear witness.

First, do no harm

*Child psychiatrist **Sarah Mares** reflects on the ethical dilemmas inherent in the 'treatment' of immigration detainees*

'First, do no harm', attributed to Hippocrates, is a familiar abbreviation of the injunction, 'Make a habit of two things – to help, or at least to do no harm'. As doctors, we practise with this in the background, behind the more formal ethical and legal codes that guide and inform practice in medicine and psychiatry. In clinical practice outcomes are hard to predict and uncertainty is a fact of life. This is never more the case than in relation to Australia's treatment of asylum seekers and refugees. While the breaches of human rights and of the Convention on the Rights of the Child are unambiguous, the best way to respond to this has not always been clear. Asylum seekers are already a vulnerable group, displaced and further denigrated by our response as a nation. How best, then, 'to help, or at least to do no (further) harm'?

Boundaries are a central issue in psychiatry. The maintenance of clear frameworks and identities is essential to protect the patient or client and the clinician, to scaffold and define the professional relationship, so that the personal and the private can be considered and contained, so that touch and connection, both physical and emotional, are not intrusive or exploitative. Of course, doctors are people with particular roles and training and obligations. We interpret the science of medicine in the light of our own experiences. It is as ourselves that we aspire to practise our art.

After my first visit to Woomera IRPC, these professional ethical frameworks and guidelines were thrown both into stark relief and out the window. I had gone to Woomera with colleagues, all of us 'experts', to write psychiatric reports, to do assessments. What we found were individuals and families who could not be assessed outside the context they were in, their distress and despair directly, undeniably related to and aggravated by their plight. What were our responsibilities to these people, who had dragged up their stories, revealed their vulnerability, their hopes to us? At first they saw us as 'saviours', overestimating our ability and influence; but as the months and years dragged on, they saw, as we ourselves did, the limits of our power in the face of a relentless political imperative. At times we were fellow sufferers in kind, if not degree: denigrated, impotent, despairing. Heartless expediency has been the rule, no matter the human cost.

Treatment of much of the disease and distress was meaningless without addressing the causes (indefinite mandatory detention, family separation, impermanent protection). Prevention always being better than cure, the options were limited. It was not enough to be sympathetic, to sit with, to listen and to nod. The only choice was advocacy. If the context was not addressed, change could not occur. The suffering and disease would spread, the numbers afflicted would increase. Children, as in many situations, were particularly vulnerable.

Mental health systems tied themselves in knots over this, and individual doctors found different solutions according to their own hearts and minds. For example, consider a man, unable to sleep, eat or concentrate, with no hope for the future, consumed with guilt at his inability to protect his wife and children from the daily brutality and harassment of detention in Woomera. This man attempted suicide. Was he clinically depressed, needing hospital admission and treatment, or was he 'responding realistically to his circumstances' and therefore suffering an 'adjustment disorder'? Some colleagues chose this path, saying this man and others like him did not have a major psychiatric illness, that he was responding realistically to his circumstances. Neither hospital admission nor advocacy followed this stance.

This is a clear absurdity for both the clinician and the person detained. It leaves no role for mental health advocacy, no justification for using the Mental Health Act to ensure treatment, or even brief respite from that particular incarceration. I see this as an abdication of responsibility, a cowardly diminution of our role and of the definition of disease and harm. Others might appreciate it as a pragmatic response to reality.

Enormous disruption did occur in already stretched health and mental health services and systems when immigration detainees were admitted to hospital, usually under state Mental Health Acts. Detainees always came with guards, whether to obstetric, paediatric, medical or psychiatry facilities. This policy had an obvious impact on the individual detainee: for example, the woman in labour, often speaking little English, separated from family, afraid, sometimes with the guard insisting on being inside the hospital room. One suffering family was admitted with a guard for each parent and one for each child, an infant and a toddler. Imagine then, the impact of four guards, (large, burly, uniformed men and women) present at all times in a small crowded inpatient unit, taking up a lot of time and space alongside the newly admitted patients. This absurdity disrupted services, and the negative impact on staff and other patients was huge. Clinicians made practical decisions about where the greater good lay, and we differed on this. Each of us lives with the decisions we made and no-one is unmarked.

At the start, we didn't know we were playing brutal politics. We were doctors, health professionals advocating for patients. We have had to learn, for example, about 'wedge politics' first-hand. To simplify what occurred, the argument over time went something like this:

'Experts say,' said the then-Immigration Minister, 'that children should not be in detention, so they will be removed from detention and placed in foster care.'

'But children should be with their parents,' we said.

'Oh doctors, can't you decide? I thought you said children shouldn't be in detention!'

Two options, both of them bad, and childhood experts and advocates arguing among ourselves, not about what was best, but about what was worse: separation from parents, or all the risks that went with more time in detention. The development of the Community Housing projects and community detention was a sort of compromise on this issue, but it has meant lengthy family separations and continued incarceration for fathers and teenage boys.

And what about another key tenet, protecting patient confidentiality? Well-meaning advocates took psychiatric reports full of private and sometimes shaming, humiliating detail and published them on the web.

They spread details far and wide in the name of advocacy, in the name of exposing the harm being done in the system; sacrificed, in effect, the individual in a shot at the greater good. One advocate said, 'This issue is bigger than the ... family'. Should we not have written those reports unless we could ensure how they would be used? They were written and left our hands, then used by well-meaning people operating under another set of ethical principles and priorities.

One man was in detention for seven years, with millions of dollars spent arguing his identity. Time and money wasted, as he was finally granted Permanent Protection. In the intervening years, his family learnt to navigate life in Australia, making the regular weekly trip to visit him. His children grew from small to big while he remained inside the fence but outside Australia, wasting away, his life in limbo. At what point should his story have been given to the press, as a way of prompting or shaming DIMIA into action? Eventually, but only after a very long time, this was done, and with effect.

Depending on the political climate, this strategy had mixed results, and was not without risk. Sometimes due and fair process, or at least action, followed publicity, but sometimes it resulted in reprisals. Before Cornelia Rau and Vivian Solon, shameless denial of harm and gratuitous denigration of asylum seekers was often the response to publicising individual cases. It is hard to know when the individual story should be made public with the aim of the greater good. In the case of Virginia Leong and daughter Naomi, this approach worked. With Shayan Badraie and his family a few years earlier it had, initially at least, worsened the family's plight [*see the stories by Ngareta Rossell, Jacquie Everitt and Junie Ong*].

This need to weigh up individual good/harm versus collective benefit arose while writing individual reports and while speaking in generalities in public forums. If we describe the damage being done to children and their families, do we use the words 'irreparable, permanent, irreversible harm, damage, loss'? Are we consigning these people to the permanent status of victim and patient, damaged goods? Many have shown great resilience and grace despite adversity. Many were not vulnerable in or of themselves before facing persecution and then incarceration in Australia. They had personal resources and strengths as individuals and families. They were motivated and organised to seek a better life. That is why they fled persecution and came here. How then should we label the harm being done, when understatement or equivocation is unlikely to have an impact or to improve their circumstances?

It worked the other way as well. Health professionals working for the companies contracted by DIMIA to run the detention centres had to sign contracts that included confidentiality clauses. They were legally bound not to disclose information about events or detainees within the system. This was officially, and with some justification, said to be in order to protect the privacy of the asylum seekers, but was distorted into a way to silence those health professionals most able to 'blow the whistle' on the inadequacy of health services in detention, the daily acts of neglect and brutality, and the ongoing corrosive and destructive effects of incarceration. Little public focus was given to these travesties before the wrongful detention of Cornelia Rau, but they became very obvious in the subsequent inquiry (which led to the Palmer Report).

Psychiatry has often been on the wrong side of the equation of human rights and mental health: consider the Soviet Union, dissidents in China today, and abuses under the Mental Health Act in Australia. This time, psychiatrists have taken a lead, child psychiatrists in particular, using our knowledge of development, our understanding of human needs and the impact of trauma to demonstrate the damage done by immigration policy and to argue for change on the basis of medical evidence and human rights principles. If the government could treat one vulnerable group so callously, who would be next?

Whatever I have done as an advocate, it has never felt like enough – a drop in the ocean when set against the stamina and grace of detainees and the courage and persistence of other advocates. They have provided inspiration, companionship and comfort. This has been a collective effort, and it continues. The law has not been changed. The willingness to use asylum seekers for political ends was no more evident than in the unsuccessful attempt by the government to reintroduce a toughened version of the Pacific Solution into Parliament after 43 West Papua asylum seekers arrived in Australia in January 2006.

Billions of dollars will reportedly be spent on a planned maximum-security prison for 800–1200 inmates on remote Christmas Island, replete in one plan with an eight-bed nursery for infants, separated from the family areas by electric doors, airlocks, cameras and security systems. The detention of children and families is clearly anticipated. The plan for this prison includes the capacity for remote monitoring (from Canberra) of bedrooms/cells. It is hard to fathom the perceived need for such a place at such expense, given that between July 2003 and May 2006, only 50 people reached Australia or offshore islands as 'onshore' refugees.

These actions are taken by our government in the name of border protection and national security. There are more humane ways of assuring that those who come here seeking asylum are who they say they are, and that their claims for refugee status are valid. This is a callous and deliberate overreaction for political purposes, with – among other things – the express intent of deterrence. The casualties are not only the asylum seekers caught up in this, but all of us. We are all diminished and ultimately threatened by policy and practice that ignore and erode fundamental human rights.

Some things have changed as a result of all our efforts in relation to refugees and asylum seekers, and yet too much remains the same. 'To help, or at least to do no harm' might well apply to everyone. To do nothing in these circumstances amounts to doing harm, or at least allowing harm to occur. We know what has been done, and we cannot say we did not. Moral indifference fast becomes complicity. Reducing the harm that is done in our name and – where possible – preventing it is our opportunity.

In a heartbeat

*Journalist **Kerrie Lee** becomes a Villawood regular and takes up a family's struggle*

When I turned on the TV in my hotel room in Ho Chi Minh City, I realised something was seriously wrong with my country. There, on BBC World, was a Norwegian cargo ship, the MV *Tampa*, laden to the gunwales with humanity, being denied entry to an Australian port. I was appalled at what was being done in my name. Paradoxically, seeing it at a distance really brought it home to me.

By the time I returned to Australia, I knew I could no longer sit by, complaining about the treatment of asylum seekers. It was time to get real. My first visit to Villawood IDC was in October 2001. This note is from my diary entry of that day:

I suppose the thing that shocked me most was the fact that these people lived, every day, in this confined space – a swathe of lawn with a few trees. Outside, stately gums moved in the breeze. That is Australia, I thought, this isn't.

As we said goodbye, we asked a 15-year-old what his little brother might like to cheer him up, trying to think of a toy or game. The boy smiled his beautiful, soft smile and said: 'You can bring him freedom.'

I am appalled – I didn't believe I could feel worse than I did already about the government and its inhumanity. I actually feel physically ill thinking about what I've seen today.

So began my long journey. My first friend in Villawood was a young woman who, with her husband, had been behind the razor wire for six months. Their gorgeous daughter had been born there. I would put her name down on my visitor form and, by the time I'd run the gamut of the security goons, I would see her waiting for me – a tiny figure in a headscarf wheeling a doll's pram. Although she had only a smattering of English, we sat companionably and I doted on the little one, with her liquid, dark eyes and tumble of curls.

It was soon after my first visit that I met the family of five, including a 15-year-old boy and girls aged 10 and 13, who became the focus of my life for nearly three years. This, then, is *our* story.

Through an interpreter, a gentle, sad-eyed Afghan man who was always available to help others - in spite of the pain of being separated from his own large family, who were exiled in a Pakistani border camp - I learned the nub of their story. (I was to discover so much more as the months and years went on, till I knew them better than friends on the outside of many years' standing.) Fleeing religious persecution in their homeland, they put themselves in the hands of people smugglers, who carried them across the world, depositing them on an island to Australia's north to await the last, most hazardous leg of a journey which was to nearly cost their father his life. During nine days at sea, crowded in with too many others, including my first friend, they were sick almost continuously. Finally, they were unceremoniously dumped on a Northern Territory beach, where the father began haemorrhaging.

The following weeks were a waking nightmare, with the family, who spoke virtually no English, being interviewed over the phone by an immigration official, through an interpreter, while their father lay comatose in hospital. Three weeks after their traumatic arrival in Australia, they learned they had been refused refugee status, and were transferred to Villawood. They appealed to the Refugee Review Tribunal (RRT), who accepted the truth of their story, but said they could simply have moved to another town to escape persecution.

This was my first brush with the foibles of the RRT and the draconian nature of the privative clause [*see Glossary*]. It had been brought in by the government immediately post-*Tampa* to ensure that, after rejection by the RRT, a person's case could never be re-examined and no new evidence could be introduced on appeal. For its part, all the government had to show was that there had been no error in law.

Despite the grandiose name, the RRT comprised only one person, appointed by the government and able to be dismissed at any time. He or she was in no way independent, and some of the decisions were more Lewis Carroll than Solomon. I was reminded at times of Alice musing about her relationship with the Red King: they were both in a dream, but whose dream was it?

Inevitably, my intimate involvement with this family spilled over into my own family life. Early in our relationship, I would return to my comfortable, middle-class home and, irrationally, rail against my life. My 15-year-old daughter, Brydie, ever upfront, said she didn't like me going to 'that place' because it made me so sad. But soon her innate compassion prevailed and she, along with my partner, Alan, and our 20-year-old son, Declan, were standing in the long, hot queue waiting for admittance to the suburban gulag. We began to appreciate how important it was to have young people among the visitors, as it gave the children an insight into the unknown world of their Australian contemporaries - one which, God willing, they would one day join.

In time, several of our children's friends joined us, and so the circle of visitors grew ever wider. As well, our older son, Shannon, a musician, performed as part of the innovative but short-lived entertainment program, 'Villawoodstock'.

The family were - and are - such charismatic individuals that they were never without visitors who, like me, fell into a pattern of being there on the same day most weeks. (It was only when I turned up once on a Monday and my friend with the baby said, in surprisingly precise English, 'You usually come on Tuesday', that I realised this was so. It was also when I realised that my visits provided more than just a way of passing a few hours in a place where time stretched interminably; they were a sanity-saving link with a world beyond the razor wire.) Occasionally I'd vary my day and meet, for example, the 'Monday friends'. This was a bonus to becoming a Villawood regular: I encountered so many extraordinary individuals whom I would otherwise never have had the opportunity to meet, and today I am proud to call them my friends.

Although I tried to avoid weekend visiting, sometimes work precluded me from making the weekday trek. These forays made me grateful for the comparatively short midweek queues, and I stopped complaining if I had to wait an hour. Sometimes on Saturdays and Sundays, the queues were so long that those towards the end didn't get to the front before the 6.30 cut-off and went home without seeing their loved ones – or only glimpsing them, wretchedly, through the wire.

While I continued to see the young mother and her baby, the number of her special friends grew, and I found I could concentrate more on the matter at hand: getting 'my' family released. Like other regulars, over the months I came to know most of the asylum seekers at least superficially, and some days it felt like a demented party – a bit like Alice at the Mad Hatter's tea party – with visitors and detainees mingling and separating, popping from one cuppa to the next, for the detainees were all heartachingly hospitable. 'My' family, for example, always had tea bags, hot water and biscuits or other treats they had managed to procure or which had been brought by other visitors. On special occasions, such as birthdays, they rustled up delicacies from their home country.

In an effort to introduce a semblance of normality into this alien landscape, birthdays were always celebrated. It was on the boy's sixteenth birthday that a particularly cruel bit of bastardry was enacted by the guards. We had bought him a Mambo sweatshirt and, as usual, didn't wrap it, as we knew it would be opened. The officer on the security door, where we were obliged to walk through a metal detector, while any foodstuffs or other items were pawed over, took one look and confiscated the gift. When asked why, he replied: 'It's property. Property can only be delivered between 10 and 12' (or whatever the hours were that week).

'It's not "property",' we responded, 'it's a birthday present.'

Finally, a supervisor presented herself and agreed to ensure that the gift was delivered safely at the end of visiting hours.

This sort of aggravation was common, and most of the time we were able to treat it with contempt, but the fact that we were trying to brighten the life of a child who had been denied virtually everything, including an education, that his Aussie peers took for granted filled us with impotent rage.

This brings me to one of the key effects the detention experience had on me and many of my contemporaries – a feeling of utter powerlessness. As middle-class Australians, we were used to having our voices heard and feeling that, through action and advocacy, we could effect change. In this, it seemed, we were lost.

Another, even more serious consequence was the emasculation of the male asylum seekers, most of whom came from societies where their role as head of the household was well defined. To be at the mercy of a system that denied them the right to work and make decisions on behalf of their families was soul-destroying.

On the other hand, I saw women who realised instinctively that if their family structure was to survive, they must stand firm, grow ever stronger – and this has stood them in excellent stead to face the challenges of life in a free, if wholly unfamiliar society.

As for 'our' family, during the long, boring months of incarceration, I became more and more aware of the strength of the glue which, in the face of unrivalled adversity, bound them together. While they had many devoted friends, Alan and I became the family's chief support in such practical matters as finding lawyers who would appear for them in their periodic, fruitless appeals. We also attended court several times, when we were finally, and irrevocably, convinced that the law was, indeed, an ass. We learnt the intricacies of the Kafkaesque privative clause inside out and became quite the bush lawyers.

The wonderful real lawyers, acting pro bono, tried every way they could to break down this law, without success. It was like trying to prove a negative. At times, we would see the judges bristling against the legal handcuffs they had been placed in but, no matter how iniquitous they considered the law, it was their duty to uphold it.

One of the low points in our encounters with the legal system was when the parents were dressed and ready to attend a hearing, but no-one picked them up. Several of their supporters, however, were in court, along with a new legal team, and we were mildly optimistic – not necessarily of getting the family out immediately, but of at least being able to introduce evidence which, we believed, would allow them another crack at the RRT. Our confidence in the legal system was proved to be hopelessly misguided and, with knots in our stomachs, my new friend Liz and I headed for Villawood to offer consolation. We figured by the time we got there, the family would have been given the bad news.

We sat at a plastic table, dust from the bare patches in the grass dancing around our feet, and waited for the family. Out they trooped, all smiles, carrying the makings of afternoon tea. 'Oh, shit,' Liz said, 'they don't know'. That afternoon represented one of the lowest points in more than two years of visiting. They were very brave and dignified, then suddenly the mother lost it. Her eyes lit up with anger and despair. She was inconsolable. The more we said we were sorry, the angrier she became. 'What are you sorry for?' she demanded. I don't think I've ever felt so utterly ineffectual. As our relationship had developed, my role had evolved: from visitor to friend, mother, sister, grandmother and, occasionally, whipping boy.

About 15 months after their arrival, the children, along with several other young asylum seekers, were allowed to go to school on the 'outside' – due, in no small part, to the efforts of individual teachers and lobbying by the Teachers' Federation. While this gave them something to fill their days, it also brought unexpected headaches for the parents, when the guards who were assigned to pick them up sometimes failed to do so.

At first, on the insistence of the authorities, the children didn't tell their classmates that they went 'home' to detention. Keeping up the lie became increasing fraught for them when new friends asked them out on weekends. They were constantly inventing excuses, and these became more fanciful as time went on – after all, how do you make up a story about a place you've never seen? As well, they felt guilty, as it was culturally unacceptable to lie. Little by little, they let the truth be known, and the students in their multicultural schools took it in their stride.

School also gave us a further source of conversation. We discussed homework, subject choices and the minutiae of classroom life. Their teachers were wonderful. The parents were allowed to attend the kids' first speech day in the school hall. We went, too. The Villawood guards, lurking by the door dressed in civvies, were uncharacteristically discreet, and we were all grateful for that. We had taken our cameras and, for the first time since arriving in Australia, the children had their photos taken. This was yet another reminder that life for this family was so far from the norm, where milestones are faithfully documented.

As the family entered their fourth year in limbo, there were signs of a softening of attitude within Immigration - or perhaps it was more to do with the fact that ever more influential voices were being raised against this pitiless system. The new Minister talked as tough as her predecessor, but she seemed to have a spark of humanity, which he so patently lacked. More and more people were being released, and each time an asylum seeker was called to the office, we held our breath. The good news spread like wildfire and everyone rejoiced. Still, there was an element of, what about us - when will our turn come?

We became familiar with the steps which led to release, one of the most meaningful being the medical check. On a hot, dusty autumn afternoon, I arrived at Villawood in time to see the family being loaded into a barred van. My heart seemed to stop, then race. I flew to the window and the driver stopped briefly so we could exchange a few words. Yes, they were being taken for their medical check. We touched hands through the bars and I looked into the radiant face of the father. 'You won!' he mouthed.

Recently, Alan and I accompanied 'our' family to their citizenship interviews, and on 15 November 2006 the family became 'New Australians'. They will make fine citizens.

This was undoubtedly the most difficult journey I've ever undertaken, and the question I am most often asked is: 'Knowing what you know now, would you still do it?'

Yes, in a heartbeat.

Un Australian

Fiona Katauskas *is a freelance cartoonist whose work has appeared in* The Sydney Morning Herald, The Australian *and* The Chaser.

Chaos

Cathy Wilcox *draws for* The Sydney Morning Herald *and* The Age.

Australia's refugee policy

***Ron Tandberg**, winner of 10 Walkley Awards, works with* The Age.

The deterrent

***Hinze** (aka David Pope) is a freelance cartoonist.*

Timeline of events

Compiled by ***John Highfield***

1992 Labor Government introduces mandatory detention for asylum seekers with 273-day limit to settle status.

1994 Labor Government, with Opposition support, removes 273-day limitation to settle status, thus laying foundation for indefinite detention.

1998 One Nation MP Pauline Hanson proposes Temporary Protection Visa for all asylum seeker claimants. Immigration Minister Philip Ruddock tells Parliament this would cause too much uncertainty in people's lives and the Howard Government will not contemplate it.

1999 Immigration Minister Ruddock announces the Howard Government has decided, after all, to introduce the Temporary Protection Visa.

1999 to 2001 Consistent reports of riots and major incidents of self-harm by detainees at the converted army base now known as Woomera Immigration Reception and Processing Centre. Water cannon used on protesting detainees - the first-ever use of it in Australia.

13 August 2001 ABC *Four Corners* program about Shayan Badraie.

26–29 August 2001 MV *Tampa* directed by Australian Maritime Safety Authority to assist small boat in distress with 438 people on board. Master of MV *Tampa* is refused permission to land people on Christmas Island (Australian territory) in breach of International SOLAS protocols, to which Australia is a signatory. Request for medical assistance denied - SAS soldiers sent as boarding party. *Tampa* refugees eventually transported to Nauru as part of the 'Pacific Solution' [*see Glossary*].

29 August 2001 The Prime Minister introduces an emergency bill, the Border Protection Bill 2001.

11 September 2001 Terrorist attacks on the World Trade Center in New York and the Pentagon in Washington DC.

September 2001 ALP Opposition votes with Coalition Government to excise Ashmore Reef and Cocos and Christmas Island from Australian migration zone.

8 October 2001 Australian navy reports foundering of SIEV 4 - a leaky Indonesian fishing boat. Defence Department falsely alleges that asylum seekers threw their children overboard, and circulates altered photographs under the direction of the office of then-Defence Minister Peter Reith ('Children Overboard Affair').

19 October 2001 353 asylum seekers drown at sea when SIEVX, an unseaworthy Indonesian fishing boat, founders after Indonesian Police allegedly helped to force overloading at a remote island off Sumatra.

October 2001 Negotiations concluded with PNG and Nauru for Australia to establish detention centres on Manus Island and Nauru in return for substantial cash payments. The operation officially named 'The Pacific Solution' by the Department of Prime Minister and Cabinet.

10 November 2001 Howard Coalition wins federal election.

November 2001 Australian Human Rights Commissioner Dr Sev Ozdowski announces that HREOC will hold a National Inquiry into children in immigration detention. Following two years of investigation and hearings, the report - 'A Last Resort?' is published in

April 2004. The responsible Government Minister, Immigration Minister Philip Ruddock, declines the opportunity to respond when the report is tabled in Parliament.

March–April 2002: Major riots and incidents at Woomera IRPC over the Easter weekend, with over 50 escapees, as protestors and activists outside encourage detainees to abscond. (For a full list of major disturbances at Woomera between June 2000 and June 2002, see the HREOC website: www.hreoc.gov.au).

August 2003: The Family Court of Australia rules that five children are being illegally held in immigration detention and orders their release into the community.

April 2004: The High Court of Australia upholds a government appeal against the Family Court decision releasing the five child detainees. The High Court declares that the Family Court has no jurisdiction to decide the validity of the detention of children, nor the power to make orders regarding their welfare. This effectively declares mandatory detention for children to be valid and appropriate, despite claims by advocates that Australia's obligations under international agreements and treaties conflict with this practice.

December 2004: Coalition wins a fourth federal election. John Howard celebrates becoming Australia's second longest-serving prime minister and declares the win a vindication of policies for strong border protection and for supporting the US in the 'war on terror', particularly in Iraq.

February 2005: Cornelia Rau identified as an Australian citizen being unlawfully held at Baxter IDC. The department admits to mishandling the case of the mentally ill woman over a 10-month period. A former Federal Police Commissioner, Mick Palmer, is named to lead an official Inquiry.

April 2005: Australian Federal Police seek assistance in the Philippines to trace the wrongfully deported Australian citizen, Vivian Alvarez Solon. The Immigration Department admits that several officers had known about the mistaken action against the mentally ill and physically injured woman for several years, but no follow-up had been conducted. A Catholic priest informs authorities that Ms Solon is resident at a Philippines hospice for the dying after identifying her in an international satellite edition of an ABC TV program.

May 2005: The Immigration Minister refers the Solon deportation to the Commonwealth Ombudsman. Another former Police Commissioner, Mr Neil Comrie, joins the Palmer Inquiry because of the increased workload.

May 2005: Naomi Leong, a three-year-old who has spent all her life in Villawood IDC, is suddenly released with her detainee mother to live in the community. Advocates welcome the release as a sign of a changing Immigration Department culture brought on by the embarrassment of the Rau and Solon cases.

June 2005: The Immigration Minister, Senator Amanda Vanstone (who replaced Ruddock in October 2003), announces that all detainee families with children under the age of 18 will be released from detention centres to live in the community. A new policy will ensure that no children are held inside immigration detention and processing centres except for brief periods in exceptional circumstances.

July 2005: The Palmer Report is released. It is highly critical of Immigration Department actions and makes strong recommendations for changes to internal culture, procedures and systems. Senior executive changes in the department include the departure of DIMIA Secretary Bill Farmer to a new Ambassadorial posting (an 'offshore solution').

October 2005: The Immigration Minister tables the Palmer Implementation Plan and the Comrie Report, which reveal the erroneous detention of over 200 Australian citizens or permanent residents. A vigorous and wide-ranging change process is to be implemented with the Department of Immigration committed to the process of reform. An official departmental apology is issued to Vivian Solon.

January 2006: Forty-three Papuan asylum seekers arrive on the Australian mainland at Cape York in a traditional craft. Initially transferred for detention on Christmas Island, 42 of the Papuans are then issued with Temporary Protection Visas. The Indonesian Government lodges an official protest with Australia.

March 2006: Fourteen Sierra Leone athletes granted a Bridging Visa after defecting from their team at the Commonwealth Games in Melbourne.

March 2006: Following a lengthy court case, the Department of Immigration reaches a confidential out-of-court settlement with Shayan Badraie. Lawyers acting pro bono for the youngster seek damages from the department on the grounds that he was psychologically harmed by witnessing suicide attempts and violence at the Woomera and Villawood detention centres between 2000 and 2002. On the same day, the department grants his family Permanent Protection (residency) in Australia.

August 2006: The Australian Government withdraws the Immigration Amendment Bill, which sought to send *all* asylum seekers who arrive by boat in Australian territorial waters for processing at offshore detention camps. Facing internal Coalition rebellion and potential defeat in the Senate, the Prime Minister announced he would drop the legislation, which many believe was a response to Indonesian political pressure.

September 2006: The Department of Immigration releases details of changed accommodation for detainees, including family villas with minimal security and self-catering at Villawood IDC. Reference groups, including prominent health professionals, are now attending regular consultative meetings to improve the delivery of appropriate care in detention centres. The department is also building low-security Immigration Transit Accommodation Centres (ITACs) for the short-term detention of unlawful non-citizens, including visa over-stayers who have agreed to depart.

September 2006: Seven Burmese asylum seekers, previously held on Christmas Island, are transferred to Nauru under Australia's ongoing Pacific Solution policy.

November 2006: Advocates release leaked copies of plans which show the Government is proceeding with the construction of a $265-million detention centre for 800–1200 people on Christmas Island which has separate accommodation for children and babies. Despite the remoteness of Christmas Island, the high-security centre is to have state-of-the-art, 24-hour electronic surveillance, including microwave movement sensors and CCTV cameras in most rooms feeding live to a central control room in the Immigration Department in Canberra.

November 2006: First report of 'The People's Inquiry into Immigration Detention' is released. The Inquiry, established by the Council of Heads of Schools of Social Work (ACHSSW) and led by Professor Linda Briskman, is a citizen-driven inquiry into the policies and practices of immigration detention arising from the incarceration of Cornelia Rau. The government inquiry into her wrongful detention was seen as narrow in scope. Following open and transparent national hearings, the final Report is to be published in July 2007.

December 2006: Mohammed Sagar, an Iraqi asylum seeker detained at sea by the Australian navy under Operation Relex in 2001 [*see Glossary*], is given asylum by a Scandinavian country after five years' detention. Mr Sagar, acknowledged as a genuine refugee, was held on Nauru and denied entry to Australia due to unspecified security concerns. His fellow countryman and Nauru detainee, Mohammed Faisal, is evacuated for treatment at a Brisbane mental hospital after becoming suicidal because of his ongoing incarceration.

December 2006: The Commonwealth Ombudsman releases three reports detailing the unlawful detention of Australian citizens and valid visa holders by the Immigration Department. In one case, a severely mentally ill man was held for 43 days without appropriate treatment. Ten children were detained, including one boy whose parent was not informed of his incarceration, despite knowledge by Immigration Officers that he was a minor. The Ombudsman acknowledges that nearly 250 similar incidents have been identified for investigation.

December 2006: Concern grows about the increasing numbers of minors (mainly Indonesian) detained by Border Protection Command (Customs) operations against illegal foreign fishers (IFFs) in north-northwest Australia. The Minister for Customs announces the commissioning of an armed trimaran to hunt down IFFs. Advocates estimate over 15 IFF children are locked up in Australian detention facilities.

March 2007: Eighty-two Sri Lankan asylum seekers, including one minor, are rescued at sea. The Australian government initially discusses returning them to Indonesia, whence they would be repatriated. Eventually they are taken to Nauru, to wait while their refugee claims are processed. The Nauru government says this must be completed within six months.

Glossary

ACM: Australasian Correctional Management, owned by Wackenhut, a subsidiary of multinational security giant Group 4 Securicor, contracted by the Federal Government to run immigration detention facilities.

asylum seeker: The terms 'asylum seeker' and 'refugee' refer to those who seek refuge as a result of persecution or war in their own country. 'Asylum seeker' most often refers to those who arrive in Australia without a valid visa, and then seek asylum. It can also refer to those who may have conditionally been authorised to enter Australia and subsequently seek to change the status of their conditional entry. Some refugees come to Australia with a visa obtained overseas under the auspices of the UNHCR.

CERT: Critical Emergency Response Team.

citizenship: all people born in Australia before 19 August 1986 are Australian citizens. If a child is born in Australia with one parent an Australian citizen/permanent resident, the child is an Australian citizen. Under current law, when a permanent resident completes two years' residence in Australia, he/she can apply for citizenship.

declarations and conventions: The Universal Declaration on Human Rights, Article 9: 'No-one shall be subjected to arbitrary arrest, detention or exile'. And: International Covenant on Civil and Political Rights, Article 7: 'No-one shall be subjected to torture or to cruel, inhumane or degrading treatment or punishment'; Article 23: 'The family is the natural and fundamental group unit of society and is entitled to protection by society and the State'. And: Convention on the Rights of the Child, Article 3: 'The best interests of the child shall be the primary consideration … [and State parties are] to ensure the child such protection and care as is necessary for his or her wellbeing, taking into account the rights and duties of his or her parents, legal guardians or other individuals legally responsible for him or her …'.

detention centres

Baxter IDF: Purpose-built facility opened in July 2002 near Pt Augusta, 275 kms north of Adelaide; nominal capacity of 1160.

Curtin IRPC: Recommissioned for migration purposes between Sept 1999 and Sept 2002; outside Derby, 2643 kms north of Perth.

Maribynong IDC: Opened in Melbourne in 1966; mainly catering for visa overstayers; nominal capacity of 80.

Perth IDC: Opened in 1981; adjacent to Perth Airport; mainly for visa overstayers; capacity of 64.

Port Hedland IRPC: Used for immigration detention since 1991; 1638 kms north of Perth; nominal capacity of 820.

Villawood IDC: Opened in 1976; in the western suburbs of Sydney; mostly used for visa over-stayers; nominal capacity of 700.

Woomera IRPC: Opened in Nov 1999, closed in September 2002; in the Simpson Desert, northern South Australia; nominal capacity of 1200, but housed over 1440 detainees in Sept 2001.

Christmas Island IRPC: Opened in Nov 2001; is a four-hour flight northwest of Perth; plans announced (in 2002) to build a permanent facility housing 800–1200.

DFAT: Department of Foreign Affairs and Trade (Commonwealth).

DIMA/DIMIA/DIAC: variously the Department of Immigration and Multicultural Affairs; the Department of Immigration, Indigenous and Multicultural Affairs; and, since January 2007, the Department of Immigration and Citizenship (Commonwealth).

donga: nickname for the prefabricated army hut used to house detainees in some detention centres.

exclusion zone: the 200-km maritime economic zone and excised territorial islands which constitute the non-migration area under Australian laws.

GSL: Group 4 Correction Services, subsidiary of UK company Group 4 Securitas, contracted by the Federal Government to run immigration detention facilities.

habeus corpus: the legal principle against arbitrary detention/imprisonment, which has been utilised by failed asylum seekers to test the legality of indefinite detention.

HECS: Higher Education Contribution Scheme, a subsidised way of paying for tertiary study.

HREOC: Human Rights and Equal Opportunity Commission.

IDC: immigration detention centre.

IDF: immigration detention facility.

IOM: International Organisation for Migration.

IRPC: immigration reception and processing centre.

Management Unit: high-security area of an immigration detention centre where detainees can be isolated in cell-like rooms equipped with 24-hour video surveillance and other restraining measures deemed necessary by officers to prevent alleged self-harming behaviours. These areas are widely regarded by detainees and advocates as places of 'punishment' for the infringement of petty rules or instructions by employees of the contractor or of the Department.

offshore processing: see **onshore processing**.

onshore processing: refers to the initial detention under the Immigration Act and the subsequent assessing and/or appealing of claims for humanitarian protection on Australian territory, according to the provisions of the UN Refugee Convention and other international conventions and treaties. 'Offshore processing' refers to such processes conducted by the UNHCR or the IOM outside Australian territory.

Operation Relex: an Australian Navy task commenced in September 2001 to deny entry to Australian territory by asylum seekers travelling in small boats, mainly from Indonesia, to demonstrate that the Federal Government was 'tough on queue-jumpers'. The navy was to intercept these boats and transport the detainees to offshore camps on Manus Island and Nauru.

The Pacific Solution: the name given to the 2001 Federal Government policy preventing asylum seekers from landing on Australian territory. The policy started with the *Tampa* Affair in August 2001 (see ***Tampa***). Asylum seeker boats are intercepted at sea and the occupants forcibly taken to detention camps on Manus Island or Nauru. Australian taxpayers meet all the costs of running the camps, and pay substantial additional amounts to the governments of PNG and Nauru to enable the practice. Several pieces of Australian legislation support the policy, including the controversial excising of hundreds of islands from Australian territory for the purposes of migration (see '**exclusion zone**').

people smuggler: person facilitating the transportation of people across international borders to a non-official entry point of a destination country for financial gain. Often connected to criminal syndicates.

permanent residence: allows the holder to remain in Australia indefinitely, but with travel restrictions in and out of Australia for five years.

privative clause: a provision in legislation aiming to exclude judicial review of decisions made under that legislation. Enacted as part of a package of legislation at a time of heightened concern about border protection following the arrival of the *Tampa* off the Australian coast in 2001.

queue-jumper: first used as a politically pejorative phrase by the Coalition Government in the late 1990s to describe asylum seekers who had arrived unauthorised and were detained under mandatory detention laws. Asylum seeker support groups reject the notion of 'queues' being available in many countries, due to limited or no diplomatic representation and the danger of civil conflict or hostility towards those seeking to flee the country.

refugee: defined under the 1951 UN Convention Relating to the Status of Refugees as a person who, because of a well-founded fear of being persecuted for reasons of race, religion, nationality, membership of a particular social group, or political opinion, is outside their country of nationality, and is unable to or, owing to such fear, is unwilling to avail themselves of the protection of that country. The concept was expanded by the Convention's 1967 Protocol and by regional conventions in Africa and Latin America to include persons who had fled war or other violence in their home country. Australia was an original sponsor of the Convention at the UN.

residential housing projects: These were set up as alternatives to immigration detention for women and children in Woomera, Port Augusta and Port Hedland.

RRT (Refugee Review Tribunal): Created in 1993 to hear appeals against decisions by the Immigration Department. Often consists of only one sitting member.

Ruddock, Philip: Federal Minister for Immigration from 1996 to 2003. Currently Attorney General.

SIEV: Suspected illegal entry vessel.

***Tampa*:** Norwegian merchant vessel that rescued 438 asylum seekers on 26 August 2001 after their boat sank. The *Tampa* was refused permission to enter Australia's territorial waters, the legality of which has been the subject of international debate.

UNHCR: United Nations High Commission for Refugees.

Vanstone, Amanda: Succeeded Ruddock as Federal Minister for Immigration in October 2003, and was removed early in 2007.

visa categories

Bridging Visa E: for people who have made multiple applications or have been illegal. Also granted for people requesting the Minister for Immigration to intervene under sections 48B and 417 (see below).

PPV: Permanent Protection Visa, granted in recognition of refugee status.

RPBV: Return Pending Bridging Visa, granted at the discretion of the Minister, allows a person to remain in the community when all other channels have been exhausted, and allows a detainee into the community while deportation or another determination is being made.

s48: if a person has a visa application refused, then he/she cannot apply for another visa while in Australia.

s48B: if the Minister decides it is the public interest to allow a failed asylum seeker to make a fresh protection visa application, he/she can intervene under s48B and lift the s48 bar on further applications.

s417: is a request to the Minister to consider substituting the decision of the RRT (see above) for one more favourable to the applicant when it is in the public interest to do so.

TPV: Temporary Protection Visa, established to deal with an influx of unauthorised arrivals. The TPV refugee assessment is not as intense as that of the PPV. The visa holder is recognised as a refugee and cannot apply for a PPV for 30 months. Under current law, the TPV holder must then prove all over again that he/she is a refugee.

Authors' notes

Page x **'Since 2001, thousands of Australians from all parts of the country and all walks of life have been moved to act in support of asylum seekers and refugees ...':** For a definition of these terms, see Glossary.

Page x **'... from 1990–1999, 92,800 applications for asylum were lodged in Australia (with 14.6 percent granted protection), compared with 374,000 lodged in the UK ...':** UNHCR (2002), Statistical Yearbook 2001: *Refugees, asylum seekers and other persons of concern*. See <www.unhcr.ch>. Also, Canada, Denmark and Norway had asylum-granting rates double that of Australia during this period. Although often described as 'boat people', the majority seeking asylum in Australia have arrived by air: in 2001, only 4000 of the 13,105 asylum applications were from people arriving by boat. Source: DIAC Fact Sheet 74.

Page x **'Of the 9500 unauthorised arrivals in Australia between July 1999 and December 2001, most were political refugees from Iraq and Afghanistan.':** DIAC Fact Sheet 75: 'Processing unlawful boat arrivals'.

Page x **'From 1992–2004, over 4000 children arrived, 300 of whom were unaccompanied, without adult care and protection':** Mary Crocks, *Seeking Asylum Alone: a study of Australian law, policy and practice regarding unaccompanied and separated children*, Themis Press, Sydney, 2006.

Page xi **'Little matter that these accounts were inaccurate and manipulated for political gain.':** See, for instance, *Dark Victory*, Marr D. and Wilkinson M., Allen & Unwin, Sydney, 2003.

Page 41 **'Daoed was found guilty of assisting in bringing people illegally to Australia on SIEVX':** For media coverage of the trail, see *The Australian*, 14/7/05, at: <http://www.theaustralian.news.com.au/common/story_page/0,5744,15930187%255E29277,00.html>.

Page 61 Hinze's work is distributed by Scratch! Media (www.scratch.com.au).

Page 115 **'Crimes against humanity require accomplices, he claims, and there is "not only the hatred that makes it happen, but the *indifference that lets it happen*".':** *Investigative Journalism: Context and Practice*, ed. Hugo de Burgh, Routledge, London, 2000.

Page 115 **'... Bell, a foreign affairs correspondent: "It's not polemical. John Pilger is too polemical for me. What I mean is a journalism which cares as well as knows".':** *The Media Online*, Kevin Bloom 02/07/04. See <www.themedia.co.za/article.aspx?articleid=133103&area=/media_insighteditorials>.

Page 116 **'But diffuse fears about speaking publicly, of being "Bakhtiarised" ':** The Bakhtairi family was publicly accused of dissimulation and dishonesty, and became unpopular in tabloid media. Other families subsequently became concerned that media coverage of their stories could have negative consequences.

Page 124 **'... a nation that had a "White Australia Policy" for decades ...':** This term refers to the Australian approach to immigration from Federation until post-World War II. In 1958 the new Migration Act abolished the controversial language test and abandoned references to race.

Page 124 **'... Julian Burnside QC was running a test case in the High Court to see if we could argue that escaping from a place as horrific as Woomera was not escaping from lawful detention.':** *Behrooz v Secretary DIMA* (2004) 208 Australian Law Reports, 271, where the court held 6:1 that the conditions in immigration detention did not of themselves constitute cruel or inhumane treatment of detainees. This made such detention lawful.

Page 126 **'Eventually all three were transferred to Glenside Hospital, but not before a trial taking days and days.':** See the judgement of Finn J in *S v Secretary DIMIA* (2005) 216 Australian Law Reports, 252.

Page 134 **'It seemed to me – and this was corroborated by the Palmer Report – that, in the department's view ...'** See the Palmer Report, in particular p. 26.

Page 137 **'... departmental officers approached the mother to voluntarily sign a Deportation Order.':** This incident was reported in *The Sunday Telegraph*, 5 June 2005, p. 4.

Page 165 **'Many suffer from Immigration Detention Stress Syndrome, as documented in *Lancet*, the prestigious British medical journal.':** See Silove, E., Steel, Z., & Mollica, R.F., (2001) 'Detention of asylum seekers: assault on health, human rights and social development', *Lancet*, vol. 357, Issue 9266, pp. 1436–1437; and Newman, L. (2005) 'Seeking asylum, losing hope', *Lancet*, vol. 366, Issue 9502, pp. 1997–1998.

Page 188 **'... but the reforms were political, not principled ...':** The government has funded reforms to the Immigration Department, recommended in response to the Palmer and Comrie reports. These include staff training in law and mental health, and the establishment of a 'Stakeholder Branch' to engage community and refugee groups in the reform process. On 7 October 2005, the government committed $230 million over five years to the reform process. See Metcalfe, Andrew, 'Implications of the Palmer Report: Future Changes', 25 November, 2005. www.immig.gov.au media release.

Page 197 **'... an advocate asked if I knew of somewhere in Sydney where a Kuwaiti Bedoon man ('Mr B') could stay.':** The Bedoon are Kuwaiti citizens who have no nationality and very few rights. This stateless minority suffers discrimination and persecution.

Page 211 **'Occasionally demands are made of them by employers that are in contravention of the APS Ethical Code':** The APS code of ethics stresses the clinician's primary responsibility to their patient and the requirement to act at all times in the best interest of the patient as opposed to any other body including employers.

Page 212 **'As the trawler sank, the then-Minister for Immigration announced to the world that "a number of children had been thrown overboard" ...':** See the Senate Committee Report at <http://www.aph.gov.au/senate/committee/maritime_incident_ctte/report/a06.htm>.

Page 221 **'The willingness to use asylum seekers for political ends ... after 43 West Papua asylum seekers arrived in Australia in January 2006.':** Migration Amendment (Designated Unauthorised Arrivals) Bill, 2006.

Page 222 **'Billions of dollars will reportedly be spent on a planned maximum-security prison for 800–1200 inmates on remote Christmas Island ...':** See Michael Gordon,'Island plan rekindles child detention fears', *The Age*, 25/1/06.

Page 222 **'... between July 2003 and May 2006, only 50 people reached Australia or offshore islands as "onshore" refugees...':** DIAC Fact Sheet 75, accessed 1/3/07 at <http://www.immi.gov.au/media/fact-sheets/75processing.htm>.

Acknowledgements

This collection is a small sample of the time, energy and love of thousands of Australians. Thanks are due to everyone who submitted words or illustrations for inclusion in the book, or told others about it, if not able to write something themselves. Ngareta Rossell and Alanna Sherry in particular made sure the invitation to contribute was passed on. Ngareta must also be acknowledged for, among other things, always knowing who to ask, or who would know or who should know, when things needed doing. For too many things to mention, we thank Ngareta.

Special thanks to Karen Cornish, Michael Dudley, Winton Higgins, Gaby Mason, Michael Wall and Sally Zwartz, our editorial group, who helped with reading all the submissions, choosing and organising the work. It would not have happened without them. Gaby, along with Jacqueline Murphy in Adelaide and Claire Jankelson in Sydney, ran the writing workshops that provided the initial idea for this project.

Thanks also to members of the Sydney Asylum Seeker Interest Group and our Adelaide colleagues, Jon Jureidini and Ros Powrie, who we have met and talked with regularly over five years of struggle and strife. They have provided support and inspiration.

Particular thanks to Zachary Steel for encouraging the academic and scientific aspects of our work and for helping with the bibliography for the book. John and Trish Highfield need special thanks. John always has the information required or knows where to get it, and he developed the Glossary and the Timeline of events for this collection. Thanks to Trish for her love and generosity: we are grateful that her fierce determination is directed at others.

Last but not at all least, love and thanks to our families and friends, in particular Sarah's husband Ian and children Ella and Jack Colley, who have given her the time and space to do this work, and her brother Peter Mares, who provided encouragement and information along the way. Thanks also to Louise's family and loved ones, particularly Serena for always having faith.

Finally, thank you to the many people who have come to Australia seeking asylum and who have trusted us with their hopes, their dreams and their stories, changing our lives in the process.

Resources

Further reading

Reportage and anthologies

Brennan, Frank, *Tampering with Asylum: A universal humanitarian problem*, UQP, Brisbane, 2003

Burnside, Julian (ed), *From Nothing to Zero: Letters from refugees in Australia's detention centres*, Lonely Planet, Melbourne, 2003

Corlett, David, *Following Them Home: The fate of the returned asylum seekers*, Black Inc, Melbourne, 2005

Dechian, Sonja, Millar, Heather and Sallis, Eva, *Dark Dreams: Australian Refugee Stories by Young Writers aged 11-20 years*, Wakefield Press, Adelaide, 2004

Higgins, Winton, *Journey into Darkness*, Brandl and Schlesinger, Blackheath, 2003

Kevin, Tony, *A Certain Maritime Incident: The sinking of SEIV X*, Scribe, Melbourne, 2004

McMaster, Don, *Asylum Seekers: Australia's response to refugees*, Melbourne UP, 2001

Mann, Tom, *Desert Sorrow: Asylum seekers in Woomera*, Wakefield Press, Adelaide, 2003

Mares, Peter, *Borderline: Australia's treatment of refugees and asylum seekers*, 2nd edition, UNSW Press, Sydney, 2002

Marr, David and Wilkinson, Marianne, *Dark Victory*, Allen and Unwin, Sydney, 2003

Moorhead, Caroline, *Human Cargo: A journey among refugees*, Chatto & Windus, London, 2005

Perini, Jessica, *Australian Focus on Issues: Refugees*, Watts, Aust. & NZ, 2004

Scott, Rosie and Keneally, Tom, *Another Country*, Halstead Press, Sydney, 2004

Shiels, Julie, *Cooking Stories*, Victorian Immigration Museum, Melbourne, 2004

Tyler, Heather, *Asylum: Voices behind the razor wire*, Lothian, Melbourne, 2003

Reports

Crock, Mary, *Seeking Asylum Alone: A study of Australian law, policy and practice regarding unaccompanied and separated children*, Themis Press/ Federation Press, Sydney, 2006

Edmund Rice Centre, *Deported to Danger* and *Deported to Danger II* : Continuing Study of Australia's Treatment of Rejected Asylum Seekers. Available at <http://www.erc.org.au/index>

Human Rights and Equal Opportunity Commission, *A Last Resort? National Inquiry into children in Immigration detention*, AGPS, Canberra, 2004. Also at <http://www.hreoc.gov.au/publications/index.html#human_rights>

Palmer, Michael J., *Report into the Circumstances of the Immigration Detention of Cornelia Rau*, Commonwealth of Australia, July 2005. Also at <http://www.minister.immi.gov.au/media_releases/media05/palmer-report.pdf>

Note: A list of research and academic publications on this issue can be found at **<www.finch.com.au>**.

Advocate organisations

AJA (A Just Australia): Launched in July 2002, AJA brings together over 11,500 individual supporters, 120 non-government organisations and over 70 prominent Australian patrons. <www.ajustaustralia.com>

Amnesty International: A worldwide movement of people who campaign for internationally-recognised human rights. <http://www.amnesty.org.au/resources>

Australians Against Racism: Established in October 2001 to counter destructive stereotyping of race and culture by actively promoting understanding and debate through the media, arts, education and the law. AAR is not associated with any political party or group. <http://www.australiansagainstracism.org>

ARA (Australian Refugee Association): Established in Adelaide in 1975, the ARA is a non-profit charitable organisation that helps refugees become settled and participating citizens of Australia. <http://www.ausref.net>

ASNA (Asylum Seekers Network Australia) Inc.: set up by Judy McLallen, Kerrie Lee and Ngareta Rossell in 2003, liaises between professional service providers to provide pro-bono support to asylum seekers and refugees. It also provides information to the media about the plight of asylum seekers. Email: ngareta.rossell@bigpond.com

BASF (Bridge for Asylum Seekers Foundation): Launched in 2003 by a broad coalition of churches, human rights groups, unions, political representatives, and individuals, the Foundation seeks donations to financially assist asylum seekers on Bridging Visa E (BE) or released under *habeas corpus* orders, who have no adequate means of survival because the visa conditions preclude the holder from seeking employment or accessing government medical or social benefits. <www.asylumseekersfoundation.com>

ChilOut (Children Out of Detention): A group of parents and citizens brought together in 2001 to oppose the mandatory detention of children in Australian immigration detention centres. ChilOut grew from its origins in Sydney to become one of the most effective national lobby organisations on the issue. <www.chilout.org>

Circle of Friends: A volunteer support group associated with the Pilgrim Uniting Church in Adelaide, dedicated to settling and supporting families released on Bridging Visas into the community. It operates under the auspices of the Australian Refugee Association (ARA). <http://www.pilgrim.org.au/groups/cof27.htm>

PEN: An organisation that advocates for writers who are unjustly imprisoned, harassed or exiled because of their writing. PEN supports freedom of expression, the freedom and responsibility of the media, and it opposes censorship. <www.pen.org.au>

Project Safecom: Incorporated in Western Australia in December 2001, its vision is for a 'safe' community for displaced persons. A section on the website deals with issues relating to refugees and asylum seekers, and acts as a resource and clearing house for information. <http://www.safecom.org.au/refugees.htm>

RAR (Rural Australians for Refugees): An informal network of community-based concerned citizens located in regional and rural Australia. Founded in the Southern Highlands of NSW in October 2001, RAR quickly spread to small branches, attracting thousands of members and supporters. <www.ruralaustraliansforrefugees.org>

Romero Centre: An ecumenical faith-based, community-funded centre in Brisbane, established in March 2000 to support refugees on TPVs and the reunited families of former TPV holders. <http://www.esjgws.org.au/issues/refugees/romerocentre.htm>

Sanctuary Refugee Foundation: A non-profit, non-denominational organisation founded in 1988 for the purpose of resettling recognised refugees, regardless of race, religion or creed. <http://www.sanctuaryrefugeefoundation.org/about_us.html>